Toxic Emotions *at* Work *and* What You Can Do About Them

Toxic Emotions at Work and What You Can Do About Them

Peter J. Frost

HARVARD BUSINESS SCHOOL PRESS
Boston, Massachusetts

Printed in the United States of America
07 5 4 3 2

Paperback ISBN: 978-1-4221-0285-5

Library of Congress Cataloging-in-Publication Data

Frost, Peter J.
Toxic emotions at work : how compassionate managers handle pain and conflict / By Peter J. Frost.
p. cm.
Includes bibliographical references and index.
ISBN 1-57851-257-3 (alk. paper)
1. Conflict management. 2. Job stress. 3. Employees—Counseling of. 4. Executives—Job stress. 5. Stress management. 6. Work—Psychological aspects. 7. Psychology, Industrial. I. Title.
HD42 .F76 2002
658.3'14—dc21

2002010612

To Nola:
Who holds space for others with great care and compassion. And for our children and grandchildren.

Contents

Foreword

Peter Frost would often say, "There is always pain in the room." His book, *Toxic Emotions at Work and What You Can Do About Them*, provides guidance and inspiration for managers who must lead organizations through inevitable pain. Frost documents the myriad ways that emotional pain is created and spreads at work. He helps us see how much of this pain can be toxic and corrosive, eating away at people's minds, hearts, and bodies. More importantly, he helps managers and leaders recognize and build strength and skills for dealing with this pain as individuals and as organizations.

Toxic Emotions at Work and What You Can Do About Them offers four important contributions to how we envision effective leadership and life inside organizations. First, the book clearly identifies and describes the different sources of toxic emotions present in organizations. Second, it argues that leaders and persons who take on the role of toxin handlers can transform these toxic emotions through compassion and skilled work. Third, the book uncovers the critical work of toxin handlers and documents the toll paid by people who assume this vital role. Fourth, the book identifies a range of concrete actions and moves that toxin handlers, leaders, and the organization as a whole can make to work with emotional pain in ways that foster healing and enable performance excellence.

The style of the book is deeply engaging. It is interlaced with real stories of toxicity and compassion that anchor the core concepts in managers' experiences. The book is also filled with practical ideas and short- and long-term strategies for managers and leaders who wish to work effectively with the inevitable toxic emotions in organizations.

To read this book is to get a glimpse of Peter Frost, the man. A year after this book was published, the cancer that inspired its writing returned and took Frost's life at age sixty-five. Frost, a South African by birth, left a remarkable legacy during his career as a professor, writing over forty articles and twenty book chapters. He also produced fifteen books including *Doing Exemplary Research*, *Rhythms of Academic Life*, *Researchers Hooked on Teaching*, *Publishing in the Organizational Sciences*, and most recently, *Renewing Research Practice*. His books and articles opened new research territories for studying the symbolism, culture, toxicity, and compassion of organizations. He was proudest of *Toxic Emotions at Work* (which won the Terry Book Award in 2003) because he felt it broke important new ground in naming a common and corrosive reality for many managers who are living in an organizational world where toxic pain is created and handled. He also believed he made progress in helping leaders see how they could work with this reality in ways that fostered healing and effectiveness.

Frost's real legacy is evidenced by the imprint he left on his students—executives, MBAs, and doctoral students. He was an openhearted and energetic teacher who modeled the subjects he was teaching. His deep passion about the subjects of organizational culture, leadership, compassion, and emotions, and his courageous and open style moved, inspired, and changed the people whom he had the honor of teaching. As you read this book, you will hear and feel his call to re-envision leadership in ways that evoke compassion as critical and necessary for healing the inevitable pain inside organizations.

—Jane Dutton

Acknowledgments

My thanks go first to the many individuals who shared with me their stories and observations, many of them painful, about life in the organizational trenches. It is with regret that in most cases, in order to protect their identities, I cannot name them and thank them personally. But I salute their courage and their generosity. Their stories give life and inspiration to many of the ideas in this book. Those I can publicly thank are Barbara Beck, Sherie Benjamin, Peter Ciotoli, George Crawford, David Crisp, Bruce Cryer, Greg Janiec, Dave Marsick, Bob McGlade, Sarah Boik, Richard Smith, and Mark Whitaker.

I offer thanks to Joan Borysenko, who unknowingly triggered for me the toxin handler insight, and to Mona Lisa Schulz, who saw the possibilities of this project before I did.

I am grateful to my ongoing "team" of health care providers, Larry Chan, Vincent Ho, Tony Wilson, and John Yeung. I am especially grateful to the Vancouver, B.C., nurses whose highly professional and empathetic behavior caught my attention when I was in their care. They sparked my initial interest in exploring the meaning and practice of compassion.

Jane Dutton has been a great source of encouragement along the way. Her counsel and her careful readings of drafts of the book made a significant contribution to the journey and to the result.

I was blessed with wise feedback and assistance from many other colleagues and friends who read drafts of the manuscript. These include Graham Brown, Sabrina Deutsch Salamon, Seonaid Farrell, Barbara Fredrikson, Yvette Hoffman, Jim Horn, Linda Krefting, Joan Lambert, Sally Maitlis, Joanne Martin, Phil Mirvis, Sid Perzow, Margaret Tebbutt, Karl Weick, Ann West, and the anonymous HBS Press reviewers.

My thanks to Sandra Robinson for her comments on the book and for her collaboration with me on the initial *Harvard Business Review* article on the toxic handler. My thanks go also to Suzy Wetlaufer, our extraordinary editor on that article.

I am most fortunate to be a member of a team of dedicated researchers and friends in the CompassionLab: Jane Dutton, Jason Kanov, Jacoba Lilius, Sally Maitlis, and Monica Worline. The CompassionLab is a joint project of the University of Michigan Business School and the Faculty of Commerce at the University of British Columbia. We started our work on the study of compassion in 1998 and over the ensuing years we have explored the experiences of pain and compassion in organizations. We meet every week virtually through our Web cameras to talk about our work, and our collaboration has been joyful and generative. My grasp of the meaning and impact of organizational pain and compassion has been deepened by our many conversations and by the generous help that each member of our team has given to me. Some of our project work inspired ideas in this book and some of our published work is cited here.

My experience working with the editorial team at HBS Press has been a delight. It commenced with my initial conversations with Marjorie Williams, who signed me up, and continued through the early guidance of Jeff Kehoe. Then followed the wise and strategic counsel of Suzanne Rotondo, who took over the project when Marjorie moved on to pursue other interests, the timely insights and advice of Genoveva Llosa, the intelligence of Jill Connor, my manuscript editor, and the skill of copyeditor Sarah Weaver. My thanks also to Hollis Heimbouch, Erin Beth Korey, Astrid Sandoval, and Julie Devoll. One of Suzanne's gifts to me was to connect me to Lucy McCauley. She is an incredibly gifted editor who intuitively grasped my intent. I deeply appreciate her contributions.

Many people gave me invaluable information and opened doors along the way. They reinforced in me the belief that projects like this one come alive because of unselfish help from others. They include Diana Cawood; André Delbecq of Santa Clara University; Ingrid Kochendorfer, Dale Sands; Martin Seligman, president of the Martin Seligman Research Alliance; Bob Robertson, CEO of Weston Inc.; and Amy Wrzesniewski, who is the leader of the positive psychology research POD on work, of which I am a member.

Julie Burtinshaw provided excellent research support throughout the project. Graham Brown and Seonaid Farrell gave me additional help checking and finding sources. Claire Hilscher, Laura Lee MacLean, and Marten Martens have done research on the toxin handler, and their findings have been encouraging and helpful.

I received invaluable technical and secretarial assistance along the way from Shirley Irvine, and Khim Mah. Cynthia Rée, my assistant, was tireless in her support.

This work was supported by funds from my Edgar F. Kaiser Chair in Organizational Behavior and from the Hampton Fund Research Grant at the University of British Columbia. I am indebted to Dean Daniel Muzyka of my faculty for his support and to former Dean Michael Goldberg whose early and enduring encouragement has been an inspiration.

Many of the ideas in this book were shaped at presentations I gave on pain and compassion. I thank the organizers and their institutions for these wonderful opportunities to think aloud and to gain benefit from the responses of my many audiences. These included presentations given for my faculty to alumni in Toronto and Vancouver (Deborah Nelson and her staff); to academics at a culture conference in Copenhagen (Majken Schulz and Edgar Schein); to managers and faculty at the Graduate School of Management at the University of

Western Australia (Stacie Chappell, Bruce McCallum, and David Plowman); to senior university executives of WEXDEV at Curtin University of Technology, Western Australia (Barbara Groombridge), and at the University of Technology in Sydney (Sally Lord, Stewart Clegg, and Philip Pogson); to academics and professionals at the University of Washington at Bothell (JoLynn Edwards and Kathleen Martin); to managers in Silicon Valley at Santa Clara University (Jan Sola) and to senior human resource managers at the Fundação Dom Cabral in Belo Horizonte, Brazil (Emerson Almeida and Aldemir Drummond); to academics at ICOS, at the University of Michigan (Jane Dutton and Diane Kaplan Vinokur), and at the fourth Positive Psychology Conference at Akumal, Mexico (Martin Seligman and Peter Schulman).

My deepest gratitude is to my family: to Nola, who created and held the space for me to write the book. I cannot ever thank her enough for her support, advice, love, and companionship over our many years together. To our children, Paul, Caitlin, and Maeve, and to Heather and Chris, who were unflaggingly enthusiastic cheerleaders for this project. Our grandchildren Áine, Aidan, Finn, and Rowan gave me solace when I felt too much of the pain that I write about in this book. Their enthusiasm for life swept away images of toxicity and suffering and replaced them with ones of joy and innocence and hope.

Toxic Emotions *at* Work *and* What You Can Do About Them

Prologue

In March of 1997, on a Friday evening, I received a phone call just as my wife and I were preparing to go out for a walk. The call was from a doctor at the British Columbia Cancer Agency. "I'm sorry to have to call you with this news," he said, "but the needle biopsy we took from your neck this afternoon has shown up melanoma cancer. It's in your lymph system." As I stood there listening to the doctor tell me I needed to call my oncologist to arrange a consultation with a surgeon—hearing him say the words "surgery" and "removal of the lymph nodes"—it was as if my body suddenly lost its skeletal structure. Everything inside me felt liquid and tractable. I could not quite believe this was happening to me. My visit to the doctor had been a routine checkup.

As I hung up the receiver and moved away from the phone, I actually stumbled. (Later, during our subsequent troubled walk, I would slip on an embankment and fall down.) I glanced around the living room; the objects there looked just as they always had. My wife, who was at the door buttoning her coat—still unaware of the news I'd just learned—appeared the same as she had before the phone rang. But everything had changed. You're never the same after a message like this. In an instant, life as I knew it had altered irrevocably.

Yet I would come to believe, over the next several months and years as I dealt with an aggressive form of cancer, that this ostensibly instantaneous alteration in my life had possibly been a long time in the making. My illness—a trigger for changes, obviously, in my personal life—also set in motion my thinking about the kinds of hidden forces that determine our well-being, even to the point of acquiring disease. And in particular, how the behavior of organizations and the people in them can affect the health of certain individuals.

A few weeks after that evening call from the doctor, I had surgery to remove the infected lymph nodes in the right side of my neck, and I took several weeks off to begin the work of healing. (There are no radical treatments for melanoma cancer beyond surgery; it isn't particularly responsive to radiation or chemotherapy. And although the odds aren't good for recovery from melanoma cancer that has metastasized into the lymph system, I'm glad to report I've had no recurrence.) During this period of rest and recuperation, I found myself trying to understand the meaning of this onset of cancer, given my life experiences in the previous few years.

I assumed no direct responsibility for having caused the cancer, nor did I feel any guilt because I had cancer. However, from my reading of the health literature, I did know that illnesses like cancer can be triggered by high levels of stress that depress the immune system and weaken the body's resistance to illness. Given that I had been working in a high-stress environment for several years prior to my cancer episode—I had been an associate dean in my school and had also been involved in numerous other demanding projects—it seemed possible that that had been a factor in my illness. I felt motivated to identify elements in my work habits and lifestyle in those years that I might need to change.

At the same time, I became alert to any practices and treatments that could keep my immune system healthy. That is how, a few months after my surgery, I found myself at a week-long seminar on health and healing. That is where my ideas about emotional pain in organizations, and its effects on people who try to manage that pain for the organization, began to crystallize.

The seminar, which was attended by a number of doctors and nurses interested in cancer treatments, was led by Joan Borysenko, cofounder of the Mind/Body Clinic at the New England Deaconess Hospital at the Harvard Medical School. Trained as a doctor in anatomy and cellular biology at Harvard, she is well known for her book *Minding the Body, Mending the Mind,* which pioneered some key ideas in mind/body medicine.[1]

About midway through the week, Dr. Borysenko spoke about the effects of emotions on people's immune systems, noting that strong negative emotions such as anger, sadness, frustration, or despair can be particularly "toxic" to the human body and affect the immune system's ability to protect it. What really got my attention, however, was something she said almost as an aside: that there are people who take on the emotional pain of others for the benefit of the whole system. "They are like psychic sponges for a family or for a work system," she said. "They pick up all the toxicity in the system." (In some societies, Dr. Borysenko noted, they have been called "sin eaters," taking on the sins of the group so that the whole community can be healed.[2])

As I wrote all this down I got goosebumps, recognizing how it tied directly into my recent thoughts: that maybe some leaders, more than others, assume the pain in their organizations for the benefit of everyone—essentially handling all the company's emotional "toxicity," as Borysenko had put it. (Of course, people other than leaders within organizations sometimes play this role, but for the purposes of this book I will focus on the particular problems the phenomenon presents for managers and leaders.)

One other reference in the workshop fed my excitement and triggered a second insight. Dr. Borysenko talked about the work of Larry Dossey, whose best-selling book *Healing Words* cited empirical evidence of the healing effects of prayer.[3] But it was his second book, *Be Careful What You Pray For,* that provided an important piece to my puzzle about leadership and emotional pain.[4] In it, Dossey's research suggests that people can also be *harmed* by prayer, if it comes in the form of negative wishes directed at them by others. Other researchers have explored a related phenomenon, the contagiousness of emotions. Daniel Goleman (author of *Emotional Intelligence*) refers to the contagiousness of emotions as having to do with the fact that how people are feeling can rub off on others.[5] For example, people in a work unit tend to pick up on the mood of their manager. If the boss is feeling optimistic and enthusiastic, those feelings can transmit to subordinates and may be observable in the office.

Emotional contagion has been examined in several studies: between individuals, in work teams, among burned-out high school teachers, and between leaders and their followers.[6] Their findings tend to support Dossey's hunch.

Dossey's observation that prayer might be a negative or positive influence was my trigger at the time and suggested to me that the whole area of pain and suffering—and any attempts to help others—was fraught with danger. I began to ask myself what the cost might be to "toxin handlers"—leaders who deal with something as potentially volatile as emotional pain in the workplace.

While Goleman's early work, at least, focused on the positive effects of high emotional intelligence (i.e., awareness of one's own and others' emotional condition and an ability to manage both), what became most salient to me after hearing of Dossey's work was that contagion could be positive *or* negative, and that emotions experienced by one person might also be *absorbed* by the person who attempts to help. Trying to ease another person's pain thus might prove a psychological and even physiological threat to the handler. This seemed to me particularly important since handling such "emotional toxins" is a competency for which most managers—unlike therapists and social workers—are not trained.

All of this implies that the people who handle the emotional pain of others might themselves become vulnerable to that very same pain. In effect, handling emotional toxins can be as hazardous as working with physical toxins. This becomes particularly true if, per Dossey's research, the person in pain associates the cause of that pain with the toxin handler himself—and thus wishes him ill. For example, if the handler also happens to be a formal leader in an organization, he might be seen as responsible for the pain and thus become the focus of negativity from both roles.

After the workshop, I began to reflect on these ideas in the context of my own experience. For four years, in the early to mid-1990s, I was associate dean in my business school. I started this job with the portfolio of faculty development (an HR-like function) and later took on the additional role of associate dean for our professional and management development programs (the executive training arm of the school). I was in a team of four senior executives in the school, led by our then-dean. It was a time of rapid change, fueled partly by many initiatives that came out of the dean's office and partly by ongoing budget cuts that hit the university. I had been a practicing manager in an earlier part of my career. Now, with my background as a professor in organizational behavior, I was having a chance to practice what I preached—and I enjoyed this new role very much, despite its pressures and fast pace. As I discuss later in this prologue and as will become evident in later chapters, it is unrelieved intensity of such pressures, especially over prolonged periods of time, that tends to wear people down and to let toxins into their systems. When at the end of my term the dean invited me to continue as associate dean, I was tempted but also felt burned out. I decided to take a sabbatical break and returned to research and teaching.

So what had I done that might be related to the ideas I was learning about toxicity? I began to see that emotional pain, or toxicity as I was now naming it, was quite prevalent in my organization. It was evident among professional staff who often lacked flexibility or sufficient funds to do their jobs as well as they wished. It could be seen (and heard) among faculty dealing with changes initiated from the dean's office. It was embedded in the debates regarding policy changes that inevitably suited some members of the organization more than others. It stemmed from many sources, among them the frustration that comes when dedicated academics have to teach and do research in an environment that is constantly being squeezed for resources—which the dean's office is powerless to provide. It came from constraints but also from opportunities: People could become angry, frustrated, or despondent as a result of what was *added* to their work as well as what was taken away. In fact, all the work of the organization seemed to involve some level of emotional pain. Toxicity, I began to realize, was simply a normal by-product of organizational life. The word *toxicity* may sound overly dramatic applied to aspects of everyday life, but in many ways it is uniquely appropriate. It suggests elements that can poison, whether a person or an entire system; toxins spread and seep, often undetected, in varying degrees. And toxins can be eliminated if you know the cure.

In my experience as a manager at the university, then, I spent a great deal of time listening to people who were upset. Sometimes the issues were work-related; sometimes they were personal. Often, I was a listening post for the pain or became involved in trying to alleviate it. Other times, as an administrator, I was the initiator of or accomplice to unhappiness. Often the intensity of the pain being expressed in my office was high, and while the visitors might leave feeling better, I often found myself carrying their pain around with me later, especially if I felt that I had somehow contributed to it.

For example, hours after the event, I might continually replay in my head a stressful encounter that took place in my office. I'd often feel a degree of sadness or frustration for the rest of the day. Or I might wake up at 3 A.M. with a visceral memory of a meeting the previous afternoon in which I had intervened in a conflict between colleagues. Whatever anger had been expressed at the meeting would keep me awake and restless in the early morning hours, thinking about how I might have dealt with the situation more effectively. Over four years, I found it increasingly difficult to let go of the pain that others presented me (though I was not really aware of the extent of that "wear and tear" until later). Issues that once might have stayed with me emotionally for only a few hours soon began to keep me awake for nights on end. Clearly, I was not dispersing the pain or the negative emotions. I was building up a residue of toxins, if you will, that made it more difficult to bounce back each day.

The more I thought about the seminar and my own experience, the more plausible it seemed that handling toxins for too long or in too intense an environment, without respite—as I'd done in my position at the university—can begin to penetrate the handlers' defenses: They take in the toxins. Faced with someone else's rage or cry for help, toxin handlers tend to confront the pain (the "fight" part of the fight-or-flight stress response). Although helping others to cope can carry its own sense of accomplishment, the bursts of adrenaline that occur in this role will, over time, wear down the helper's immune system. The result? Physical and mental ill health. (This is apparently true even for experienced pain handlers such as therapists and social workers, who despite their training can burn out and become very sick as a result of this toxic contamination.[7]) So, while the supportiveness of my dean and my family were important modifiers of this effect, they were not enough to protect me from the long-term result of working so intensely with the emotions of others.

I recall vividly the first time I spoke publicly about these ideas. I was ending a morning session on leadership with some thirty managers, from a variety of countries, who were attending a three-week residential program at my school. All had successful track records in their companies and were being groomed for senior management posts. I decided to take the last ten minutes to sketch my ideas about toxicity in organizations and on the role and costs of toxin handling. The room went very quiet, and I wondered if it was because they were intrigued or because they thought I was crazy! I offered to continue the conversation over lunch with anyone who was interested. I added that I was starting to interview managers about their experiences with toxic situations and that I would be happy to include anyone in the class who wished to volunteer for the study.

At the end of class, I was mobbed by participants wanting to talk about these ideas. Many volunteered to be interviewed, and they typically had powerful stories to tell about toxicity in their organizations. The source of the pain might be other managers, organizational interventions, or simply change. Sometimes they saw themselves as a source of the pain and were astute enough to have caught the situation and dissipated the pain. Often, they described situations in which they were toxin handlers. Their backgrounds confirmed my hunch that the people who fill this role include line managers running projects, people in charge of operational units, and people who champion a product or service in their companies. Several participants recounted examples in which the toxin handlers themselves were "contaminated" by the emotions they were working with. Eventually, they became ill or they burned out.

Later, I began to distinguish between the formal and informal leaders in organizations who handle others' pain, and those leaders who actually *create* pain for their subordinates and peers—whom I call "toxic bosses." But I also began to see that sometimes there's an inherent duality in this whole phenomenon: that it's possible for a leader to be both a handler of emotional pain *and* a source of that pain. This is an important point: Handlers of toxins can become so infected with others' pain that they, in a real sense, become "toxic" themselves, and begin inflicting pain on others. As I began to include these ideas in my presentations to management groups throughout Canada, in Australia, and in the United States, I found people connecting emotionally to the topic again and again. That encouraged me to expand the reach of our developing sample of interviewees, and soon the first publication of these ideas appeared in the *Harvard Business Review*.[8]

The Inevitability of Pain in Organizations

THIS BOOK focuses on the pathological effects of organizational toxicity and how to handle them. It also examines the compassionate actions of managers and leaders who strive to deal effectively and humanely with toxicity. However, it is critical to recognize that toxicity, or emotional pain, is a *normal by-product* of organizational life. All organizations, and indeed all managers in organizations, generate emotional pain as part of the normal process of conducting business—creating new products or services, setting new benchmarks for performance, and so on. Getting there is rarely painless. A decision by a company to go in a new direction or to acquire a competitor, or even to disperse benefits in a new way, may hurt some employees. A manager under heavy pressure to deliver results may come down hard on his team when the numbers aren't showing on the scoreboard. Another manager may start to micromanage her employees in the middle of a crucial new project, driving her subordinates to distraction.

While none of these events need be serious or enduring, they all produce some level of distress or disruption that needs attention if the system is to stay healthy. At "normal" levels of toxicity, the people on the receiving end may feel discouraged or deflated for a short while and then simply absorb it themselves. ("Joe's grouchy at the moment—he must be getting heat from the top. He'll get over it!") Or a manager herself might recognize that she has caused pain, and awaken in one of those "3 A.M. moments" to think: "Oops, I really didn't listen when Mitch was trying to make a point. I shouldn't have jumped in with my opinion right away!"

But even though emotional pain is a normal by-product of life in the workplace, organizations that want to stay healthy need to learn to handle such toxicity effectively—or prevent it in the first place. Many biological systems demonstrate just that. While processing inputs, such as food and liquids that help it survive and get work done, the human system, for example, produces toxins—and then when functioning healthily, discharges or absorbs the toxins effectively. The kidney and the liver, among other components, act to eliminate toxins produced when a person eats, drinks, exercises, and so on. The problem arises, in any system, when the levels of toxicity become too high and remain at that level for a long time. In humans, ongoing stresses make it difficult for the natural toxin removers such as the kidney or the liver to function well. Over time they may wear down and become damaged, or the immune system may become compromised. Illness or even death can ensue.

In the case of organizations, the problem of toxicity generation, especially when it is intense and enduring, is magnified because most companies don't see the role that debilitating pain can play in undermining their success. Or they often sweep it under the carpet as quickly as possible. They are even less likely to recognize the valid role of toxin handlers in the organization or to acknowledge and support the handlers when they need it.

This book, then, examines the various ways toxicity is handled in the workplace and offers ideas about how leaders, through compassionate actions, can help foster the health and productivity of their organizations and their people. Chapter 1 sketches a picture of the debilitating effects of emotional pain on individuals in organized settings—and what both compassionate and harmful responses to that pain look like. Chapter 2 examines the various sources of organizational toxicity, while chapter 3 looks in depth at the actual work of toxin handlers. The resulting emotional toll that managing toxins takes on handlers is the focus of chapter 4. Chapter 5 examines specific ways in which handlers can protect themselves from the toxins they help manage.

Chapter 6 describes how handlers can educate their organizations about the value of what they do and the ways in which they need support. This chapter also examines what organizations can do to protect these valued employees. Chapter 7 focuses on the compassionate role that leaders can take to manage toxicity in their organizations, and includes hands-on lessons for distributing the load beyond the designated toxin handlers. Chapter 8 looks at how organizations can create and sustain compassionate workplaces. This chapter offers specific steps that the organization itself, through its policies and practices, can take to prevent high toxicity by intervening effectively and enhancing the recovery of people affected by the toxins. Chapter 9 explores a variety of salient issues related to toxicity and presents a specific case to illustrate the potential of using emotional pain as a diagnostic or a lens into the sources of toxicity.

Given the opportunities and challenges facing organizations in the twenty-first century (including physical attacks unlike anything we've seen in recent times), good leadership more than ever requires the ability to anticipate pain and the skill to deal with it effectively and compassionately. At the very least, leaders need to understand how to clean up toxicity once it has been created. We can't prevent emotional pain in the workplace, but leaders who recognize that that pain indeed exists—and have compassionate systems in place for dealing with it—can create healthy organizations. It is my hope that this book offers the tools and the recipes to do just that.

CHAPTER ONE

Emotional Pain in Organizations

Harry, the CEO at the Australian office of a multimillion-dollar consumer package goods company, had just seen his organization through its second merger in two years—with predictably painful results.[1] *The sudden turnover of leadership at the U.S. headquarters left the direction of the company in a confusing array of hands. Equally disturbing, the IT systems and manufacturing supply chain that the company had always relied on were now flawed as a result of the merger and new company. Top financial managers were forced to do their periodic reports—adding up hundreds of thousands of dollars, for hundreds of product lines—on computer spreadsheets.*

Just when it seemed as if things couldn't get worse, the new bosses at the home office began demanding performance results that Harry felt were unrealistic, given the economic climate—not to mention the unsettling effects of the mergers. In addition, the company's existing go-to-market strategy of selling through its traditional retail distribution chain needed significant rethinking; it was becoming costly and uncompetitive, compared with the competition's highly effective e-business strategy. Harry and his team strenuously signaled their concerns and recommendations to the head office managers, but the new managers wouldn't budge—and the pain of the last two years' upheavals quickly turned toxic. (In the prologue, I describe in some detail, the meaning and nature of toxicity in organizations.) Harry found himself spending more time trying to fix internal problems and managing the demands of HQ, rather than focusing on the retailers, customers, and staff.

It didn't take long for the pressure to take its toll on company performance, and ultimately on Harry himself. Moreover, the frustration and anger that Harry's staff felt as a result of the performance demands eventually became debilitating. "I remember walking into a quarterly outlook meeting where people all had their heads in their hands. 'We're going to miss by 20 percent,' they said. 'The numbers just aren't there,'" Harry said. "At one point a VP, someone who was a very strong person, came into my office and broke down in tears." The relentless pressure from the head office eventually wore down the intellectual and emotional vitality of both the staff and the CEO, who had done his best to buffer staff from the corporate mandates. The company's financial results continued to worsen and although people were loyal to Harry, they began polishing their resumes.

PAIN IS A FACT of organizational life. Companies will merge, bosses will make unrealistic demands, people will lose their jobs. The pain that accompanies events like these isn't in itself toxic; rather, it's how that pain is handled throughout the organization that determines whether its long-term effects are positive or negative. What turns emotional pain into toxicity, especially in organized settings, is when others respond to that pain in a harmful, rather than healing, way. Such was the case when the new corporate team at Harry's company did nothing to acknowledge the cumulative effects of the mergers, much less reexamine the financial demands they were making on the Australian office.

The consequences of such harmful responses are far from benign. Toxicity, the outcome of emotionally insensitive attitudes and actions of managers and of the practices of their companies, doesn't simply ruffle a few feathers. Rather, it acts as a noxious substance, draining vitality from individuals and your entire organization, potentially causing everything from missed deadlines to a mass exodus of your key staff. And as Harry's head office learned too late, the effects of toxicity don't stop at these sorts of outcomes, which disrupt the workflow. Left unchecked, toxicity will seep into your organization's performance and right down to your bottom line. Despite the pervasiveness of emotional toxins in organizations and their negative effects on people and on profits, no one will raise the subject since, as most of us have experienced first-hand, the discussion of emotion and pain in work situations tends to be seen as "weak" or "soft," leaving those who do see it—and help to resolve it—with their mouths shut and their heads down.

This is a book about what organizations and their leaders do to produce emotional pain, how that pain can become toxic, and the effect that pain can have on individuals and the workplace. It is about the managers and professionals who deal with this pain—people I'm calling "toxin handlers"—who work, often unobtrusively, to help people who hurt and keep them focused on their work. Moreover, it describes what happens to toxin handlers when their important work goes unacknowledged and unsupported in the workplace—and how organizations suffer as a result. Rather than being a field guide, *Toxic Emotions at Work* describes the role of compassion in organizations and the task of handling toxic emotions in the workplace, as well as the importance of both contributions. It illustrates how individuals can improve their toxin-handling competencies, and how compassionate companies can embrace these same practices.

Most important, perhaps, this book looks at what companies and their leaders can do to prevent toxicity from demoralizing employees, damaging performance, and, ultimately, contaminating the health of the organization.

The Costs of Organizational Toxicity

THE FACT IS, emotional pain exists in every organization at some point, and it takes a heavy toll. Recent books such as *White-Collar Sweatshop* report the frequency with which hardworking, valuable employees have negative experiences in the workplace or hear bad news that leaves their hopes dashed, their goals derailed, or their confidence undermined.[2] The sources of the pain vary, but much of it comes from abusive managers, unreasonable company policies, disruptive coworkers or clients, or from poorly managed change. I call this confidence-sapping, esteem-draining pain *organizational toxicity*. It is a by-product of organizational life that can have serious negative effects on individuals and their organizations, unless it is identified and handled in healthy and constructive ways.

This kind of pain shows up in people's diminished sense of self-worth and lost confidence and hope. It is destructive to performance and morale. And it is at a level and intensity in many companies today that can no longer be ignored: The tangible consequences include lost profits resulting from things like diminished productivity or, worse, mass exodus. According to a study by the U.S. Bureau of Labor Statistics, organizational change at any level—be it downsizing, mergers, or a change in leadership—can lead to a loss of 75 percent in productive work time.[3] More significantly, job stress resulting from bad management and inhumane organizational practices adds directly to the cost of doing business. "Job stress is estimated to cost U.S. industry $300 billion annually, as assessed by absenteeism, diminished productivity, employee turnover, direct medical, legal, and insurance fees, and workplace violence," writes Joel H. Neuman of the State University of New York at New Paltz. "The market for stress management programs, products, and services was $9.4 billion in 1995 and was projected to be $11.31 billion for 1999."[4]

Sometimes, however, the costs of employees' frustration and anger can prove even more serious. When people believe they've been treated unfairly (especially by their supervisors), they can turn on their organizations, attempting to "even the score" in any number of ways—at great cost to the organization.

Apart from quitting, which carries its own set of costs to the company, acts of revenge, sabotage, theft, vandalism, withdrawal behaviors (withholding effort), spreading gossip, or generally acting cynical or mistrustful can all represent direct and indirect costs to the organization. In a six-year longitudinal study on workplace sabotage, researchers found that 65 percent of all acts of sabotage stemmed from discontent with management and its perceived unfair behavior toward workers.[5]

Another study suggests that this dissatisfaction with management leads to reduced loyalty, and "once that loyalty has been destroyed, an employee is more likely to commit an act of sabotage."[6] The authors of that same study point out that events such as the Union Carbide plant explosion in Bhopal, a Pacific Southwest Airline crash in California, and a devastating hotel fire in San Juan, Puerto Rico, "were allegedly initiated by disgruntled employees with a score to settle."[7]

Other incidents, such as the recall of Firestone's tires in 2001, reveal similar patterns. Examining detailed data on Firestone, two economists from Princeton University, Alan Krueger and Alexandre Mas, found "circumstantial, but broad and consistent evidence that a disproportionate number of flawed tires were made at the firm's Decatur, Illinois, plant when labor and management were battling" (referring to a 1994–1996 labor dispute).[8] The economists also pointed out that those tires were more likely to fail than tires made at a nonunion plant. In a *Wall Street Journal* article on this incident, David Wessel wrote, "No one factor explains the Firestone catastrophe. The new Princeton work strongly suggests that squeezing workers even in an age of weakened unions can be bad management, especially where employers abruptly change the rules . . . brute force can backfire and the consequences can be severe."[9]

Other kinds of threats to organizations reflect our society's increasing reliance on computers. For example, computer viruses may be planted with ease, and their effects can be extremely costly to organizations and individuals. According to Neuman, who conducted an extensive study of the effects of organizational injustices on profitability, "[T]he same factors that lead to increased incidence of aggression and bullying may often lead to decreases in employee performance or costly acts directed against the organization. . . . Clearly, the costs associated with unfair treatment can assume astounding levels in both human and financial terms."[10] This proposition has received support from C. B. Wilson, who estimated that $5 billion to $6 billion is lost every year in the United States economy because of real or perceived abuse of employees by employers.[11]

Organizations cannot, obviously, survive such kinds of abuse indefinitely. Fortunately, when leaders recognize emotional pain when it occurs and act to intervene, potentially lethal situations in the workplace can be reversed.

Toxin Handlers: The Organization's Hidden Asset

WHETHER ORGANIZATIONS and their leaders are aware of the fact or not, they rely on toxin handlers to deal with the pain that results, almost as a matter of course, from doing business every day. These toxin handlers can and do work in many different levels of the organization, offering compassion and practical help to troubled employees.

Harry, in the opening example, was a toxin handler who happened to be CEO. As a company leader, Harry felt responsible for the emotional well-being of his people, and he did what he could to mitigate the most damaging effects of the pressure coming in from the head office. He listened to his staff, he sympathized, he tried to negotiate with headquarters for more realistic goals. And although his efforts didn't bring the organizational changes he'd hoped for, by all accounts his compassion went a long way to alleviate the worst effects of a toxic situation. When, after a year of relentless pressure from headquarters, Harry decided to leave the company, he did so amid kudos from his staff, his customers, and even his competitors. The head office managers never understood or valued what he had done for the company.

It bears repeating that, while emotional pain is an integral component of organized life, it is the human *response* to the pain that determines whether it becomes toxic or generative, focusing people on ways to harness, absorb or to overcome it, whether it endures as a debilitating poison or is transformed into a force for health. Consider, then, two more examples of toxic situations: one that is transformed through compassion, and one that spirals downward when compassion is withheld. To draw the connection between pain and the power of a healing response even more clearly, both stories are set in a hospital.

Several years ago, I was one of four men in a postoperative cancer ward. Although I was healing well, the patient in the bed across from mine, a man in his seventies, had had his stomach and esophagus removed and was having great difficulty coping. On this particular morning, with several different tubes attached, he'd made an unsuccessful attempt to get to the bathroom. A nurse near the end of her shift quickly helped him, shaken and humiliated, back to bed. He looked near death's door.

The new nurse who came in for the morning shift was remarkable. She made sure the other patients were comfortable and then spent most of her day caring for this suffering person. She did all the technical things one expects: She brought in the doctor and someone to check the machines that supported him; she contacted his family to come and visit him. It was the extra care she gave him, however, that caught my attention. She checked in regularly, held his hand and spoke words of encouragement; she pulled the curtains around him from time to time to give him privacy. By the end of the nurse's shift, late in the day, the man was sitting propped up by pillows and reading the newspaper. He had some color in his face.

I walked over and told him I was pleased to see him looking better. He smiled and said that in the morning he'd felt so helpless, he didn't think he'd last the day. I'm not sure how he fared in the long run, since I was soon discharged, but I had no doubt that the nurse's caring attention had saved the man's life that day.

That story illustrates not only how bleak the world can look to people who are suffering but also what a profound—even lifesaving—difference a compassionate, competent response to pain can make. Contrast that story with the one that follows, which also takes place in a hospital setting—but with a very different outcome.

A health care employee was in the hospital after delivering a stillborn baby. Her pain and grief were magnified by the fact that she had been trying to conceive for many years, suffering a miscarriage before the latest pregnancy was brought to term. When her boss stopped by her hospital room, the woman assumed he was there to offer his condolences. Instead, he'd come to ask her when she would return to work.

Not only did his lack of compassion compound the woman's grief; his actions so shocked and angered the woman that she later applied to be transferred to another unit. The thread of loyalty that she felt for her boss had been broken. And the boss—who ran a very busy and overextended unit—lost a valued employee with more than ten years of experience.[12]

How Pain Grows into Toxicity

As this last story shows, an unfeeling response undermines people's confidence, esteem, dignity, and sense of connection to others.[13] It *disconnects* them from the capacity to respond competently to their painful situation. It removes the desire and the ability to do their jobs. Perhaps most problematic, a toxic response decreases people's sense of hope—a critical component in feeling connected to life around them.

In a study of individuals with Lou Gehrig's disease, published in the *New England Journal of Medicine,* researchers distinguished those patients who were also clinically depressed from patients whom they identified with a condition they called "hopelessness"—meaning they felt they had nothing to look forward to. When both groups of patients were asked if they would consider euthanasia as a way to end their lives, if it were a legal option, only the patients who felt hopeless said yes.[14]

Part of the disconnect that leads to feeling such hopelessness is the result of what Daniel Goleman describes as a "neural hijacking," in which the amygdala ("an almond-shaped cluster of interconnected structures perched above the brainstem, near the bottom of the limbic ring") triggers emotional reactions before the thinking brain has any chance to pick up a signal or evaluate it.[15] While such hijackings often manifest as explosive emotional responses (that the individual often regrets almost as soon as they occur), the emotional mobilizations of the amygdala also sound the alarm for the brain, drawing on the body's flight-or-fight hormones. Thus the cardiovascular system is activated and the hormone norepinephrine is secreted, heightening the sensory circuits. Among other things, these activations put a fearful look on the person's face and raise the blood pressure. Everything becomes focused on the perceived or real danger the person faces.[16]

A man who is emotionally abused by a boss, shaken by news of a layoff, or told he has cancer will find that such hijacking will immediately disrupt a creative work groove as he struggles to process his flood of reactions. If, in addition, the responses of people around him are less than empathetic, he'll be left with few resources other than fight-or-flight through which to resolve his dilemma.[17] Pain that is mishandled will more likely lead to grief. People whose pain is left untreated will avoid future situations that resemble the pain-inducing incident. When people are hurting, when they are shocked by what happens to them or by what they hear about themselves from others, they become disconnected from hope and from a sense of belonging to a supportive community. They may subsequently enter a phase of denial followed by anger and depression (following the cycle of grief that Elisabeth Kübler-Ross and others have discussed).[18] But the immediate reactions are likely to be confusion, disbelief, and shaken confidence. As we all know, people burdened with those feelings cannot easily attend to their normal day-to-day tasks and responsibilities.

That day in the cancer ward at the hospital, I saw my fellow patient feeling just that kind of shaken confidence—with a potentially fatal outcome. Similarly, the employee who had delivered a stillborn baby was in a state of intense grief; the thought of when she'd return to work was the furthest thing from her mind. The boss's response to this employee's pain only exacerbated her sense that she was alone with her grief, a wide gulf of pain separating her from the world around her—and certainly from her job. The difference between the outcomes of the two situations lies primarily in how someone with professional responsibility (the nurse in one case, the boss in the other) handled the disconnection of the person in pain.

Lack of compassion, or the inability or unwillingness to empathize with the plight of another and then to act accordingly, impairs all kinds of relationships. The dynamic can occur between coworkers, between teacher and student, or between parent and child. For example, a parent preoccupied with work may fail to notice when his child is having difficulties at school and needs a sympathetic ear—rather than a dismissive gesture that undermines the child's confidence. Or a coworker, blind to the emotional plight of a colleague struggling with conflicts at home, might criticize his attendance record or his effort at work.

Although each took place in a hospital, the stories of the nurse in the cancer ward and the insensitive boss hold important lessons for the wider world of work. Emotional pain can completely debilitate the people who experience it in organized settings, disconnecting them from their normal healthy responses to difficult situations.[19] Healthy responses encourage those experiencing emotional pain to try to overcome it—to treat pain as feedback that can spark learning, and to make constructive changes.

The Healing Impact of Compassion

A CONSULTANT was conducting a high-pressure, two-day seminar for a group of senior managers. At the end of the first day, it was clear to everyone that it was not going very well. Feeling despondent and at a loss about how to proceed, he was gathering up his notes when the CEO came over, put his hand on the consultant's shoulder, and said: "This is a game of halves. I'm sure you will do just fine in the second half tomorrow." That simple remark restored the consultant's confidence to the point that after making several adjustments to the seminar and working long into the night, he delivered a highly successful session the next day.

When emotional pain is handled well, it is often accompanied by a willingness to reenter situations that might be painful and confront them head-on. There can even be feelings of satisfaction and pride if one sees the pain as the necessary price to accomplishing some valued outcome in the long run. For example, when a work team reaches its target, creating a breakthrough product after working around organizational roadblocks, turf battles, and misunderstandings, the distress felt along the way is considered worth it. "No pain, no gain," goes the saying. But to reach that kind of positive outcome, the team needs to feel hope along the way—confidence and belief in the worth and achievability of the goal. And when inevitable emotions such as frustration or despondence surface, the team needs a leader who can recognize the need for intervention and deal with the pain appropriately, as the CEO did for the consultant in the previous example.

As the next story in the section The Compassionate Manager suggests, however, there are specific skills that can markedly diminish or even remove an individual's pain, in this instance helping a new manager to regain her confidence. This point of reconnection is very similar to what Edward Hallowell has called the "human moment" that can occur in any interaction between two people.

The Human Moment

Writing in the *Harvard Business Review,* Edward Hallowell describes a human moment at work as one in which a manager gives her full attention to an employee or a colleague who has come to her in distress. "The human moment has two prerequisites," he writes, "people's physical presence and their emotional and intellectual attention."[20] Providing such human moments requires a commitment of energy, says

Hallowell: "[A] human moment doesn't have to be draining or personally revealing. . . . A five-minute conversation can be a perfectly meaningful human moment. To make [it] work, you have to set aside what you are doing, put down the memo you were reading, disengage from your laptop, abandon your daydream, and focus on the person you're with."[21]

The levels of healing that can occur during such close interactions extend to the very chemistry of our brains. Hallowell cites the well-known study from the 1940s by Rene Spitz that showed how infants who were not held and cuddled suffered retarded neurological development. Later research confirmed this finding. As Hallowell reports, current knowledge about the chemistry of the brain's reaction to human-to-human contact shows that positive contact "reduces the blood levels of the stress hormones epinephrine, norepinephrine, and cortisol." People can also emit the hormones oxytocin and vasopressin, which promote trust and bonding, he continues. Moreover, contact between people "stimulates two important neurotransmitters: dopamine, which enhances attention and pleasure, and serotonin, which reduces fear and worry." When people are in pain, therefore, the efforts of someone else to reach out and help can physiologically reduce fear and stress and enable them to begin to function effectively again.[22]

It's important to remember that people at all levels of the organization can and do play the role of toxin handler, providing such human moments to others. Office assistants, for example, sometimes become listening posts for frustrated workers, and their attention can help relieve the pain. They also have been known to skillfully reframe the concerns of others and draw them to the attention of higher-ups, giving management the insights and opportunity to act on information otherwise kept under wraps. Serving as this critical link in the chain meets a basic need of every organization—for senior managers to stay in touch with the day-to-day concerns of employees.

Still, managers and other company leaders are often in the best position to extend "human moments" to their people, preventing toxicity from growing and spreading. Such managers regularly place themselves between the source of the pain—a boss, company practice, or change initiative—and those affected by it. They deflect, filter, dissipate, or absorb injustices and frustrations so that people can focus on their jobs. For example, they can anticipate when the organization is generating some kind of pain (such as layoffs) and can try to protect those who might be targets by speaking to them privately and helping them prepare for the news.

The Compassionate Manager

At an offsite meeting of three hundred of Cisco's managers, Janet Skadden, a new manager in human resources, wanted to try something different. She had come to Cisco from Tandem, a company whose relaxed, interpersonal culture encouraged employees to participate in activities like trust-building games. Skadden hoped such games might help the Cisco engineers loosen up a little, especially given the beachfront atmosphere of the meeting. But, to put it mildly, Skadden's exercises didn't go over well. When the attendees returned to the office, they were still talking about Skadden's "beach games."

Skadden was despondent. But CEO John Chambers, who'd witnessed Skadden's efforts at the beach, came to her office and told her what a great job she'd done in pulling the offsite together. When Skadden pointed out that her exercises had bombed, Chambers said: "The minute you stop trying to do things like that, I'm going to be really disappointed. If you're not taking risks and trying new things, you're not trying hard enough. I loved the fact that we tried something different."[23]

Such a compassionate response from a leader can have enormous power in signaling to others in the organization that their efforts, even when they fail, are going to be met with understanding and encouragement. Being responsive to organizational members as people, rather than as a factor of production, creates a climate in which they know that their efforts to improve the organization's performance will be appreciated. Chambers did not celebrate Skadden's failure. Rather, he sensed her embarrassment and praised her courage and her effort. By thinking first about the person and her feelings and then assessing her performance, a leader can create a culture in which compassionate responses to pain become a natural part of doing business. Put another way, handling toxins becomes one of the things that leaders at all levels routinely do for one another and for their employees. The "residues" of toxic actions or events are more rapidly dispersed and people can get on with doing their jobs well.

In 2000, a Gallup study of two million employees at seven hundred companies confirmed the value of such compassionate management. The study found that most people rate having a caring boss higher than how much money they earn or the fringe benefits they receive. Indeed, how they related to their immediate supervisor determined both their productivity and how long they stayed in the job. According to one account of the Gallup poll: "The study confirms findings by a 1999 Lou Harris Association/Spherion poll that found 40 percent of those who rated their supervisor as poor were likely to jump ship, compared to 11 percent who rated them as excellent."[24]

What specific skills enable a manager to help someone in distress in a compassionate, positive way—in effect, to become an efficient toxin handler? I will address these competencies more substantively later in the book, but foremost is the ability to notice that someone is in pain in the first place. Then it becomes key to listen empathetically and be emotionally present for the other person, which requires full attention to the feelings the person is expressing.[25]

The basic skills that compassionate managers employ are to

- Read emotional cues (their own and others') and anticipate their effects in work situations.[26]
- Keep people connected. They make a habit of engaging in "human moments" with their colleagues and their staff.
- Empathize with those who are hurt and listen to them with care.
- Act to alleviate the suffering of others.

- Mobilize people to deal with their pain and to get their lives back on track.
- Build a team environment where acting compassionately toward others is encouraged and rewarded.

As we've begun to see in this chapter, managers who possess such skills often can keep their people happy and productive, even in the face of major organizational shifts. On the other hand, managers who regularly ignore or bumble pain management can pay a high price. In this era, the competitive edge goes to those companies that harness and magnify the intellectual *and* the emotional energy and commitment of their workforce. Creating or ignoring human suffering detracts significantly from these advantages.

Take, for example, the case of Dave, a manager of several office administrators at a large corporate headquarters, who was approached by a staff member to intervene in a dispute. Despite the employee's obvious distress (a coworker had criticized her, unfairly she felt, and in front of her peers), Dave made it clear that he had little time for such interpersonal matters. He urged her to work the problem out herself or talk to the coworker directly. The coworker, however, who had a reputation for this kind of behavior and had already caused two other people in the office to resign, refused to discuss the incident. When the staff member, frustrated, approached Dave to negotiate a meeting with the coworker, his response was: "She will never apologize, so there is no use having the meeting." Her frustration and anger unabated, the employee soon found her work starting to suffer—and she began looking for another job.

Clearly, a manager's ability to handle the toxic feelings of even one staff member can affect the organization as a whole. Had Dave made more of an effort to address the situation, regardless of who was at fault, the disgruntled employee could well have been appeased—and the company wouldn't have lost a productive and conscientious worker.

But organizations themselves—not just managers—can also act in ways that encourage compassion rather than indifference, producing healthy rather than toxic responses. The example of HeartMath LLC, based in Boulder Creek, California, illustrates the transformative power of organizations that are adept at handling pain.

The Compassionate Organization

HEARTMATH is a multinational training and consulting organization that helps individuals and organizations neutralize the effects of human stress as it relates to quality of health, performance, and creativity. In 2001, not long after Bruce Cryer took over as CEO and president from the company's founder, Doc Childre, the company had an opportunity to "walk its talk" in its own organization. Orders were reduced and training programs were cancelled as HeartMath began to experience the effects of the declining U.S. economy. First-quarter results in 2001 were disappointing, with revenues down significantly. Staff were becoming disheartened.

"We are a patient organization," said Cryer, "but as the year was shaping up it was evident that we needed to address this change in fortunes." What followed was a series of conversations with all employees over several weeks in April and May 2001 to decide what to do.

Childre was fully involved. "He wanted to ensure that everyone in the organization was heard. We held many of our meetings after work, at times when people could easily attend. That way there were no distractions and no one was left out. We kept drawing people back to our mission and to our concern for the welfare of our employees and our clients."

At the same time, new business realities required definitive action, and soon it became clear that some layoffs would be necessary. Long-time staff were understandably hurting at the prospect of leaving the organization after many years of loyalty. But through it all, HeartMath as an organization acted true to its values, retaining the trust of its people. "We were concerned about those being laid off as well as those left behind to carry on the mission and work of HeartMath," Cryer said. "For example, we worked out an arrangement for a husband and wife team that allowed one of them to work with us as a consultant while the other stayed on as an employee. They told us that they were deeply touched by our efforts. I know others saw this gesture and were heartened."

The organization's compassion was also evident in the way it dealt with information. "We shared all the company's financial data with everyone," Cryer said, "so when our profitability almost immediately started picking up, staff could see this and be encouraged by it too."

By September 2001, the company had restructured and a new strategy was in place. "We now had to focus better than before, to appreciate the power of our technology, and to reinspire ourselves to move forward. We adopted the theme 'A change of heart changes everything,' which became a symbol internally and externally of this new energy. That vision has given us renewed focus, and it has tapped our enthusiasm for the work we do and the way we do it," said Cryer. And although the terrorist attacks of September 11, 2001, had an additional impact on revenues, the company was nevertheless left with a healthy profit at the end of that year. HeartMath leaders attribute the turnaround to the company's renewed focus on strategies that matched the values and mission of the organization.[27]

Like compassionate managers, then, compassionate organizations such as HeartMath promote a culture and a set of policies that produce generative responses from its people and thus ripple through all levels and aspects of the company. We will look at these practices in more detail later in the book, but in general the compassionate organization

- sees a clear link between the emotional health of employees and the organization's bottom line
- recognizes and rewards managers who are good toxin handlers
- hires for attitude as well as technical skill
- maintains a fair-minded workplace, recognizing the direct connection between consistent values such as loyalty, responsibility, and initiative, and the health of the organization overall

- has intervention strategies in place for times of distress or change (such as layoffs, personal trauma among staff members, or natural disasters) and rehabilitation strategies to ensure long-term recovery of hope and vitality in the workplace
- builds a company culture that values compassion and community as beneficial to productivity and to people

Organizations that ignore the principles of toxin handling risk more than just losing people; their performance can be affected as well. Consider the following example of how compassion directly affected one organization's ability to meet its goals.

How Compassion Affects Organizational Performance

THE HEARTMATH story provided a sense of the linkage between a caring response to organizational challenges and company performance. The following story offers another example of this link.

When Sarah Boik came aboard as head of the physician billing department at Foote Hospital in Jackson, Michigan, it needed a significant overhaul. Performance, measured by "days in AR" (the number of days that it takes the organization to collect a dollar from accounts receivable), had reached an all-time high of 187 days.[28]

Boik's mandate: to get the number below 92 days. The unit was further challenged by the hospital management team to beat the industry level of 81.5 days. By July of last year, just twenty-four months after Boik came on board, the department's figure was below 80 days, surpassing industry benchmarks. In the health care industry, where reimbursement is notoriously problematic, Boik's results were considered top-of-class.

Both Boik and her team attribute the success to several factors, all reflecting the best attributes of compassionate organizations and leaders. For example, Boik recognizes that one source of pain for workers is when their contributions aren't valued. "I believe that people want their workplace to work well," she says, "so I give them responsibility and I make sure that they have the resources they need to get the job done." She takes time to listen to their concerns and ideas. "I try to put myself where they are. I learn what works and what doesn't, and remove roadblocks so that operations run more smoothly."

Boik's skills go beyond task-focused leadership to understanding the value of acknowledging people's efforts. "We do fun things and celebrate when we reach goals," she says. She also understands the benefits of being firm and of pushing limits. "If someone isn't mad at me, I'm not doing my job," she adds. But she also knows that this drive needs to be seen as fair and necessary to get results. "I don't respond in anger," she says. "I try to take twenty-four hours off before addressing heated topics. And I try hard to help my staff see the reasons for what I am proposing or what I am doing."

When people are struggling, Boik moves to help. She cuts some slack for the employee who has lost a family member or who has a sick child. She allows coworkers to take time to help other staff members in difficulty. She ensures that routine details such as completing sick leave forms are taken care of so a person who is suffering doesn't have to worry about such intrusions. Moreover, since many of her staff live on limited income, Boik sometimes brings extra groceries to the office to share with those in need. Occasionally she even helps with money to tide someone over during a difficult time. Such interventions of food and finances are always done with discretion.

Perhaps as important as anything else that she does to be responsive to employees' pain, however, is the climate of support she's created in the unit. The staff feels empowered to step in and provide support and consolation to other coworkers who are in need of compassion. It is part of the way work and life are lived in the department.

As noted, Boik's actions at Foote seem to have directly affected how well the group was able to reach performance goals, as measured by "days in AR." But other leaders such as Harry, the CEO whose story opened this chapter, also recognize a correlation between compassion and performance. Harry used his toxin-handling skills—listening to people's grievances and advocating on their behalf to the home office—out of a personal sense of responsibility to his people. But he also recognized that dealing with these grievances was in the best interests of the company. "You want to protect your people emotionally so that they continue to do their job," Harry said. "If they're awash with toxins from frustration and stress, then they're not going to do their job."

In fact, study after study has shown a distinct correlation between a harmonious workplace and a company's profits.[29] For example, in reporting a study of 136 nonfinancial companies, Jeffrey Pfeffer and Jack Veiga highlight the effect of management practices on performance.[30] Each of these companies initiated public offerings in 1988, but within five years only 60 percent of these companies were still in existence. The researchers' careful empirical analysis, controlling for size, industry, and profits, showed that the value the firm placed on human resources was significantly related to the firm's survival: "The difference in survival probability for firms one standard deviation above and one standard deviation below the mean (in the upper 16 percent and the lower 16 percent of all firms in the sample) on valuing human resources was almost 20 percent."[31] I would add that the HR department is important to an organization's survival because it acts as a critical toxin-handling resource.

Despite its many benefits to the organization and the individuals in it, toxin handling carries its own set of difficulties, of course. Success stories such as the one at Foote Hospital are not common. In most companies, the work of toxin handlers such as Boik—in a real way, essential to an organization's success—is usually overlooked. At the end of the day, when a successful project is assessed, most companies don't consider the contribution of the toxin handler. It's no surprise, then, that so many organizations struggle to repeat a winning strategy. Why? Because they're missing an important, unsung component in the equation: the effective management of emotions. And it usually *remains* unstated.

Moreover, as hard as toxin handlers such as Boik or Harry (the CEO in the chapter opening example) work, their actions aren't always able to permanently solve company problems. Although the pain may be healed and the toxins temporarily absorbed, the causes of the pain still persist since it's rare that companies recognize their toxic actions, their effect on performance, and their impact on the handler. Unsupported and overwhelmed, the toxin handler eventually burns out. Such was the case of Michael, a senior project manager at a public utility company.

The Problem of Handler Burnout

FOR YEARS, Michael led a team of engineers who worked quickly and effectively together, developing creative ideas that helped advance the organization. All that changed, however, when the utility's board brought in a hard-charging CEO and made Michael one of his direct reports. Not only was the new boss unpredictable—his expectations and demands seemed to change daily—he also took any opportunity to ridicule and intimidate his staff. The effects on people's loyalty, and even health, were almost immediate. One project manager was hospitalized with ulcers and decided to take early retirement; many others in the organization began to seek work elsewhere.[32] Morale sank and with it, performance. "People felt betrayed and scared. The copy machine was busy churning out resumes," said Michael.

For three years, Michael acted as the office's self-selected toxin handler, demonstrating compassion in the face of others' pain. For example, he would step between the CEO and his colleagues, making it possible for people to vent their frustration behind closed doors. He stood up for coworkers at meetings when the CEO picked on them and, as a result, sometimes took the verbal abuse. Sometimes he played the role of the CEO's front man, translating his often irrational or hostile directives so that people heard only the instructions—not their debilitating effects—and could put them into action.

But over time, shouldering all the sadness, frustration, and bitterness in his unit began to take its toll. Although Michael's actions helped "keep the ship afloat," he also reported that he wasn't always able to process all the pain effectively. He became exhausted, physically and emotionally, and began getting sick more often. Just as he was considering leaving not just the company but his profession as well, the board fired the disruptive CEO. "When he was fired," Michael reported, "I felt as if an enormous load had been lifted off my shoulders." As a result, Michael stayed in his job—and the company was lucky enough not to lose an effective leader and toxin handler.

A main theme in this book is that there are ways for organizations to support toxin handlers so that they can avoid burnout and continue their important role. Had someone noticed the amount of pain that Michael was processing for the organization and worked to remove both the pain and its source (the toxic CEO), Michael might not have begun to burn out. As it was, the organization's total lack of response was yet another toxin and eventually eroded Michael's resourcefulness.

Such scenarios occur again and again in organizations. Too often, people like Michael soldier on, and the toxins they absorb eventually begin to affect their day-to-day interactions with others—not to mention their own health and well-being. Moreover, handling toxins drains time away from other projects, which can harm the handler's performance. Deadlines may be missed or targets undershot. This in turn prompts other toxic outbursts (from the handler's manager) or else requires the handler to work overtime to keep up with his workload, sapping his energy even further.

Companies that *don't* support the toxin handler—that don't acknowledge the inevitable toxins of organizational life and the importance of removing or reducing them—pay a high price: The handlers burn out, leaving no one to manage the emotional pain that companies generate every day. The result? Morale suffers and productivity drops—along with the company's profits.

Burnout happens even if the toxin handler happens also to be the CEO, as was the case with Harry in the opening example of this chapter. In fact, burnout might be even greater for handlers who are top leaders in the organization. Even though Harry was seemingly in a position to tell others what to do, in reality, like others at every level of organization, he was a manager caught in the middle. He was responsible to the board, to the head office, to shareholders, to his staff, and to customers. "It is almost like being the center of the hourglass," Harry said. "You've got an open funnel up top where the pressure pours in. And then you've got this person in the middle—that's me—who acts as that funnel where the grains of sand pass. And then you've got an open funnel at the bottom pouring out to staff, the market, and customers."

Not surprisingly, the pressure of trying to keep everyone happy eventually took a toll on Harry physically. He found it increasingly difficult to maintain concentration, and was getting colds more often. "People would look at me and say, 'you're looking tired, you're looking older.' But you know what? Through all of this, you're still the CEO and you still have to suck all the toxins up for everybody. The most crushing aspect of this is that you have no control over what's happening. You help others in pain but you cannot really help yourself."

The messages in this chapter are simple yet profound in their implications for a healthy and productive workplace. Emotions are part of the human condition and thus inherent in any organizational setting, and they have an impact on function and performance. Despite this fact, managers and their organizations—in their relentless drive for bottom-line results—frequently overlook or dismiss the impact of emotions. This is a costly mistake for everyone, since people who are unhappy disconnect from work, turning their attention to their suffering and its causes rather than to doing excellent work.

Toxin handlers are a key source of healing and reconnection for people in pain. Compassionate managers and compassionate organizations can share this role and lead their systems to greater health and better performances. But such managers and organizations continue to be the exception rather than the norm. That needs to change if we wish our organizations to reap the many benefits of compassionate practices that we've begun to look at in this chapter. This work is too important to the well-being of people and to the success of the organization to be overlooked, dismissed, or left to only a few committed individuals.

Now that we've taken a glimpse at what emotional pain in the workplace looks like—and the difference that a healing response can make—the question remains: Where does all of that emotional pain come from in the first place? In chapter 2 we'll examine the specific, potent sources of toxicity found in most organizations.

CHAPTER TWO

Sources of Toxicity in Organizations

Ryan was a senior manager who kept two fishbowls in the office. In one were goldfish; in the other, a piranha. Ryan asked each of his staff to pick out the goldfish that was most like themselves (the spotted one, the one with a deeper color, and so forth). Then, when Ryan was displeased with someone, he would ask the person to take his or her goldfish out of the bowl and feed it to the piranha.

RYAN MAY BE an extreme example of a manager causing toxicity in his work unit and even his company, but the behaviors and attitudes of managers are often a main source of pain in organizations today. Other sources can be traced to a company's policies and practices; sometimes there's a direct connection between how individuals create toxicity and the way the corporation conducts its business. Some degree of toxicity at work, however, is simply inevitable, stemming from the changes, traumas, and crises that people and companies experience from time to time.

Let's look now in more detail at the various ways that toxins are generated in the workplace. The forms they take could be thought of as the seven deadly "INs":

- INtention
- INcompetence
- INfidelity
- INsensitivity
- INtrusion
- INstitutional forces
- INevitability

Intention: The Role of Malice

PEOPLE LIKE RYAN, the goldfish-killing manager in the opening example, intentionally create pain in others. The actions of such managers are designed to degrade others, or to undermine the confidence or self-esteem of subordinates.[1] Creating pain may serve as a mechanism of control, so that there are no challenges to the boss's authority. Another good example is Michael's boss, the CEO of the public utilities company, described in chapter 1. This CEO was so abusive, he regularly sought out staff members for personal attack, degrading employees in front of their colleagues.

Some bosses develop grudges toward particular individuals and direct most of their vindictiveness to encounters with them. A manager may not like a staff member who has been transferred into his unit, even if highly recommended. The staff member may find herself picked on, her performance criticized at every turn. Over time, such attacks begin to have an effect: The staff member's enthusiasm and confidence diminish. Her performance starts to match the manager's assessment of her as incompetent. A self-fulfilling prophecy is in the making, and without intervention to deal with the poisoned situation, the worker will eventually be fired or quit.

Sometimes, however, the focus of the boss's abuse includes everyone. No one is spared the personal invective. What often makes matters worse is the unpredictability of such an attack. Employees never know who will be the next "victim."

One CEO we encountered, who typifies this kind of behavior, made it a practice at senior-management meetings to pick on someone in the room as the meeting began and harangue that person for several minutes—for actions real or invented. The CEO seemed to be intentionally setting a tone, creating a level of fear and intimidation in the group that carried over into the agenda discussions. Another CEO fired a senior manager in the latter's glass-walled office where the rest of the staff, who had been tipped off about the event, were able to look in from their desks in the open office. Despite the fired manager's request that this be done privately in another room, the CEO persisted. The manager felt humiliated and many of the staff members were angered and demoralized by the spectacle as well. The result? A chain reaction of poorer performance and general discontent—the exact opposite effect the manager was presumably hoping to trigger with this public act.

The purpose of malice is to deliberately harm someone else. Its reasons are many and varied: a need to control or dominate; a dislike of individuals from a particular gender or ethnic background; past experiences with staff that were themselves painful, leaving the abusive boss distrustful of his current staff. Or the malice may stem from a belief that this is how to motivate people and get the best out of them.

Whatever the reason, the typical emotional responses from those on the receiving end of malicious behavior are fear, anger, confusion, and resentment. By using the fish to demonstrate his negative judgment of an employee, Ryan created a great deal of toxicity in his organization. People who worked for him focused much of their energy on "playing it safe" and covering their tracks. They also left the organization as quickly as they could, creating a very high turnover. These are the kinds of outcomes that most often accompany malice in the workplace. Yet, despite his actions, Ryan kept his job for a number of years. The fact is that malicious, abusive behavior frequently goes unnoticed—or undisciplined—in some organizations. In particularly toxic companies, such behavior isn't seen as undesirable! On the contrary, senior managers often condone it, operating under the same misguided presumption that punishing, coercive behavior like that of the CEO leads to improved performance. However, my studies and others' research show again and again that just the opposite is true.[2]

It is important to recognize that many people on the receiving end of abuse find ways to protect themselves from attack. Some try to shrug off the malicious behavior, at least in the short run. But the effect of such abuse persists long after the triggering event; even in resilient individuals, there is a cost to maintaining a constant defense against aggressive personal attacks. The toxins that cause emotional pain tend to leave a mark. Over time, the persistence of abuse, and the uncertainty of when it might rear its head, wears down its targets, as well as the people who work around them. They are in a constant flight-or-fight response, making it difficult to function productively over the long haul.

In fact, data collected by George Fieldman and his team at Buckinghamshire Chilterns University College in High Wycombe, England, suggest that the way employees experience their boss directly affects their blood pressure, and ultimately their overall health. Using twenty-five health care assistants as a sample, Fieldman's team tested their blood pressure each day and had them describe their feelings about their bosses on a questionnaire. (All of the assistants had two different supervisors for whom they worked on alternate days of the week.) "The assistants who had one boss they liked and one they didn't had higher blood pressure than a control group who had two supervisors they rated equally," the study found. In fact, the assistants' average blood pressure leapt from 113/75 to 126/81 on the days they worked for a boss they disliked—"high enough to cause a significant health risk over time," said Fieldman.[3]

Incompetence: Managers with Weak or Inadequate People Skills

MANY MANAGERS lack systematic training in the art of creating productive relationships with their staff. Often they've been moved through the ranks or hired from outside based on their technical skills. No one checks on the manager's competency for working with people, or if they do, they may not give as much weight to weak or modest interpersonal skills when stacked up against strong sales or IT skills and a record of delivering product.

The pain that incompetent managers create takes a number of forms. Some vacillate too much, driving staff "up the wall" with their inability to make a decision or to stick to one once they have made it. Managers' indecisiveness can leave staff exasperated and even immobilized. A related source of toxicity stems from managers who are unpredictable. Although they may appear to be decisive on a particular issue, the inconsistency of their method of decision making leaves the staff bewildered. Take a manager who, in one instance, tells her staff to use their initiative on a decision. Then the next time, in a similar situation, a subordinate who takes the initiative is sharply reprimanded for not checking in before taking action. This kind of mixed message is exhausting and ultimately undermines the subordinates' sense of their own ability to make good decisions.

Indecisiveness can also take the form of a manager who asks for careful advice and analysis from his staff on a key decision. After putting in extra time to meet his request, they may find their inputs are as easily rejected as accepted—without explanation. Such an inability to predict a manager's direction or actions leaves staff unable to act with confidence in themselves or in the process. Diminished individual self-esteem and plummeting group morale results.[4]

Other managers are "control freaks" who micromanage their people, nagging them to the point that they're unable to accomplish their assigned tasks. Worse still is the manager who steps in and takes a task away from someone before she has even had a chance to begin. "We can't breathe!" the staff of such a manager will say. "He's all over us, constantly looking over our shoulders." Or: "Nothing gets done around here without his fingerprints being all over the job. And then he wonders why people are feeling down, unexcited about 'using their initiative.'"

In such a workplace, where the boss has to approve every little thing, logjams occur as work becomes tied up in his office until he has time to get to it. And the pain is shared all around: When one person's work is backed up, other people in the unit find their own projects stymied as well, awaiting the boss's careful attention. The resulting delays from an overcontrolling supervisor can frustrate competent staff, leaving them feeling out of control—a feeling that correlates highly with excessive stress.[5]

Infidelity: The Act of Betrayal

A HIGHLY TOXIC form of infidelity or falseness by managers is betrayal of coworkers. Betrayal by a supervisor destroys trust and always engenders emotional pain. Take Fred, a gregarious new CEO with an open manner, who encouraged his managers to talk with him about their concerns. Some of his managers became sufficiently confident in their relationship with Fred that, when pressed, they gave him their views on two of the VPs who, while technically competent, created disruption and severe unhappiness among the staff. Fred shared these views with the VPs, including "who said what about whom." The VPs retained their positions and found ways to punish the managers who had talked with their CEO.

Another common form of betrayal is when a boss promises an employee—or leads the employee to believe she will get—a promotion, but instead gives the job to someone else. Other managers betray trust by taking the best ideas of their subordinates and passing them off to the organization as their own. Once the word gets out about the manager's ploy, enthusiasm for "showing initiative" shrinks among the staff, along with their sense of hope. Although betrayal is most familiar outside the workplace—after all, much of great literature and the arts is built upon the powerful emotional responses betrayal can elicit—the fact remains that it also happens within the context of work. Managers who abuse their power over subordinates through betrayal trigger intense emotional reactions, as anyone who has experienced it can attest. The effects include long-term bitterness, a mistrustful work team, and fear. Reestablishing trust once it's been broken can be next to impossible, thus setting the stage for deteriorating boss-subordinate relationships and paranoia—both highly detrimental to the organization.

Insensitivity: People Who Are Emotionally Unintelligent

IN THEIR BOOK *Primal Leadership,* Daniel Goleman, Richard Boyatzis, and Annie McKee define emotional intelligence in terms of four domains: *self-awareness* (knowing one's own emotions, strengths, and limits—and recognizing their impact); *self-management* (keeping disruptive impulses under control and displaying honesty and integrity); *social awareness* (which includes showing empathy with others as well as being aware of organizational politics); and *relationship management* (including the ability to motivate others with a compelling vision, develop people through feedback and guidance, and manage conflict).[6]

Put in an organizational context, managers with a high level of emotional intelligence should be able to "read" the way staff members are feeling, particularly when they display symptoms of emotional distress. They typically are also able to gauge the emotional impact of their own actions on others. Later we will discuss these qualities as ones that effective toxin handlers exhibit. We'll also explore how the pain we create as managers needs to be "mopped up" to minimize the level of toxicity in the workplace. The issue here, however, is how the *absence* of emotional intelligence in managers harms the organization—particularly when it translates into a lack of empathy for the feelings of others and a lack of awareness about how their own emotions affect other people.

Vivien, an office worker in a branch of a national financial institution, tells the story of approaching her boss for permission to attend the funeral of a family member, a young nephew tragically killed in an accident. When told that the funeral was on the following Monday afternoon, the manager, preoccupied with company deadlines, initially refused the request. He needed her to attend a meeting Monday afternoon, he said; he urged Vivien to try to get the family to change the funeral to another day. Vivien, who had been close to the young boy, was devastated by this response. Eventually, her boss reluctantly allowed her to go to the service, but the hurt and the anger she felt toward him lingered long after the incident.

One can understand the pressures that many managers feel as they try to meet deadlines or get key people with busy schedules into the same room for a meeting. As this example illustrates, however, some managers cannot separate work from the emotional needs of their staff. They have trouble identifying with a staff member's distress, or else they operate from a belief that everyone's emotions (including their own) should be "checked at the office door." Such managers don't understand why anyone's personal life, even emotional pain, should take priority over workplace tasks and commitments. As a result, they respond insensitively to a colleague's cry for help—and lose the loyalty and willingness of that person to go the extra mile for the manager or the organization.

Other managers engender toxicity in the workplace because they regularly express rage, disappointment, or negativity. A human resources staff member recalls the meetings he attended some years ago, when the head of the unit would pepper their monthly meetings with "doom and gloom" projections about the company and the unit's own prospects for turning the situation around. "He was an incredible pessimist," recalls the staff member. "He'd dredge up all kinds of statistics and stories about how everything was going to fall apart in the company. We knew most of it was 'BS' but everyone slunk out of the meetings depressed. It would take days for us to get our energy back and then, soon enough, it would be time to hear it all again." The staff member added that this manager seemed oblivious to the effect he had on everyone, even when they tried to tell him how unhappy his "sermons" made them.

Toxicity from one manager is bad enough; when it's generated by the behavior of several managers in an organization, it can wreak havoc—and be extremely costly. In a particularly ironic case, a recent survey of the staff at Canada's Human Rights Commission revealed the staff's high dissatisfaction with the organization's six-member senior management team. In an organization whose mission ostensibly was to protect abuses of human rights, staff complained that senior managers paid no attention to their feelings or good ideas, nor did they empathize with employees' efforts to do good work, often in very difficult circumstances. These six executives, they said, "publicly criticized their work; cast blame on others for mistakes; never consulted workers . . . and failed to offer recognition or feedback."[7]

The survey had been ordered by the agency's chief commissioner in response to soaring staff turnover: 65 percent of employees had left in the past two years, and 37 percent of workers and management remaining were actively seeking other jobs. The report also indicated that staff (rank-and-file)—in contrast to how they felt about the six managers in question—were generally happy with their working relations with their peers in the organization. As this example illustrates, no organization is immune to toxic emotions. The good news is that if CEOs and other managers pay attention to the messages employees are sending, toxicity can be identified and addressed before problems such as the one the Human Rights Commission experienced begin to surface.

Intrusion

EVERYONE CAN NAME a charismatic leader who inspires his followers on behalf of his or the organization's goals. But sometimes those same magnetic personalities contain a flip side that draws followers into an intense work regimen that creates an unhealthy balance between their work and personal lives. They get seduced into the leader's agenda, hooked on an unsustainable workload. Then, when the charismatic leader quits or fails, the followers are often left with regrets and burnout, or else this learned work addiction keeps them permanently off balance.

Jack worked for a very charming and highly energetic boss who "lit up the room." Most of his staff would go to incredible lengths to please him and to meet the targets he set for them. Jack recalls having made special arrangements to spend one December holiday season with his family at an island resort. He had learned that if you didn't book your time off and create some "walls" around it, you could easily find yourself giving it away to meet the latest urgent assignment. This year, as he was packing his computer and readying to leave for the break, his boss walked in. "Something's come up Jack, and we need to get it sorted out in the next few days. I know you'd planned to take this time off, but you really are the only one I can trust to do this right." With his disarming smile and a hand on Jack's shoulder, he implored, "Won't you please do this for me? Perhaps we can sort out some time off for you early in January!" With a sinking feeling in his stomach and a realization of what he'd have to face at home, after a few mild protestations, Jack agreed.

Of course, Jack should have said no. But the power of a charismatic boss is insidious and is often very hard to resist, particularly if intrusion is integral to the relationship between the manager and his subordinates. Intrusion works by building up the apparent irreplaceability of the "victim," the importance of the particular task to the company and to the subordinate's career, and the impossibility that this task can be deferred to another day. Even if Jack had said no, it is doubtful that he would have escaped feeling guilty or uneasy about doing so, and it would have weighed on him while away. The unique toxicity of intrusion is that those who are captured by it work so hard to please their charming boss that they eventually burn out. The manager's charisma and drive blinds employees to their own health and welfare, and they discover this only when things go wrong or when the manager moves on. By then, it's often too late to prevent the damage.

Institutional Forces: Contemporary Corporate Agendas

At Enquiry B.C., a toll-free information service in British Columbia, female telephone operators must wear skirts or dresses; they're forbidden to wear even dress pants. The operators, however, who provide information by telephone about the provincial government, are never seen by the public. Gillian Savage, who quit in the summer of 2000 because of the policy, reported in a newspaper interview that the call center has several such bizarre rules that have led to poor morale, diminished service quality, and huge staff turnover. Another employee still on staff reported that the operators feel so demoralized by the company's policies that many have lost interest in their jobs, even failing to provide the right phone numbers in response to public requests. But despite the fact that ten people out of a total staff of about twenty-five had recently quit, the company's owner defended the dress code in the newspaper article and said she was unaware of any worker discontent.[8]

Toxins, then, can flow from everyday company practices that hurt the people who carry them out. This includes everything from company policies to competing visions within the firm—or worse, lack of vision—that cause confusion and emotional fallout. Such toxicity is frequently unintentional, but it's exacerbated when the organization is insensitive to the ways it affects the people who try to make the system work. Unfortunately, that's exactly what often happens: Top management, like the company owner in the previous example, will appear surprised and even defensive when the toxicity is exposed. If their subsequent responses don't deal with the pain in a constructive fashion, the pain endures and the negative effects on morale and performance continue.

Similarly, companies with inconsistencies between stated policy and what happens in practice foster emotional pain. For example, management may extol the virtues of teamwork as the path to success and even provide mechanisms that celebrate it, such as team-building workshops and team logos on T-shirts. Yet, when the time comes for salary increases, bonuses, and promotions, it becomes obvious to many employees that the spoils go to the individual stars in the company. Loyal staff members are left feeling demoralized, their efforts to collaborate and share their talents with others undervalued. Along the same lines, internal conflicts about budget size for individual operational units can generate resentment and sap initiative, perhaps inevitably. But when these conflicts are used to manipulate and undermine managers, they can be corrosive to relationships and to productivity in the workplace.

Another source of institutionalized toxicity is company policies that are dishonest or misleading. Recruiters sometimes paint pictures of what a job will be like and the endless opportunities awaiting those who can perform well—but in reality that vision might not square with the situation. Then, when the new recruit finds she has fewer resources than promised and less discretion to act effectively, her resulting dissatisfaction and confusion can send her emotional and intellectual commitment to the job spiraling down.

Other kinds of unrealistic expectations—common especially in high-tech companies—can lead to similarly debilitating emotional pain. Demanding schedules and almost impossible "stretch goals," while keeping alive a staff's competitive fires, can also wreak havoc, especially when they keep coming in relentless waves. Employees have no time to recover from their exertions or to renew their creativity, and they often have little or no life outside of work—and burnout ensues. In her book *White-Collar Sweatshop,* Jill Fraser describes as "corporate water torture" the seemingly endless rounds of "cost-cutting, lagging raises, declining benefits, and increased workloads" that white-collar workers experience in corporate America.[9]

Even technology itself can create toxicity in the workplace, especially given the deluge of new technologies that are continually introduced. Dan Stamp, founder of a worldwide training company, Priority Management, calls this "digital depression and IT rage." A full 83 percent of IT managers report having to deal with enraged workers, according to studies that Stamp cites. The damage they inflict on computer equipment includes "everything from ripping out the mouse to hurling laptops against the wall."[10] The source of the frustration? The never-ending flow of electronic items into the workplace that increasingly tie people to the office and to their work. Indeed, because of the growing dependence on computers, cellular phones, and the Internet, the opportunity for disruptions to service (e.g., a server that goes down can interrupt e-mail access for hours) has increased exponentially, and usually comes without warning. While the impact ranges from inconvenience to disaster, IT workers suffer the most, having to deal with other employees' frustration, anxiety, and anger.

Moreover, increasing electronic surveillance of employees through company access to voicemail, e-mail, and other Internet activities is another potential producer of frustration and anger.[11] A recent study of U.S. businesses by the American Management Association, a New York–based training and consulting group, reveals that "three quarters of U.S. businesses now electronically monitor employees in some fashion, double the rate of five years ago."[12]

Although electronic advances are inevitable and contribute positively in many ways (including the understandable need for company vigilance, through surveillance, about illegal use of systems), the resulting intrusion on people's personal privacy, and on their sense of autonomy and life balance, is often experienced as toxic.

Inevitability

SOME KINDS of emotional pain are simply unavoidable, no matter how enlightened an organization's policies or emotionally intelligent its individual managers. Let's look now at some of these inevitabilities of organizational life.

The Impact of Trauma

A clerk in a financial services branch of a large Canadian chain described how a few years before, his immediate supervisor, a man in his early forties, passed away suddenly of a heart attack over the weekend. The supervisor had been at work the previous Friday, but when the staff showed up on Monday, he was nowhere to be seen. When the store manager gathered everyone together for the morning meeting, they could tell by the tone in his voice that something was wrong. "Still, I was unprepared for the shock when he announced that my boss was dead," the clerk told me. "Some of my coworkers, who'd worked with him many years, wept openly. Others went off to be by themselves."

Traumatic situations like this arise from time to time and can cause a great deal of emotional distress. Be it the death of a coworker or an injury to a staff member, everyone feels the painful effects. Other kinds of workplace trauma include unexpected downsizings, especially upsetting for a staff that has been together for a long time. Or trauma can arise from an external source such as a fire, an earthquake, or even, as the people of the United States learned on September 11, 2001, a terrorist attack.

No one can forecast such life-altering events, so naturally no one can blame a particular manager or company policy for the upheaval that results. Nevertheless, even pain that arises from trauma becomes toxic when it undermines people's confidence and hope. While managers cannot control the onset of a natural trauma that affects them or their staff, they can help determine the level and duration of the toxicity. In chapter 3 we will address specific ways that leaders can handle painful situations.

The Exercise of Leadership

A significant and inevitable source of toxins in organizations arises from the fundamental work of leaders. Carrying out change initiatives or redirecting the company's energy and talents is never safe or easy. Nor are the outcomes predictable—including how employees will respond. Colin Powell defines leadership as "the art of accomplishing more than the science of management says is possible."[13] To do this means taking risks, bending and sometimes breaking rules, and more often than not pushing, persuading, and even manipulating others to accomplish things whose end result they may not yet understand. Frequently, this requires leaders to push the limits of what has been done before by an individual, a team, an organization. Consciously or not, leaders create conditions of discomfort and even pain for those who are led.

For example, in his effort to save a crew stranded in space, Eugene Kranz, NASA's manager for the Apollo 13 space project in April 1970, decided to switch ground crews, regardless of expectations and seniority (or feelings) of his staff.[14] Like the surgeon who, despite the discomfort experienced by the patient, removes a cancerous growth to save the patient's life, the leader may need to take pain-inducing actions to create a successful outcome. She'll put intense pressure on her team if a project is falling behind schedule. He'll cut off discussion in meetings and press a particular course of action if he believes it will accomplish the company's goals. Followers may get hurt in the process, and the resulting toxins are a by-product of any push that leaders make for performance or change.

In fact, leaders who do their jobs effectively will always produce a certain amount of toxicity, and even competent leaders have their "off days." What manager has not been inconsistent or insensitive in some situation during his or her career? Who has not micromanaged under duress, when a less intrusive approach might have been more appropriate? Given the difficult jobs that managers are often asked to do, they might sometimes appear short-tempered or abusive. They might make promises they can't keep, or share a confidence unwisely, or underplay someone else's contribution to an idea—all things that create emotional pain.

But what distinguishes good leaders is their *response* to the inevitable pain they create. Good leaders recognize the discomfort they create and construct ways to dissipate toxicity.[15]

The Nature of Organized Life

As we've seen, some kinds of traumas are simply a fact of organizational life. Even organizations with thoughtful, reasoned policies have induced suffering through the unexpected, unintended consequences of those policies. For example, a performance management system overlooks the creativity of some contributions in its efforts to recognize others; a hiring system overloads the organization with skill sets that unexpectedly become redundant, leading to terminations of committed employees.

Sometimes organizational policies and practices constrain the kinds of information staff receives, stimulating frustration or disappointment in the system. When someone is fired or denied a promotion, for instance, often the organization conceals the real reasons to observe legalities or to protect those involved. Nevertheless, the pain of the individual at the heart of such controversy may become shared by others if he was well known and well liked, or if others see the company's action as unjust.

What organizations can do through the acumen and actions of their toxin handlers, and by other, more systematic means, is to deal with the pain as honestly as they can. They can do this either before or after emotional pain arises, dispersing these toxins in a healthy way—just as other healthy systems, such as biological organisms, rid themselves of naturally produced toxins.

Other Sites of Toxins

THE SOURCES OF TOXICITY discussed thus far have focused on the behaviors and impact of managers and the organization at large. But malice, interpersonal incompetence, and insensitivity are all potential characteristics of people—whether or not they hold management or leadership positions. Subordinate employees, customers, boards of directors, and shareholders can become sources of toxicity as well.

Toxic Employees

Art is one of the brightest and most energetic people that his company has ever employed. He was hired into the organization's research and development laboratory two years ago and he has made a number of important contributions to the company's product line. At the same time, he's managed to alienate most of the staff. He bullies the secretaries and other support staff, and he can be quite dismissive of some of his colleagues. "He doesn't suffer fools lightly," says a colleague, and lately it seems that most people in the organization fall into that category, as far as Art is concerned. He's become known as much for his tantrums as for his good ideas. Worst of all, no one seems willing or able to confront him about the toxicity he's producing.

Individuals or groups in a work unit or organization who behave this way are being uncivil. Indeed, a study by Christine M. Pearson and her colleagues found abundant evidence of this kind of workplace incivility, whose perpetrators exhibited the following characteristics: They are rude and show little respect or regard for others. They can make life uncomfortable for their managers and colleagues, intentionally or unintentionally. They can be temperamental; they can sabotage work procedures to settle a score; they can indulge in emotional outbursts that are abusive to their supervisor or colleagues. They can spread gossip, creating factions and setting up scapegoats who are the victims of their careless talk. They can distort or frame language that feeds on others' insecurities or prejudices, poisoning the workplace.[16] And despite the decline of guaranteed employment in many business sectors, there continue to be uncivil employees who avoid doing the "heavy work" of their unit or who otherwise don't contribute effectively to new directions and initiatives. Over time, a single employee can do any or all of these kinds of things, fostering a workplace that is unhappy indeed, because employees who are uncivil are toxic.

The origin of some of this behavior resides in the psychological makeup of the uncivil individual. However, the sheer complexity and fragmentation of the workplace (and of work and information overload) is also to blame.[17] Many people feel there simply isn't time anymore for the "niceties" of a civil life. We are too busy and too pressured to stop and acknowledge our colleagues as human beings. We are too distracted to be mindful of what they are doing. As a result, our words and actions are often hurtful rather than helpful to others.

Not surprisingly, Pearson and her colleagues found evidence of a link between incivility and organizational performance. More than one-half of the employees in their sample (775 employees from widely diverse organizations in the United States) reported that they "lost work time because they were worrying about the uncivil incident that had occurred." More that one-fourth acknowledged that they "wasted work time trying to avoid the instigator. . . . They rerouted former paths to avoid hallway encounters, and they withdrew from collaborative efforts in which the instigator took part." Several of those in the sample (nearly 25 percent) said they "stopped doing their best" as a result of experiences of incivility. Nearly half the respondents contemplated leaving the organization, and in 12 percent of these cases people did eventually quit.[18]

What is particularly disturbing about the impact of this form of toxicity is that it sapped the spirit of supportiveness in organizations. "Through all phases of our study," Pearson reported, "people told us that after being targets (of incivility) they ceased voluntary efforts. Some stopped helping newcomers, others stopped offering assistance to colleagues." Still others quit working on task forces and committees or pulled back their commitment to these and other assignments.[19]

What often compounds such toxicity is the inability or unwillingness of managers or the organization to confront the problematic employee. In some cases, toxic employees are perceived as being too valuable to terminate; in others, they are protected by regulations that make them impervious to sanctions, including termination.

Often an employee's toxic actions result directly from toxicity that they themselves are experiencing from above—from a manager or the organization in general. In fact, a recent survey discovered that 81 percent of workplace bullies ranked higher than their target.[20] So pain begets pain, and the toxicity leaches down through the organization. Trust, difficult to win in the first place, evaporates as workers feel progressively more abused by their colleagues and disconnected from their work. And it is sometimes difficult to uncover the possible organizational prompts for employee-generated toxicity. That same survey showed that toxic workers are usually adept at disguising their incivilities from their superiors, and are often viewed as valued workers possessing unique talents.

Toxic Clients

Sally, a customer service manager in a public relations firm on the West Coast, talks about one particular client, the biggest for her firm, who thought nothing of calling his company contact at any hour of the day or night. Then, often belligerently, he would demand a progress report on a particular project. He would also berate his contact in front of others when that person attended meetings at his organization. "Everyone dreaded working with him," Sally said.

Not all toxicity, then, is generated inside the company. A common external source of pain is unreasonable demands from clients, and the abusiveness that tends to accompany them. Often managers overlook unreasonable client behavior in their eagerness to keep their customers happy. Sometimes companies even lead their clients to believe, through advertising, that employees will respond to irrational behavior graciously.

Some industries—for example, airlines—have institutionalized toxicity. Flight attendants, as the frontline representatives, are expected to personify friendliness to an often highly stressed client base. Travelers expect five-star service provided by happy, eager-to-please flight attendants. So, even in the face of blatant abuse, these service providers "grin and bear it," in part in the interest of safety: No one wants a disgruntled passenger creating a dangerous situation on an airplane. Abuse experienced by flight attendants, then, is regarded as the cost of doing business.

Again, that kind of pain is exacerbated when employees feel unsupported by their organization. For example, when guitarist Peter Buck of the rock band REM was cleared of "air rage" charges made by British Airways, airline executives said they would welcome Buck back as a passenger. The announcement angered the airline staff, some of whom allegedly had been injured by the guitarist during a flight from Seattle to London. Buck hadn't denied his attacks on staff and equipment in the first-class cabin of a British Airways jet. His successful defense rested only on his statement that a combination of sleeping pills and red wine had left him with no recollection of his unruly behavior. But when the airline apparently had no words of condolence for its own employees who were affected by the incident, Amicus, the union representing the cabin crew, considered legal action against British Airways. Union officials said that "BA should have been 'more sympathetic' to staff's feelings before announcing that it would accept Buck back." "That was not a very tactful thing to say—and many staff will be unhappy about it," a spokesman added.[21]

Incidents such as the one at British Airways breed precisely the kinds of toxicity that lead staff to burn out. And when staff burn out or otherwise lose their initiative, they are replaced. In the process, organizations lose capable people and cost themselves thousands of dollars. Indeed, an exhaustive study by Arlie Hochschild, detailed in *The Managed Heart,* examined how airline companies seek to control the emotions of their flight attendants. Workers are taught methods to "prevent an angry response through 'anger-desensitization.'" But labor that involves suppressing one's emotions comes at a high price: Eventually the flight attendants become "alienated from an aspect of self—either the body or the margins of the soul—that is used to do the work."[22]

Other kinds of workers who are expected to curtail their emotions include secretaries, waiters, sales staff, telephone operators, and almost anyone else in the service industry. What all of them share, says Hochschild, is a job that entails (1) face-to-face or voice-to-voice contact; (2) a mandate to produce a particular emotional state (namely, comfort and satisfaction) in the people with whom they come in contact; and (3) an employer who exercises a degree of control over the emotional activities of employees.

Few jobs that require such "emotional labor" offer formal coping mechanisms, so people create their own. Wall Street traders and investment bankers trapped in high-stress jobs have a telling way to cope with the toxicity in their working lives. In a game called "What's our number?" traders target a number that represents the amount of cash necessary to leave their jobs and "begin living." According to writer Ellyn Spragins, the game is played throughout corporate America and includes top managers, "road warriors" who see their families on weekends, and staff lower down the corporate ladder. As long as the money is good, Spragins writes, these workers "[defer] real life, and its unpaid, pedestrian pleasures."[23]

Toxic Hybrids

Frequently, toxins produced in companies come from both the qualities of particular individuals *and* organizational factors. For instance, an inconsistent senior manager may have been promoted based on company practices that celebrate technical competencies, such as financial skills or IT know-how, over a manager's ability to motivate and retain staff. A CEO with a laserlike vision of where the company needs to go may have an equally astonishingly low level of emotional intelligence. While he drives his organization to success in the marketplace, his interpersonal style alienates his team, severing lines of communication that could help him in the future. As a result, staff members learn to keep their heads down and to avoid raising tough issues. And although the bottom line might come out looking great, the leader's tactics, unabated, can create a toxic workplace, stripping the organization of talent and reducing what remains to essentially a company of conformists—a dangerous position for any organization in today's competitive global environment.

A particularly noxious form of toxicity stems from broken promises, which again can come from a combination of actions by a leader and the organization. A January 2001 newspaper report on the United Nations Office for Drug Control and Crime Prevention (UNDCP), in Vienna, illustrates this point well. "The UN office responsible for combating drugs and organized crime," read the leaked letter of resignation by the agency's director of operations and analysis, Michael Schulenburg, "is a façade of meaningless international conferences and broken promises." Schulenburg accused the agency's head, Pino Arlacchi, of traveling around the world "announcing multimillion dollar projects, then quietly canceling them." Schulenburg continued that the staff became "demoralized, intimidated and paralyzed" by Arlacchi's management style, and the organization as a whole was "crumbling under the weight of promises that it is unable to meet."[24]

Not long after Schulenburg's resignation, UN Secretary General Kofi Annan ordered Arlacchi to leave the organization when his contract finished at the end of February 2002. "The move follows months of controversy over Mr. Arlacchi's management style that has put in doubt the future of the UN's programme of fighting the international drugs trade," read an article in the *London Financial Times*.[25] Indeed, the ripple effects of the allegations spread to European donors, including the Netherlands, who decided to cut off their funding of the UNDCP following allegations of Mr. Arlacchi's mismanagement, which were the focus of a damning UN investigation. UN internal overseers who inspected the agency described its decision making and operational system as "more appropriate for a task force than for an established organization that needs clearly defined responsibilities and lines of authority. . . . Mr. Arlacchi, who has said in the past he has been unjustly singled out, could not be reached for comment."[26]

Combined sources of emotional pain—in this case, allegedly both management behavior and deep-seated dysfunction in the organization—clearly affect the way that business gets done every day. Although in themselves not toxic, such sources can produce pain that forms the roots of toxicity, especially when that pain is ignored or mishandled.

The Roots of Toxicity

As we've seen, toxicity is produced when an individual's attitudes or an organization's policies, or both, fail to take into account the emotional attachment people have to their contributions to work. They discount the human qualities of people at the receiving end of an initiative, intervention, or retort. Unfortunately, this lack of sensitivity to others (consciously or otherwise) is an all-too-common trait among people who hold high levels of power and influence, where the name of the game is surviving, prospering, and acquiring control. In themselves, these goals aren't inherently toxic, but they tend to become so when the players ignore how their actions affect others.

One veteran senior manager from a major U.S. corporation put it this way: "The toxic producers, disconnected from their humanity, deliver practices that create damage to others, who are hurt in the process." Another manager I interviewed (who wishes to remain anonymous), a senior HR executive in the retail industry, had this to say about the pain-inducing practices of top management: "Fish stinks from the head! The higher up the toxic person is, the more widely spread is the pain, the more people there are who behave in the same way as that person. All the lieutenants begin to talk and act the same way as the toxic boss. If you have a CEO who delivers public lashings—when he, in effect, does his performance appraisals in public—then you will find that the lieutenants begin to join in."

The key point here is that top managers influence the attitudes and actions of a wide circle of subordinates. Jack Welch observed, "I always told our business leaders their personal intensity determined their organization's intensity. How hard they worked and how many people they touched would be emulated thousands of times over. The CEO sets the tone."[27] When a leader's behavior is dictatorial, is dismissive of the feelings and value of other people in their organization, that style becomes a model in the culture.

But how is a culture of toxicity created in organizations in the first place? It stems in part from the way managers rise to the top, and in part from how they're treated when they get there. To reach the top in many organizations, managers feel they have to turn a blind eye to the toxicity they see and cause along the way. They become dulled to the painful emotional elements of their work. Moreover, as people rise higher and higher in an organization, they find themselves with fewer reality checkpoints and mentors. Noted one senior executive: "By the time you are a CEO, you have no sounding boards. It's hard to express your fears and concerns to people around or below you. You don't want to appear stupid or uncertain." Managers, then, are always at risk of losing touch with what is really happening in the organization and with how their behavior affects others. "All of us in the organization have a part of this," this same executive observes. "We foster the myth that 'the boss must know best' and so we pat him on the back for the good decisions and we don't mention the poor ones. And then we fall into the trap of believing our own PR for the boss, so we get into the habit of turning to the boss."

This absence of corrective feedback for top leaders can enable even more toxic behavior. When the people around them fail to tell leaders how they affect people, it only reinforces the sense of certainty and control they already feel. In the absence of healthy correction, even the most emotionally intelligent of leaders can lose their human touch. Since followers essentially collude in this pattern, in a sense organizations get the toxicity that its managers and practices deserve.

In these ways and others, organizational toxicity is insidious. People learn to lie, and the perpetrators are often unaware that they are doing so. The integrity of their communications becomes lost in "corporate speak" and in the need to cover up the real intentions of their actions. At other times, the lying is intentional. "I was lied to many times by the VP of Operations in our manufacturing company," said one senior executive. "The VP told me over and over again that he was not going to close down our operation. But he knew from the start that that was exactly what was going to happen. He blindsided me." As they try to rationalize their actions and do whatever they can to further their own interests, organizations and their managers become lost in their own fog of lies. They lose their integrity and they risk the reputation of their organization—and they spill toxins into the system along the way.

Finally, the core of toxicity resides in organizations' own drive to survive. "One needs to remind oneself on a daily basis that if you're not contributing to the bottom line, you'll be disposed of," says a senior manager in the automotive industry. "This is true despite the company's and the HR department's assertions that 'we are about people.' Meanwhile, with one snap of the finger, people are gone!" This executive added that it would be healthier if top managers were more honest about the true nature of the company–employee relationship. "If they ask me to swallow 'crap' and they tell me it's 'crap,'" he continues, "I can deal with that, at least for a while. But they tell me it's candy, and it isn't! And they expect me to keep eating it and to be happy." Under such toxic circumstances, people eventually lose heart, with all of the predictable consequences: They make only lackadaisical efforts at work or else they leave their jobs altogether.

We've seen in this chapter that emotional toxins are inevitable in organizations, and that they stem from many different sources. Managers create their fair share of them—something that cannot be avoided entirely, given the stresses, strains, and expectations of getting work done through others. It is true that good leadership by its very nature engenders pain. It pushes people out of their comfort zones—which is necessary to get things done in a world of competition and change. Even so, some managers are malicious, or lack good decision-making or people-managing skills, and therefore unduly contribute to the frustration, anger, and low morale of their employees. These are the managers who betray others and sow distrust, or who buy commitment through the force of their charismatic flair, thereby robbing their followers of critical judgment and their ability to say no when they should.

Not just managers but organizations themselves create conditions for toxicity through policies and practices that fail to include the human factor in their execution. Their modes of production, especially the ever-changing technologies of work, squeeze out time for humanity, for civility, for people to reflect on their actions. The flow of toxicity can also come from outside the organization—from customers and clients who make demands on organizations and their staff that are unreasonable, unprincipled, or just plain abusive. Still other kinds of toxicity simply cannot be avoided, such as illness or a death in the family, an earthquake, a fire, corporate failure, or even a terrorist attack.

We need to recognize that the values we reinforce in our organizations often are a prime source of toxicity. Unbridled attention to the bottom line, regardless of what it takes to achieve a given return on investments, blinds us to the possibilities of even more long-run effectiveness, if we take into account the value and emotional health of our workforce. The toxicity that flows from managers who ignore the emotional costs of their actions (to themselves and to others) can poison the wells of innovation and goodwill in the company. Corporate lies, distortions, and manipulations that cover up mistakes and foster self-aggrandizement do little to benefit any of the stakeholders.

So while pain is inevitable in organizations, it is often destructive to human beings and their relationships. And although companies will always have insensitive people or particular organizational practices that create and spread toxins, there are people and practices that can help to alleviate that pain. Most organized settings employ what I've been referring to in this book as "toxin handlers"—people often working unobtrusively—who mitigate the effects of emotional pain.

In chapter 3 we will look more in depth at the work of these toxin handlers and the critical role they play in organizational life.

CHAPTER THREE

The Work of the Toxin Handler

Soon the Ragman saw the woman sitting on her back porch. She was sobbing into the handkerchief, sighing, and shedding a thousand tears. Her knees and elbows made a sad X. Her shoulders shook. Her heart was breaking. The Ragman stopped his cart. Quietly, he walked to the woman, stepping around tin cans, dead toys, and Pampers.

"Give me your rag," he said gently, "and I'll give you another." He slipped the handkerchief from her eyes. She looked up, and he laid across her palm a linen cloth so clean and new it shined. She blinked from the gift to the giver.

Then, as he began to pull his cart again, the Ragman did a strange thing: he put her stained handkerchief to his own face; and then he began to weep, to sob so grievously as she had done; his shoulders shaking. Yet she was left without a tear.[1]

THERE ARE MANY possible interpretations of the meaning of this story, but in the context of this topic it captures eloquently some of the workings of the toxin handler. The handler sees another person in pain, moves with empathy to remove the suffering, and, in the case of the Ragman, takes it on himself.[2] The woman who was immobilized by the hurt becomes reconnected to hope and can move forward, freed of the pain's debilitating effects that prevented her from functioning.

The work of toxin handlers is about responding compassionately to pain in their organizations in order to either minimize or prevent it, to identify it, contain it, remove it, or find ways for people to live with it constructively. Their compassion takes the form of noticing and feeling the pain of someone else and then acting in a way that is intended to help the other person heal.[3] Their work can help restore hope, confidence, and even joy. Jean Baker Miller and Irene Stiver call this the "zest"—the empowerment and increased self-esteem that people feel when they become connected to someone who demonstrates care and empathic attention.[4]

Why do toxin handlers do the work they do? Surely their motivations come from many complex psychological and emotional roots besides sheer altruism. But it is safe to say that, at the very least, toxin handlers are motivated by a desire to help others recover from pain, to keep work units free from emotional distress that undermines performance, and to help people accept unavoidable pain and thereby create a healthier workplace.

Toxin handlers have a complex profile: They are not only caregivers who help heal people who hurt; they are also leaders who work with pain in ways that are designed to sustain or enhance performance in the workplace. Moreover, they are social architects who contribute to the creation and maintenance of their organizations as healthy, compassionate, and productive systems of relationships.[5] As such, they focus on the emotional needs of individuals and on the emotional linkages and relationships within organizations.

Toxin handlers respond to pain in many ways, small and large, but their work tends to reflect five major themes:

- Listening
- Holding space for healing
- Buffering pain
- Extricating others from painful situations
- Transforming pain

Listening to Pain

A CORE COMPONENT of effective toxin handling involves listening with compassion to someone else's pain, providing a moment of human connection. In the case of Michael from chapter 1—the project manager who worked for the toxic CEO—staff members regularly burst into his office, on fire with anger and frustration. Michael's response was to point them toward a chair while he closed the door. There, he would let them cool down without interruption. "I didn't say much," Michael recalls. "But I would look them in the eye and do a lot of nodding." Just being emotionally present in this way for someone in pain can help them feel that they've been heard and their feelings validated.

Managers who act as toxin handlers, then, not only gain valuable information for resolving the issue at hand; the act of listening itself also can salve the wound. By consciously taking the time to connect with a person in pain and listen to the person's story, the handler helps the healing begin.

That is one reason why Orit Gadiesh, chairman of the international management consulting firm Bain & Co., keeps an open-door policy. "I always have time for almost anybody who comes by. . . . It doesn't matter what the topic is, if somebody wants to talk to me then I am completely focused on them, not on what needs to get done. If that is what is most important to them, there must be a good reason."[6]

At other times, listening entails directing the conversation more strongly so that the person in pain can mobilize a recovery. William Kahn of Boston University describes the case of an office manager in a department store who is upset at her own ineffectiveness at supervising one of her staff. When she brings her problem to the business owner, the owner listens patiently, then asks a few probing questions while withholding judgment. He then validates the office manager's efforts by telling her how impressed he is that she's trying to learn how to be a more effective supervisor. He shows further compassion with her struggles by sharing with her a similar situation he faced in the past. Finally, the owner supports the supervisor by offering feedback about how to reframe the situation in a less constraining way.[7]

What makes toxin handlers such good listeners? Like their professional counterparts (nurses, therapists, and counselors), they have what Patricia Benner describes in highly skilled nurses as the competency of *attunement,* which is the ability to discern the real condition of their patients, despite a contrary diagnosis from a doctor or even from test results. Paraphrasing, we can understand attunement this way: A nurse who is attuned to the condition of a patient can tell when a patient who looks OK according to the charts actually needs help, or conversely, she will pick up underlying strength and healing in a patient who has all the characteristics of someone who is very ill.[8]

Attunement comes from long experience working with people, particularly those who are hurting, and from reflecting on those experiences to discern the cues of what particular kinds of pain look and feel like. It means mentally storing these cues and later retrieving them to help in another situation. Accordingly, a key aspect of attunement is being able to empathize with others, to "imaginatively put oneself in [the] other's place and [to] identify with others' experiences."[9] Indeed, toxin handlers attune to others by conjuring in their minds and bodies what their colleague or subordinate might be going through. They then harness this set of images and feelings to communicate to the other person that they've "got the picture" of her pain. The business owner in Kahn's example draws on a painful story from his own experience that parallels the office manager's story, fashioning a bridge between them for further communicating what's being felt. The person with the problem feels truly heard and will more likely listen to any advice he might offer.

Many toxin handlers report feeling actual physical sensations of other people's emotional pain. For some it's in the gut; for others it's in the chest, neck, shoulders, or elsewhere in their body. This visceral component to toxin handling isn't so unlike the Ragman's sobbing when he took the handkerchief of pain from the woman on the porch.

A manager in a consulting firm described his discomfort when listening to a colleague who was depressed and had lost his confidence: "I felt for Rob, who was really hurting. He didn't look well to me. I did all I could to try to bring him back to life. [Rob eventually recovered from this condition and told the manager that his support was of considerable help to him when he was feeling so "down."] But by the end of that session with Rob, I felt exhausted, as if I'd absorbed some of his negative energy. I could feel it in my belly."

Rob's pain came not from anger or someone else's attack on him but from his own deep despair. Handling Rob's agony, like working with other forms of pain, engaged the manager's mind ("He didn't look well to me") and affected his own emotional and physical responses ("I felt exhausted"; "I could feel it in my belly"). We will discuss in the next chapter the need for handlers to let go of this empathic response, but for now the story illustrates just how toxin handlers are affected by the work they do and yet are still able to do their work so effectively.

In an extensive study of social workers in the United States, William Kahn pinpointed the qualities that make caregivers (which toxin handlers certainly are) such good listeners.[10] Foremost, they are accessible: They are easily located (in their offices or elsewhere, via reliable electronic or other connections) by someone in need. Once found, they reliably allow the time and space to make a meaningful connection. They also ask about what is going on, obtaining information that will help them understand the emotional, physical, and cognitive needs of the other person by probing for his experiences, thoughts, and feelings. They then pay attention, using verbal and nonverbal gestures to demonstrate that they are listening acutely. They validate the other person's worth, showing respect, regard, and appreciation for the person. Moreover, as we already discussed, they empathize with the other person, putting themselves in his place and situation, and letting him know that they understand how he's feeling. They provide support through offers of appropriate information, feedback, insights, interpretation, and protection. They convey compassion through displays of warmth, affection, and kindness. And finally, they are consistent, providing a steady stream of resources—compassion and physical, emotional, and cognitive presence.

As listeners, then, pain managers provide consideration and attention that allow the person in pain to feel heard, respected, and helped. And although such listening lies at the core of the toxin handler's work, it is far from the only task of the handler.

Holding Space for Healing

ORGANIZATIONAL ROUTINES and priorities focus (relentlessly in many cases) on such instrumental ends as meeting targets, completing projects, or delivering service to customers and clients. Managers are rarely attentive to the emotional states of the people doing the work. Continual pressure for high performance and commitment often desensitizes the corporate response to people who may be hurting—be it from an unexpected job loss or demotion, an accident, sudden illness, or even the death of a colleague or loved one. Instead, management looks for (though may not get) "normal" behavior from these employees.

Yet pain of this nature frequently calls for a time-out—for space that provides an opportunity to grieve and regroup. Toxin handlers understand this reality. They pick up on the hurt of those around them, empathize with them, and anticipate how the distress will likely affect their state of mind. They then find ways to create and hold a space that will provide respite—"breathing room"— in the workplace. The space can be both physical (such as a private office where problems can be discussed) and emotional (the toxin handler's own listening ear and compassion). There, people who are hurting have the opportunity to recover their balance and begin reconnecting to their capacity to make good decisions and function effectively.[10]

Of course, while all of this is going on, the work of the organization still needs to get done—which raises another aspect of the toxin handlers' role. "Holding a space" for others to heal often requires the handlers to pick up the slack, covering others' assignments or redistributing their tasks, at least for a while. Often this means they must argue for formal support from superiors, requiring the handlers to find ways to convey the human dimension as well as the facts of what's happening in the painful situation. The job is doubly sensitive, of course, because usually handlers also need to maintain a degree of confidentiality. This takes extra effort, especially if it means redistributing the person's workload without revealing the real reasons why to those who acquire the new assignments. But done successfully, such maneuvering facilitates very positive outcomes for both the people involved and the organization. Tasks are accomplished, and the company retains the vitality of its workforce.

The kinds of emotional pain or trauma that require a "healing space" often come from intentional management actions, such as layoffs, mergers, or the firing of a staff member. Astute organizations that anticipate the resulting emotional fallout hire outplacement specialists or counseling consultants to provide such a space for anyone who needs it. But even such systemic helping mechanisms are often distant from employees' day-to-day emotional experiences, or else the operation is so short-lived that the toxin handler is still needed for the trench work.

Many traumas are unexpected, however, and creating and holding space to allow others to heal is more improvised than planned. In chapter 2, we described how the manager of a retail store told the staff that a supervisor had died suddenly over the weekend. The manager's subsequent actions provide a good example of the space-holding behavior of toxin handlers. The young employee who recounted the story told me that when the store opened for business that day (and for several days afterward), the manager handled the lion's share of the work, including all the deceased employee's appointments. On the day of the funeral, the manager supervised workers who came in as temporary replacements from other branches. Rather than attend a lunch that the staff organized to celebrate the life of the deceased supervisor, the manager stayed behind to clean out the dead man's office. That way, when the doors opened to staff and customers the next day, everyone could start fresh. "It made getting on with our normal business so much easier," the employee told me. "I also found out later that the 'day off work' was not normal company policy. Our manager had fought hard with his bosses so that the entire staff could attend the funeral and gain some closure."

When an event happens unexpectedly, as did the death of the supervisor, it shocks people, upsetting their equilibrium and sense of order. The toxin handler's efforts to deal with the pain in such situations are largely improvised or invented, with little time to rehearse, to consult widely, or to lobby to ensure higher-level support and authorization. The work is guided by what he learns from a sensitive reading of the emotional and practical components of the particular situation; the work is sustained by compassionate and organizationally attuned responses that unfold as the handler intervenes.

Sometimes an organization has systems and policies that facilitate a handler's work, offering a set of procedures for dealing with so-called compassionate cases. But even when such enlightened mechanisms exist, they provide at best only broad guidelines. They do not equip handlers with ready-made practices, and they do not identify the subtleties of a particular emotionally charged situation. Nor can they. The ways that people respond to pain are not universal. Some people become numbed or otherwise uncommunicative and need help to discuss their feelings. Others need to emote, to cry or rage against the situation they're experiencing. Still others need to be directed toward specific actions in order to cope: to go home, see a doctor, or talk to friends. What all of these scenarios have in common is what the toxin handler provides: the healing space in which to process pain.

Incidentally, by providing a space for healing, handlers begin to ease their own pain as well. Like the people around them, toxin handlers are shocked by unexpected events such as the death of a colleague. The handler's own sadness will give him added empathy for others in the same situation, but it will also leave its mark. If intense, it will require at some point that he find ways to work through the pain to allow him to leave it behind. The act of handling pain for others is actually a step toward assuaging this pain.

Creating a healing space, even when improvised, involves the toxin handler in two instrumental activities. One is anticipatory: Leaders who are effective toxin handlers must make a judgment call on the severity of the shock experienced by the staff. They then need to decide on the form and duration that a held space entails and the steps that the organization should take to provide it. Space for one person may mean granting a day off; for another, some quiet time in an office with the door closed; for someone else, a release from work responsibilities for a few weeks.

For example, when Orit Gadiesh from Bain & Co. noticed that one of her long-time managers seemed unhappy, she called him into her office. "I don't need to know what's going on, but I'd like to make it easier for you," she told him. "Would it be better if we halved your case load for the next couple of months?" The manager seemed relieved and took Gadiesh up on the offer. Two months later he returned to tell her he was ready for more work—"and I probably would not have been here now if you hadn't helped me out," he told her.[11]

Buffering Pain

When an organization's leaders issue instructions, edicts, or opinions to people lower down in the ranks, the messages often have an "edge" to them that reflects a negative or discriminatroy opinion or value judgment aimed at the recipients. They may carry performance expectations and deadlines that are unrealistic that, if heard in a particular way, would make staff members feel angry or demoralized.

Toxin handlers often step into such situations quite effectively, drawing on several competencies that make them particularly good buffers. These include the ability to

- reframe toxic messages
- draw on political capital to get desired results
- build relationships
- display personal courage

Reframing

When an organization has difficult information to communicate, toxin handlers often become the official message bearers or may informally intercept and amend the messages to decrease the emotional pain they might cause. For example, one toxin handler at a transportation company was told by her boss: "Tell those idiots out there to get their act together and finish the job by Friday, or else they'll be sorry!" Her response was to pull her staff together and put the directive in a form that conveyed the task but not the sentiment. "The boss needs us to complete this task by Friday," she told them, "so let's put our heads together and see what we need to do to meet this deadline." By taking the sting out of the boss's message, the toxin handler helped everyone to focus on the challenge rather than seeing the directive as an attack on their capabilities.

Like empathetic listening, such reframing of toxic messages helps to buffer their potentially damaging effects. Reframing focuses handlers on the emotional and technical aspects of a message in order to deflect or prevent pain from reaching its intended audience. The handler zeroes in on the meaning of the message itself and how it may affect people. He reads the message or situation and hears and feels the toxin in it—and then dissipates the toxin.

People with high levels of emotional intelligence are particularly good at such buffering. They are tuned to the emotional tones of language and its malleability, spotting reframing opportunities where other people do not. They work from a premise that several possible meanings can be crafted from most organizational information—and they know how to choose the one that will best buffer pain. In this sense, the toxin handler uses "emotional common sense" to ask, "How can I construct this message so that it removes the pain and makes what the words say more hopeful and workable?" The underlying goal: to say what needs to be said while leaving people's self-worth intact.

The boss at the transportation company intentionally sent three messages: "The work must be done"; "the workers are idiots"; "failing to get the job done will lead to punishment." Knowing that the original messages might demoralize the staff or make them resist the instruction, the handler reframed the boss's messages to become: "The boss needs us to get a job done"; "there is a deadline of Friday"; and "let's see what we need to do to complete the job." A potentially disruptive and destructive message was transformed into one that could even energize the staff with a renewed sense of motivation.

To buffer pain effectively, the toxin handler needs to be able to read messages coming through the system and to sense the barbs in them, intentional or otherwise. This attunement is visceral. The handler feels the meaning of the message or evolving situation as it might be experienced by those who will be affected by it. She can visualize and feel the anger, fear, or demoralization that derogatory statements or actions would trigger if they were directed at people personally. The handler is also often particularly quick at recognizing such situations and stepping in to serve as a buffer.

Joyce Fletcher, who was studying engineers in a high-technology company based in the northeastern United States, tells the story of Abby and Sam, two lab partners who were hard at work when their boss walked in and asked Sam a question. Sam, who was harboring resentment toward the boss over a recent lost contract, responded in a derisive way, without looking up from his work. Before he could finish, however, Abby jumped in with the answer for their boss, who then thanked them and left the room. "Sam sometimes twists the knife in harder and harder," Abby explained to Fletcher. "So I just jumped in and answered the question. So I'm the middleman who [is] sort of like a tension breaker, solving two problems at once I guess."[12]

The emotional negativity of a message or action can be fairly obvious—such as Sam's response to his boss—and almost anyone who observes well will sense that this isn't the best way to act. But the difference between the toxin handler and most other people observing a negative situation is that, like Abby, the handler not only knows how to intervene; she is also willing to take the time to do so.

Drawing on Political Capital

Handlers are also adept at creating and using political capital to get the desired results. As good judges of what is possible politically in an organization, they know when to push messages or initiatives back to the sender to be "detoxified," when to simply cut the toxins out of the communication flow, or when to prevent an order from being carried out. The toxin handler also catches more subtle politically motivated sources of pain and nips them in the bud.

Savannah, a project manager in a transportation company, led a team implementing a new promotion program that was based on performance rather than seniority. Resistance within the organization was enormous, but in this case, the program went through. In the process of implementation, however, many employees verbally attacked Savannah's team members. "It was a case of 'kill the messenger,'" Savannah says. "All the anger and bitterness that people felt for top management was directed at us."

As a toxin handler, however, Savannah worked hard to protect her team from the worst pain of the attacks. A senior manager who opposed the new policy, for instance, sent a personally insulting letter to one team member. Savannah intercepted it and sent back a memo that instructed him to send all future correspondence directly to her. The tactic worked. Another senior manager opposed to the policy tried to punish Savannah's team by moving it to smaller, less attractive office space. Savannah deflected the move by calling in some political IOUs in the organization. She had enough support in a management meeting to get the move overturned—and her team stayed put.

Building Relationships

Buffering also entails being willing and able to use one's influence to change the nature of an intervention. Toxin handlers are often good at building relationships and working with people. They have strong interpersonal skills, and their ability to listen well to others and to frame their own messages in constructive ways builds political points with people throughout the organization.

"I take the time to find out how my colleagues are doing, and I file away mentally issues they mention that I may be able to help them with later," said one handler. Said another: "I feel that being part of a team is very important if we are to succeed as a company. When calls for support come my way, I do what I can to keep this spirit alive by being responsive with resources and anything else that might help." Knowing what is going on for other managers helps handlers keep a pulse on the emotional climate in the organization. Moreover, developing relationships by being helpful to others builds capital for times when handlers need to create and implement interventions that protect their own staff. Thus handlers build networks of colleagues who will in turn listen to them and who can be persuaded to support the handler's initiatives. That was precisely Savannah's advantage in heading off the people who tried to sabotage her project.

Displaying Personal Courage

Finally, pushing back to buffer pain is often an act of personal courage. Handlers fight battles and take stands to help others that can put their own positions at risk. They are doing, in fact, what good leaders and managers should do to help their staff. With their innate attunement to others' pain, toxin handlers harness their concern for people—or their moral justification in defending a project—to stand up for others, often risking their own careers. As was the case with Savannah, they understand the cost of *not* intervening.

Harry, the toxin-handling CEO we discussed in chapter 1, believes this kind of buffering intervention should come from the top. "I don't believe that toxicity should run downhill," he said. "I believe you should suck up the bullshit and then present a problem to the staff that they can handle and be held accountable for." Harry was also clear about the need to buffer emotions that can destroy good working relationships. "The CEO should contain the bad emotions so they don't get through to the rest of the organization. I don't want to yell at somebody else because I was yelled at by my board or by my managers."

BOX 3-1 BUFFERS BETWEEN NATIONS

There is another form of buffering that deserves attention here—the important work of peacekeeping. Peacekeepers can be found at all levels of the organization. They're often the people mediating behind the scenes when there's a major dispute between a boss and subordinate or a feud between coworkers.[13] But peacekeepers also operate on a grander scale—as sanctioned buffers between warring factions in conflicted regions of the world (e.g., between Tutsis and Hutus in Rwanda)—offering valuable lessons for the microcosm of the organization.

Obviously, peacekeepers operate with a different mandate than do toxin handlers in corporations or other organizations. But they resemble organizational handlers in that they act to reduce emotional and physical pain so that conflicts can be explored in constructive ways. Their typical mandate is to prevent or reduce fighting and bloodshed between parties and forestall the infringement of human rights.

Like toxin handlers in organizations, peacekeepers witness much pain (albeit of greater intensity than their corporate counterparts see), and they try to deal with its effects even when they're unable to remove its sources. Rather, they act as "safety valves"; they work within the situation they inherit to prevent further pain when possible, and to absorb pain that is generated when parties in conflict act out their aggressions.

An important point is that, although the pain handler's acts of courage feature in large and small ways throughout the organization, often they go unnoticed. Which is usually just what the handler, always acting with utmost discretion, prefers: to help in ways that don't embarrass others or draw undue attention to someone's pain.

The Toxic Tandem

An intriguing form of buffering pain can occur in a relationship I call the "toxic tandem": a toxic boss who has a toxin handler regularly by his side. Whether by intention or accident, the toxic boss finds a partner to prevent pain or to mop up the pain she causes. The boss has no interest or competence in managing interpersonal relations, and she's indifferent to the pain she inflicts. Her toxin-handling partner, however, has the emotional intelligence and the predisposition to deal with it. The handler also has the interpersonal skills needed to convince the toxic boss that he, the handler, can deal with the toxic fallout from the boss's actions.

The handler deflects, dissipates, or absorbs pain caused by the boss, thereby effectively providing an antidote to the boss's "poison" and becoming, in a real sense, the boss's personal pain manager. As effective as the toxic tandem can be, however, it can also be overused and abused. Later I shall discuss in detail healthier alternatives to the tandem. These include having the toxin producer dispose of his or her own "waste," ensuring that pain disposal is the job of more than just a few toxin handlers, and introducing a healthier set of policies and practices for dealing with people in the organization.

The tandem is something of a "bad cop/good cop" configuration, but the two managers rarely articulate this strategy to each other. It is an emerging and rather tacit relationship. Usually it begins when a handler realizes that a malicious, incompetent, or insensitive boss needs to be managed; the pain-generating boss might then notice that "things go more smoothly" when she listens to the handler or lets this partner do the "people work." By teaming up with a toxin handler, a toxic boss implicitly acknowledges that she needs someone to soften her blows or pick up the pieces after her emotional storms. The boss's intentions thus are communicated to staff without the disruptive effects of her toxic style. The pairing is not unlike those found in families where one family member steps in to smooth the dysfunction generated by an abusive or troubled parent or child.

This organizational partnership is not surprising, since toxic managers without competent handlers alongside them alienate and demoralize their staff in the long run. Some toxic bosses realize that if their abusive tendencies became known by their board or by those who assess their performance, they might face censure or even be fired. Their toxin-handling partner protects them against these outcomes. (Many toxic bosses are highly adept at managing their superiors, however, and they can present themselves in ways that mask their toxicity. Often it takes years, if ever, until they're "found out.")

Occasionally, the partnership between toxic boss and toxin handler lasts for years. In one case, a toxic boss brought his "chief lieutenant" with him from one job to another for fifteen years. This toxin handler routinely filtered the boss's anger and prevented chaos. After meetings filled with belligerent tirades, for instance, the toxin handler would walk from office to office, explaining the boss's "real" opinions and assuring people he was not as angry as he seemed. Thus the organizations they worked for continued to function.

However, many toxic bosses don't fully appreciate the extent of the toxin handler's interventions or recognize the benefits that result from them. Or, they eventually take this protection for granted. If the handler burns out and leaves the organization, the boss's toxicity then begins to leak out directly on the staff, leading to low morale and high turnover. Eventually the word gets out that the organization is "not a good place to work," and it then fails to attract high-caliber recruits.

Sometimes the symbiotic relationship between boss and handler becomes counterproductive. When toxin handlers enable people and organizational systems to continue generating pain, year after year, with no corrective consequences, they in effect "cover up" the sources of pain—to everyone's detriment. For example, Justine, a toxin handler in a government agency, continually covered up for her boss and protected her own staff from the boss's criticism. But later she decided that may not have been what was best for the organization or the staff:

"I think it might have been a mistake to act as a buffer for so long. In hindsight, was I doing the boss any favors? Was I doing my staff any favors? Maybe I should have told them: 'This is the way it is. I have no idea what he wants. Go and see him and see how you get on.'"

If they're not careful, then, handlers may prolong and even encourage the generation of pain from the abuser. Because toxic bosses have been protected from the negative emotional consequences of their behavior, they have no need, or appreciation of the need, to change their behavior. Dangerously high levels of toxicity are therefore masked in the system, delaying diagnosis and remedies. Handlers in this kind of relationship "fly very close to the sun" and, like Icarus from the fable, risk being burned out or "contaminated" by their constant proximity to the source of the toxicity. They tend to lose their perspective on what is fair. Their constant reframing of the boss's toxic behavior becomes a rationalization of it. Tactical positioning of the abusive messages to get work done becomes uncritical acceptance of his actions. The line between toxin producer and toxin handler becomes blurred—affecting the handler's judgment, health, and, eventually, effectiveness.

It is important to reiterate, however, that this tandem relationship can and often does serve a useful function. Pairing a boss who has strong technical or financial ability but weak "people skills" with someone who is adept at interpersonal issues can create a healthier situation than if the toxin producer worked alone. To keep the arrangement healthy, however, the boss needs to be aware of his limited emotional intelligence—and of how he is harnessing the handler's skills to benefit staff and to meet organizational objectives. The boss then consciously delegates the responsibility for the emotional well-being of the staff to his handler, while retaining accountability for the result.

Extricating People from Painful Situations

GREG, a senior manager in a Canadian national bank, was concerned about a young, promising clerical staff member who'd been moved several months earlier into a new department. The department's manager hadn't wanted the new employee, and things were not going well. Greg was hearing reports from the manager about how incompetent the transferred clerk was. "I was told she was a rising star," said the manager, "and all I see is errors and lack of initiative."

Greg, however, remained convinced of the employee's potential. He also knew that this manager was a hard-driving, bottom-line type who did little to develop his subordinates unless they behaved just like he did right from the start. Working behind the scenes with the HR manager, Greg arranged for the clerk to be moved to another area with a manager who had a good track record as a mentor. The transfer was framed as a "developmental opportunity" for the clerk and as a chance to meet an urgent need in the new area. Greg commented later, "The whole thing had to be done very tactfully and with political sensitivity—including getting buy-in from the HR department—or else the woman would have been labeled a whiner and a loser, and I would have been accused of meddling by her boss. In the end, everyone won." The clerk settled into her new position quickly, blossomed, and in later years became a senior manager herself.

As this example shows, sometimes the only way to help people stuck in a toxic situation is to get them out of it. One expects that someone in such a predicament would remove himself from the situation, and many do. But sometimes people lose the confidence or the courage to act on their own behalf. Toxin handlers, then, can play a rescuing role by identifying sites where valuable employees may be floundering.

For example, a manager in a particular unit might let a worker know, through direct or indirect feedback, that her contribution isn't valued. Perhaps the manager inherited the worker from another manager and then found that their styles were incompatible. Even though the employee may have considerable potential, the manager's lack of confidence in her over time makes her doubt herself, creating a self-fulfilling prophecy. A staff member's self-confidence can similarly deteriorate when units or organizations merge, and what was once a constructive working climate becomes a poisonous one. The managers of these merged units may not be inherently toxic, but they're often not attuned to the qualities of the staff they inherit—and thus don't value people's contributions as much as they deserve.

As we just saw with Greg, the senior bank manager, toxin handlers' work in these situations can be tricky. Usually they succeed only if they happen to be in a staff function such as human resources or are otherwise senior to the toxic site's manager. The handler must operate well behind the scenes to intervene, because a manager who has somehow poisoned a site cannot easily be confronted. Confrontation may lead to a backlash against the worker or the toxin handler, who can become labeled as interfering or undermining. Because bad bosses can and often do produce high bottom-line performance in their units despite their harmful behaviors, toxin handlers have to demonstrate real harm to a particular employee if they hope to extricate her. The move must win acceptance by both someone higher in the organization as well as the manager of the new unit to which the employee will transfer.

Handlers (again, usually HR people in these cases) therefore often work without the unhappy employee's knowledge, spending time negotiating with others (including a prospective new boss) to move the employee to a more supportive atmosphere. Such transfers require buy-in from several key players and require tact from the handler. Neither the manager of the toxic site nor the worker in pain tend to know all the reasons for the move. In fact, in the case of the clerk that Greg stepped in to assist, the clerk herself never learned the real story behind her transfer. As we also saw in that example, the way that the handler frames the situation is key to successfully removing the person from a painful site. The transfer needs to be seen as a win for everyone. Handlers cast the employee in a positive light, minimize the personal negativity of the current boss, and help the managers of both units to see the benefits to them and their departments.

Transforming Pain

TOXIN HANDLERS don't just try to remove the pain around them. They are often adept at helping people to view it in a more positive light, thereby transforming the toxicity and enabling people to move beyond a painful experience. Handlers do this by drawing on a set of skills that includes

- framing pain in constructive ways
- changing the view of painful experiences
- empathic teaching

Framing Pain in Constructive Ways

Alexandra, a vice president at a large financial institution in New York, was responsible for commercial and small-business accounts, but in reality she spent at least 50 percent of her time counseling coworkers. Most often, the staff issues stemmed from encounters with the newly minted M.B.A.'s the bank hired periodically.

"They always came in acting like they owned the world. Let's just say they tended to be pretty arrogant and heavy-handed with the secretaries and clerical workers," Alexandra recalls. Her first job, then, was to explain to her staff that these young professionals were really good people inside, just seriously lacking in interpersonal skills. Then she had to pull the M.B.A. recruits into her office and help them understand that being a boss didn't mean bossing people around. "And I had to do that without getting their backs up," she recalls. "Otherwise they would have panicked, and that would have killed productivity. It was incredibly delicate stuff."

Handlers can create and hold space for others to deal with their pain; they can buffer it and even help people get out of toxic situations. Sometimes, however, they must deal with pain that cannot be encircled or buffered or escaped. The toxins that arise through ongoing emotionally unskilled behaviors and from inevitable side effects of organizational policies or actions are often simply realities everyone must accept. The handler's job, then, becomes resolving these situations in ways that help people see these inevitable sources of pain in a constructive light—in a real sense, transforming the pain.

Alexandra embodies this kind of toxin handling. She deals with the ill will generated by professionals' treatment of secretaries, framing each side to the other in a helpful way (to staff, "these young professionals are really good people inside," and implicitly to the M.B.A.'s, "staff do important work here, and you need their services"). She also coaches the M.B.A.'s to develop more respectful responses toward staff and a more emotionally sensitive perspective on being a boss. Neither the staff nor the young managers are removed from handling this situation, but the reasons for their behavior are explored and cast in terms that make their relationship more workable. The sensitivity of such toxin-handling work is affirmed in Alexandra's reference to the delicacy of the interactions she initiated to change the way the M.B.A.'s treated administrative staff.

Changing the View of Painful Experiences

Many potentially toxic situations in organizations cannot be changed in the short run and therefore require the constructive "translation" that toxin handlers can offer. For example, difficult CEOs or senior managers will rarely change their styles even if they understand that they're hurting people. Similarly, pain resulting from the prospect of a merger or layoffs often can't be avoided. Alexandra, the VP in the previous example, also had to deal with just such a scenario at her bank. "I spent hours on end talking other managers through their fears and insecurities around our possible merger with another bank," Alexandra says. "It was in the newspaper regularly, and people would come running to my office. Everyone was terrified they were going to get fired. One by one, I would calm everybody down so they could get back to their real jobs."

Much of the toxin handler's work to transform situations, then, occurs through changing the view of painful experiences. And in fact, very little of what goes on in organizations can be reliably defined by a single interpretation of what has taken place and why. Writes Jane Dutton, "Even events, developments, and trends that have clear beginnings and endings, such as the precipitous drop in the stock market on one Monday during October, 1987 or the [then] upcoming unification of European markets in 1992 can be interpreted differently."[14] The language we use, therefore, and the labels we provide for what we believe has happened in a particular organizational event become powerful tools. They direct our own and other people's attention and motivation toward what comes next in the process. Dutton goes on to say that managers can choose to construct situations as possibilities instead of as problems, as opportunities rather than threats. Toxin handlers can help people facing painful situations to transform them into ones that can be managed, that allow for empowered action rather than paralysis and despair.

David Crisp, recently retired senior vice president of human resources at the Hudson Bay Company in Canada (one of the country's leading retail chains) helped his staff to see difficult situations constructively by encouraging them to create a plan of action that could help them through stressful times at work as well as give them a realistic appraisal of the situation they all faced. "I tell them that this is a tough period, and workwise we have to get through it. We have to put things in the right priority so we get our butts kicked as [little] as possible and we can feel proud that the right things got done," he told me. Crisp (currently a leadership consultant) also reminds staff of the importance of making time for themselves and their families.[15]

"So you are helping your staff put together a plan to deal with the circumstances. And sometimes a staff member might go home saying, 'That was a crappy day, I didn't get done the key things. I know I'm going to get yelled at but it's absolutely OK. I am on plan as best as I can be.' And so they can turn it off and go do something recreational." That way, he says, his people can sleep at night understanding that a bad day doesn't mean everything's lost. "They know they'll have to adjust the plan instead of agonizing over things that can't totally be fixed."

Crisp's attitude corresponds to a distinguished and growing body of research that demonstrates the benefits of constructing experiences that people view in a positive light, rather than a negative one. One early review of this approach cites research showing a connection between positive emotion and creativity, risk-taking and problem-solving strategies, stronger motivation to perform, greater persistence on the job, and more efficient and speedier decision making.[16]

Another provocative stream of studies has been undertaken over many years by Shelley Taylor at the University of California, Los Angeles. In studying people who look at painful situations through "rose-colored glasses," Taylor and her colleagues found many health-giving effects.[17] Study after study showed that people who deal with pain and illness through "positive illusions" are more likely than their pessimistic counterparts to recover from their condition or to experience greater peace and well-being—even if their actual circumstances don't change or even deteriorate. That is, they discount a so-called hard realities diagnosis of a painful situation ("This is your condition and here are the facts about the unlikely chances of recovery"), and instead favor a more optimistic set of beliefs and practices ("I will find a way to overcome this problem") that could be considered illusionary, given the person's actual condition.

People who handle the pain of others in organizations intuitively understand the benefits of such positive thinking and harness this potential to help people in emotional pain anticipate more hopeful outcomes. Thus even though some hurtful actions and decisions in organizations cannot be avoided, the way the pain is viewed can be changed. The meaning of the experience and the reasons for it can be revisited and given a more helpful and empowering interpretation. A senior manager in charge of human resources in a large corporation describes his approach to uncontrollable sources of pain when they arise in his organization: "I sit down with my staff and examine with them the nature of thc assignment. We identify the sources of pain, but I also tell them that we can't avoid doing the job. It's going to be painful, but let's not get 'bent out of shape.' We will get through this. What can we do to make it less painful and more constructive?"

Clearly there are dangers in helping people to accept pain that they experience in the organization. This smacks of condoning unfair and disruptive behavior, and it could be argued that it enables and sustains toxicity. Indeed, we will look later at these kinds of dysfunctional effects of toxin handling. For now, however, the point is that all sources of toxicity cannot be removed from organizational life, and that positive reappraisals of the situation can help people deal with the pain constructively and creatively.

Empathic Teaching

Consider the following vignette in which, by reframing an experience, a toxin handler acts as a kind of coach, helping someone recover his effectiveness on the job. During a monthly meeting, Andy, a new staff member in a service organization, found himself barraged by angry questions from the CEO. Bewildered by the attack, particularly since he felt he'd done a good job in the time frame he'd had, he left the room visibly upset. Soon after, one of the managers who observed the attack approached Andy's boss, who'd also attended the meeting. "Is Andy OK?" he asked. "Are you going to speak to him?" Andy's boss replied that he already had; he had explained to Andy that this was not about him at all. The CEO was frustrated about the pace of implementation of his new policy, and he was sending a message to everyone about his displeasure. "I told him that the CEO uses this tactic a lot," Andy's boss said, "and that I probably should have warned him, [Andy], before the meeting, and I apologized for not doing so. I mentioned that we know how this works and how we have all adjusted to it." Andy seemed relieved at hearing this, and the boss decided he'd also put a word in the CEO's ear that "he might want to lighten up on new members of the team or pick on someone more experienced next time."

In this case, the handler—the newcomer's boss—reinterprets the event in such a way that the latter has a way to understand the source of his pain, to put it in a different context and then let it go. The handler also says he will push back at the source of the pain (the CEO) and try to coach him to be less toxic in his future behavior. This case also includes the action of yet another manager, who ensures that someone is attending to the hurt employee.

By working with the dismayed staff member to restore his confidence and empower him to move forward again, the boss in this example did what Joyce Fletcher calls *empathic teaching*. This process, which focuses exclusively on the needs of the person in pain, "takes the learner's intellectual and emotional reality into account and focuses on the other (what does s/he need to hear) rather than on the self (what would I like to say?)."[18] Handlers thus make a potentially toxic experience less threatening or painful. Alexandra, from the earlier example, did this in two instances: when she taught secretaries to manage the new M.B.A.'s (and the M.B.A.'s to become more responsive bosses) as well as when she gave distressed staff special attention during the proposed merger.

While much of the work of the toxin handler goes on behind the scenes and is therefore mostly tacit, often those who are helped later come to appreciate what has been done. Their loyalty toward the handler—and often, the organization—is enhanced, and they can even internalize the handler's actions so that they too learn to respond effectively when they see people in pain. "I would go through a wall for my boss," said one manager, who worked in a management consulting firm. "When my mother died suddenly, my boss, who is an exceptionally busy man, not only came to the funeral, which I sort of expected, but he also came to the burial and to the wake. He gave up a morning for me and my family, without any fuss or fanfare. I have never forgotten his kindness." The branch employee who told the earlier story of the manager's actions to create breathing space for his staff after the death of a colleague also hoped that "one day I'll be able to manage this way with my own staff."

Clearly, then, the positive impact of toxin handling on those who are helped can go well beyond the immediate situation.

The work of toxin handlers, as we have seen, is complex, subtle, and demanding. It is a necessary and often inevitable part of the healthy functioning of organizations. A whole repertoire of skills and competencies—listening, holding space for healing, buffering pain, extricating people from painful situations, transforming pain—is employed in toxin handling. When these skills are executed well, they can help people who are suffering to better cope with painful situations. The use of these skills can prevent toxins from flooding the workplace. But beyond the impact of handling techniques, such as those described in this chapter, is the sheer effect of the presence of a toxin handler in the organization. Simply knowing that someone has this role can have a

BOX 3-2 TRANSFORMING PAIN THROUGH EXAMPLE

The forms that transforming pain takes can sometimes be very subtle—but nevertheless extremely effective. Sometimes people handle toxins around them almost without being aware that they're doing so, through the simple but powerful example of their own inner strength, or the compassion they embody, or both. I came across one such person when I was receiving treatment for cancer at a naturopathic outpatient clinic.

For several hours each day, I would sit in a common room, hooked up to an IV alongside other patients receiving similar kinds of treatment. On one occasion, I struck up a conversation with the woman next to me. She was someone who exuded great warmth to everyone around her. As we talked, she told me of the long battle she was having, first with ovarian cancer and more recently with brain cancer. She had had several bouts of surgery. Her regular doctors had said she had little time left to live—but here she was, working with a doctor of naturopathy using an alternative therapy.

Despite her medical condition, she embodied profound inner strength and positive energy. One would never have known the extent of her illness and the direness of her condition. She looked frail, but her eyes never showed it. They were so bright and so clear that you could almost see her spirit through them. There was no sense of her being a victim of these cancers or of her being vanquished by them. Nor would they dampen her joy for living. She so moved and inspired me that I found myself thinking, "If she can handle her situation with such grace and such vitality, then I can deal with my condition well, too."

When she died in January 2000, two and a half years after we first met, I was asked to say a few words at her funeral, and I told this story of how she'd inspired me. Afterwards, many people in the church audience approached me with their own stories of how this woman had similarly inspired them in their daily lives. She was simply a person who, by the way she lived her life, had a healing and uplifting effect on those she met.

Perhaps, then—like the contagious aspect of emotions that Daniel Goleman writes about—people's displays of resilience can help enable similar responses in those around them, transforming pain into hope.[19]

calming effect for others in the organization. An employee in a bank expressed it to me this way: "When you know there's a doctor on board a plane, you feel safer making the flight. Knowing there's a toxin handler in my organization has the same effect on me." The toxin handler steps between sources of pain and its targets in the organization. At its most productive, this work protects an individual or group from the impact of pain or even removes it, so that everyone can continue their tasks with their self-esteem intact or restored. When successful, the toxin handler can feel extreme joy and satisfaction in the work as she observes the people she's helped to begin to heal.

Of course, considerable costs and risks may also lie in store for people who do the difficult work of toxin handling. In chapter 4, we examine these side effects and the reasons behind them.

CHAPTER FOUR

The Toll on Toxin Handlers

In 1990, Dave Marsing, a plant manager for Intel, was assigned to turn around one of Intel's microprocessor fabrication plants near Albuquerque, New Mexico. The situation he inherited was dire: The plant's yield rates were bad and getting worse, and senior management was pressing very hard for a quick solution. Employees were in pain, too, saying that unrealistic pressure from above left them anxious and frustrated. "I was trying to be a human bridge between all the parts of the company and cope with all the emotions," Marsing recalls. "On the outside, I was soothing everybody and work was getting back on track, but on the inside, I was in turmoil. I couldn't sleep, couldn't eat."

Two months after Marsing arrived on the job, at thirty-six, he suffered a near-fatal heart attack. "The heart attack was the result of a hereditary condition that got pushed over the edge from the stress," said Marsing. Later, when he became Intel's vice president of the technology and manufacturing group and general manager of assembly/test manufacturing,

Marsing made important lifestyle changes, such as incorporating stress-management techniques into his workday.[1]

ONE OF THE BIGGEST DANGERS of handling toxins is becoming toxic to yourself—as Marsing learned, and as I did in my own experience as a manager (recounted in the prologue). Too often, handlers become so immersed in the work of healing others that they are unable or unwilling to recognize the toll being taken on their own mental and physical health. The negative repercussions of toxin handling are particularly high when (1) the role is played for too long and the toxic condition becomes chronic (when handlers must deal with a continuous stream of others' emotional problems); and (2) when the level of toxicity is acute (because of a particularly painful episode, or more typically, as in the Marsing case, because too many different toxic events converge on the handler simultaneously).

The result? Toxin handlers, over time, experience a number of negative effects that if untreated begin to dull their sensitivities as handlers, the effectiveness of their technical work, and the health and quality of their own lives. They become overwhelmed by all the pain they are trying to cope with and to heal; it numbs them to their own and other people's feelings. And because handlers usually work alone, keeping to themselves the pain they're managing, they become isolated and trapped in the role. The confidential, behind-the-scenes work they do rarely allows them opportunities to unburden themselves to others or otherwise dissipate the toxicity.

HR specialists, in particular, are often in the most danger. By handling one difficult situation after another, usually with no respite or any tangible organizational "win" to claim and enjoy, they soon burn out. Still, dealing with people's emotions is often considered an implicit part of an HR person's job. So what about toxin handlers in other areas of the organization? They sometimes end up feeling anxious or guilty about this role, since helping people in pain takes time away from their assigned tasks—be they preparing budgets, writing reports, or getting a product out the door.

Managing Pain: Not in the Job Description

"I FEEL THAT HELPING PEOPLE with their emotional issues is work done *in addition* to my regular tasks," said one manager at a lumber company. Many handlers, in fact, told me that they frequently work late into the night and on weekends to "catch up" with their technical assignments, since the work of handling toxins consumes a great deal of their day.

Of course, toxin handling has its intrinsic rewards; otherwise people wouldn't do it. Many handlers, in fact, have very positive images of their work. One such person described herself as a "human modem"; another as a "human bridge" (also the term that Marsing used). Moreover, people in formal handling roles, such as HR specialists, usually find ways to derive satisfaction and motivation from the work itself rather than looking for acknowledgment from the organization. For others, helping people can be a means to a satisfying end when it helps the handler herself get her own work done. For example, a project leader who somehow removes or contains pain among her team members will more quickly meet her goals.

But apart from whatever kind of personal satisfaction a handler might feel, working to alleviate the pain of others in organizations is rarely rewarded, encouraged, or supported. As one handler, a former vice president in the banking industry, observed: "You have to get your reward for doing this kind of work within yourself, because you rarely get recognition from the corporation."

Emotional work, then, gets bootlegged onto the manager's agenda. As a result, even she doesn't give it the weight it deserves as a valued contribution to the company's well-being. Moreover, she feels little hope for ever receiving support for this work, since in most organizations "emotions" is a taboo subject: Leaders too often equate emotions and emotionality with weakness, something to be dismissed or even ridiculed (or both). The vital work of handling pain is therefore discounted by both the handler and her organization—and so disappears from sight.[2]

The cumulative effect of working regularly with organizational pain—and receiving little support for that work—is that handlers wear down physically, mentally, and emotionally. To understand this phenomenon better, let us examine three sources of burnout:

- the nature of the work of toxin handling itself;
- the handler's own behavior; and
- the organization's actions, policies, and attitudes.

The Toll from Toxin Handling Itself

ONE OFFICE WORKER at a government institution that was being squeezed of resources described his unseen role this way: "People come to me and 'throw up' their problems all over me," he said. "I do what I can to help or involve someone higher in the organization. Then, when I've had enough, I go find a manager and I 'throw up' all over him." The metaphor of feeling "thrown up on" is a powerful image of the way that toxicity can be experienced in organizations—and of its effects on the handler.

Not surprisingly, the most common toll of toxin handling—whatever its cause—is *burnout,* psychologically, physically, and professionally. For example, Michael, the project manager with the difficult CEO (described in chapters 1 and 3), had to take a year off from his job to recover from the stress of dealing with a toxic boss before he could rejoin the company in another capacity. And while professional pain managers such as psychiatrists are trained to look for the warning signs of excessive stress in their bodies—such as stiff necks, nausea, and headaches—toxin handlers in organizations are amateurs. Like untrained workers at a radioactive site, they toil in danger zones. Without protective procedures of some kind they can become very sick, or at the very least lose their zest and their capacity to perform.

Savannah, the project manager at the transportation company cited in chapter 3, is a case in point. Assigned by company leaders to head a team implementing a new promotions program, she faced much resistance within the ranks of the organization. For the most part, she was able to buffer her team from the worst of the toxins. However, she wasn't able to protect herself quite as well. After several months, she recalls, the stress began to get to her. "At work, I would be strong for my team, but at home, I cried a lot," she said. "I slept away from my husband, although I didn't actually sleep very much, and often felt terribly depressed. The worst part, though, [was] the panic attacks, which would come on so suddenly. My heart would pound, and I would lose my breath."

Another toxin handler, who spent much of her time protecting her staff from her own abusive boss, talked about how she felt continually angry. She eventually quit. While she was between jobs, she was invited to join her old colleagues for dinner—and was reminded again of why she left. She captures the toxicity of her former workplace this way: "I just looked at them and I thought, 'That was me!' Stressed out, unable to concentrate, returning obsessively to the latest crisis, not being able to follow the flow of conversation. They were in a terrible state. And two weeks before, I had been the same way."

These are stories I've heard again and again from toxin handlers in managerial positions, in particular. They told me of bouts of depression, severe heart palpitations, hyperventilating, chronic sleeplessness, and cases of pneumonia. Two of the managers I interviewed were diagnosed with cancer. But these cases aren't just anecdotes. Scientific evidence has demonstrated a strong link between stress and illness, first documented in the 1950s by Dr. Hans Selye, the renowned Canadian medical researcher who was professor and director of experimental medicine at the University of Montreal. Selye found that overwhelming stress leads to a breakdown of the protective mechanisms in the body—in other words, that stress compromises the body's immune system.[3]

More recent studies have shown similar results. In 1993, an analysis of two decades of research on the connection between stress and disease concluded that stress can compromise the immune system so severely that it hastens the spread of cancer, weakens resistance to viral infections, increases the risk of heart attacks, and raises blood pressure.[4] Incidentally, the report says, stress puts intense pressure on the biological areas most susceptible to attack. Thus, if a person's cardiovascular system is prone to weakness, his response to stress might be a heart attack; in someone else with, say, a particularly weak intestinal system, chronic stomach ailments might appear.

In the short run, stress can cause fatigue and irritability, diminishing the toxin handler's effectiveness. In the long run, however, the toll of stress on the toxin handler redoubles, aggravating heart problems, raising blood pressure, and lowering immune systems.[5] Studies at East Tennessee State University have shown that mental stress "can double or even treble the chance of death for individuals already at risk for heart disease." Doctors at the State University of New York at Stony Brook have linked stress to prostate cancer, while researchers at Carnegie Mellon University have shown that people under stress "are more likely to develop infections."[6]

Moreover, research shows that the negative effects of stress last a surprisingly long time. In one study, published in the *Journal of Advancement in Medicine* in 1995, researchers asked groups of healthy volunteers to focus on one of two emotions: anger or compassion. Measures were then taken of a key immune system antibody, secretory immunoglobulin A—called IgA—which helps the body resist invading bacteria and viruses. When the volunteers spent just five minutes remembering an experience that made them feel angry or frustrated, their IgA levels increased briefly, then dropped substantially and stayed low for five hours. When volunteers focused on feelings of care and compassion, IgA levels rose and remained at a high level for six hours. These findings suggest that simply remembering an emotion can strongly affect a person's health. Toxin handlers, then—who often later mull over the emotional pain they've encountered during the day—most certainly experience a drop in their IgA levels that can last for hours.[7]

BOX 4-1 STRESS AND GENDER

A recent review of stress literatures on rats, primates, and humans suggests that the response to stress may be different for women than for men. Shelley Taylor and her coauthors argue that while the primary physiological response to stress—the fight-or-flight response—occurs for both men and women, the *behaviors* of women tend to follow a pattern of "tend-and-befriend."[8] So, for example, when a woman senses danger, rather than staying to fight or running away, she is more likely to run to tend her children and to gather together with other women. She thereby reduces her own distress by ensuring the safety of her offspring and by gaining support and comfort through her bonds with women.

Taylor and her colleagues believe that the female response triggers hormones that support caregiving rather than fight-or-flight behaviors. They therefore identify the pattern as a factor of natural selection and as an explanation for the different levels of investment that males and females often have in parental responsibilities.

Even so, the authors do not say that *all* women respond to stress this way. What this research does suggest, however, in the context of the themes of this book, is that toxins can be particularly destructive when someone responds to a woman's emotional difficulties with no compassion. Leaving a woman alone with her pain when the prescription for healing is care and attention can be destructive indeed. Further, given that many, though not all, toxin handlers are women, it suggests that female toxin handlers may feel the isolation of this undercover work acutely, and may have a particularly difficult time letting go when the toxicity in the situation becomes highly stressful and warrants that they fight back or withdraw.

Another study of IgA was done recently by Dr. Jos Bosch, a researcher at the Ohio State University and an expert on neuroendocrine immunology. He and his colleagues have found that "short, sharp bouts of stress produce high concentrations of 'defense' proteins, against the secretory immunoglobulin A chemical in the saliva." Their study, published recently in *Psychophysiology*, demonstrated that acute stress will activate the immune system—something toxin handlers may experience when helping others to resolve difficult situations. Nevertheless, says Bosch, "at a certain point, too much stress will depress [the immune system]."[9] This observation proves consistent with the experiences of toxin handlers who wear down over time.

Stress impairs not only the immune system, however; stress triggered by negative emotions can also influence the brain's neural pathways. As the activity of thinking about what makes one angry is repeated, stronger and stronger circuits are built in the brain.[10] The level of emotional distress therefore increases until there is literally a neural architecture that supports that state. That pathway becomes easier to activate the next time distress occurs, in effect making it a personal "hot button."

For toxin handlers, who shoulder the stress of others in addition to their own, the implications are clear. "Caregivers are human, too," Dr. Michael Myers, a psychiatrist and clinical professor at the University of British Columbia, told me. As a specialist in physician health, Myers treats physicians for clinical depression, and has found that many of their complaints center around the difficulties of coping with the problems of their staff—doctors and other health professionals. As Myers put it: "These administrators have lost their ability to keep their armor in place."[11]

Thus the work of dealing with toxins, by its very nature, can exact a high personal toll on the handlers. But that toll can be even greater, depending on how the toxin handlers themselves behave and the kinds of strategies they adopt.

The Toll from Handlers' Own Behavior

PAUL, a human resources manager in an educational institution, recounted the difficulty he has leaving work at the end of the day—particularly if he's been working closely with employees who are in emotional pain. "I'll sometimes have a problem physically getting myself out of the office," he said. "I'll get all ready to go, bags packed, computer shut off, coat on. And then I'll start to fiddle with the personnel files in my in-basket. 'I'll just go through Joe X's case one more time,' I tell myself. Or else I'll tell myself I should reply to somebody's request for assistance, or find a reason to leave someone a voicemail." These are all things that Paul knows could wait until the next working day. But, as he says, he becomes "like a deer caught in the lights of an oncoming car. It's as if there's an invisible bar across my office door. I simply can't make myself leave."

Immersion in managing or handling the pain of others can cloud our capacity to help ourselves. Indeed, Daniel Goleman says that "emotions are contagious."[12] Toxins from others, then, seep through our defenses, and we take the pain home with us. We spend time thinking, even obsessing, about the situations we are trying to heal. The effects of the pain we've witnessed wake us up at 3 A.M. and we can't easily go back to sleep. We aren't attentive to our relationships with those who are close to us, since we carry our colleagues' pain wherever we go.

Part of the problem is that handlers aren't always aware they're doing these things in the first place. Like Paul, when handlers are burning out, an invisible bar seems to hold them hostage to the toxins around them. But really they're imprisoning *themselves*, having lost perspective. Unlike managers who aren't toxin handlers, pain managers are so empathically attuned to others' suffering that they're unable to easily detach themselves, and often refuse to "leave the grounds of engagement," to use Robert Solomon's evocative term.[13] In so doing, however, they squander their own emotional energy, saving their skills for diagnosing others, not themselves. They seem blindly indifferent to what their efforts to help others cost them personally.

Why do so few handlers seem to know how to handle themselves? Because handlers aren't professionally trained to do this kind of work. After all, few organizations recognize this role in the first place. Handlers therefore lack valuable skills that could help protect them from burnout. But there are other reasons that handlers' own habits get them into trouble—the roots of which are reflected in the reasons why handlers take on this work to begin with.

For example, people may handle toxins as part of their formal job, as is the case for many HR managers. But often these managers view the "human" part of their title as more important than the "resources" component. Other toxin handlers simply get drawn into the work bit by bit by their colleagues who trust them for their calmness, their sensitivity to the emotional needs of others, and their willingness to listen and to help. Still others take on the work for instrumental reasons. They see a direct correlation between helping others with their pain and getting results. They act to get pain out of the way so that employees can proceed with their work and contribute effectively to the needs of the project or assignment. Similarly, some people are drawn to the helping role as a way to help themselves. Handling the pain of others feeds their own emotional needs as well as those of others. And finally, for some, helping people feels like a calling. They will find situations that need attention and care wherever they go, and they will become engaged in healing efforts almost in spite of themselves.

Clearly some of these motivations, more than others, contain in themselves the seeds of burnout. People who see toxin handling as a means to an end—such as completing a project—will less likely take the toxins into their psyches and bodies as much as, say, people who see handling others' pain as their "calling." Indeed, handlers most often feel the wear and tear of their work when they have a high personal investment in handling outcomes and an attachment to the issues involved. Investment and attachment tend to draw handlers into the emotional problems of others, and they lose the ability to let the problems go. Handlers, particularly those in organizations that have instrumental agendas of bottom-line accomplishment, have a high vested interest in the success of their efforts. They want their efforts to work. They want their people to heal and to be free from emotional pain, at least to the point that they can focus on meeting the organization's needs.

All that is well and good—at least for the organization. Handlers, on the other hand, by identifying with the pain of others, are drawn more and more into an emotional involvement that, as we've seen, can lead to burnout and even physical illness if they don't have the tools to deflect that involvement. "When suffering is at stake, and we've offered ourselves to its relief, we naturally have an interest in how situations evolve," write Ram Dass and Paul Gorman in their book, *How Can I Help?*[14] But over time this interest can become compulsive; handlers begin to spend too much of their own emotional energy on the outcome of their interventions—and eventually they wear down.

This downward spiral worsens if the outcome of the handler's work is particularly ambiguous—as it usually is, by its very nature. Working with others' pain is essentially a fluid process, with few clear-cut results that signify a "win" or offer a feeling of accomplishment. In Savannah's case, for example, her buffering activities saved the project and protected her staff, to an extent. But several of her staff quit at the end of the project in protest for the battering that the unit took and, as we know, Savannah burned out. She said later how she had often agonized over whether her efforts to handle her staff's pain were sufficient.

Handlers with a compulsive need to know the outcome of their work, then, simply create more frustration for themselves. "Did I really help?" they ask themselves. "Could I have done something else?" "Was it really for the best?" "How do I know [what I did was right]?—God, it's somebody's life [I'm dealing with]!"[15]

Another personal trap for handlers is having an *agenda* for the person being helped. Handlers have high emotional competence, including being adept at sensing others' emotional states. But that competence crosses the line into unhealthy behavior when handlers lose their perspective—for example, by jumping in to "steer" a person in a particular direction.

In a sense, this is an inevitable pitfall of handling toxins in organizations. Managers with pressures for results are organizationally primed and personally predisposed for actions they think will make a difference. In chapter 3 we described a senior manager who extricated a promising staff member who was languishing in an unhelpful work unit. The staff member wasn't consulted and likely couldn't be told why she was transferred. The intervention worked in the sense that the staff member blossomed and the organization benefited. But that kind of intrusion of a handler's agenda into a painful situation can become seductive. Unchecked or overplayed, the handler's actions can be seen as manipulative (which inevitably they are) and therefore resented, even if they achieve healthy outcomes. The handler then becomes defensive or feels embarrassed by the outcome, pressing even harder to make amends. A "cycle of reactivity" therefore begins, which doesn't help anyone and eventually wears down the handler.[16]

Perhaps the most insidious personal trap for the handler, however, is an excessive need to be liked, a frequent need for approval for his or her hard empathetic work. Handlers are highly sensitized to the importance of healthy relationships in organizations. They are also strongly attuned to people's feelings, making them vulnerable to their own and others' hearts as well as their minds. The real danger comes, however, when a handler does this work to compensate for low self-esteem. People with a poor sense of themselves have few resources to keep them from being drawn into the toxicity of a situation—especially if these are the only situations where the handlers experience approval. Like the other personal traps already discussed, a need to be liked weakens the handler's ability to stand back from the toxins they work with and to let them go.

Despite all these examples of how the toxin handlers can create problems through their own habits and attitudes, often the greatest toll on their emotional and physical health comes from the organization itself.

The Toll from Organizations' Actions, Policies, and Attitudes

JOHN, a senior manager in a health care assessment organization, told me how his job as head of a division suddenly turned sour when he got a new CEO—and "politics entered the organization like you've never seen," he said.

The new CEO changed the whole direction of the organization, and John suddenly felt very constrained in everything his division did. "We were constantly asked to prepare reports and to defend our decisions. It put a huge strain on my team of managers who had large caseloads and needed to spend time with their clients, rather than doing 'urgent paperwork,'" he remembered. He soon found himself continually stepping in to protect his team from the suffocating demands. He looked for ways to simplify the reports; he argued frequently with his bosses. In general he felt a great deal of pressure and no supporting structure. But things got worse still when the CEO was fired, and shortly after, so was his boss. "The new CEO was also a very political animal," John said. "Everyone was unhappy, and I spent a lot of my time dealing with other people's stress. Meantime, I was neglecting everything else in my life, including my health." On one occasion, he became so ill on a flight to the East Coast that when the plane landed, he was rushed to an emergency room. He awoke two days later after doctors had removed a cancerous tumor from his kidney. "They said I should have been dead with this condition." That was four years ago, and although John now pays more attention to nutrition and taking vitamins, he said that people continue to bring their problems to him. "But I wonder: Maybe I shouldn't do so much advice-giving to others. Maybe I need to get better at taking care of my own needs."

As I've pointed out before, organizations by their very nature create a regular supply of emotional pain, be it from a new boss, a merger or layoff, or policies for promotions, raises, and bonuses. As in the case of John, in the preceding example, someone always feels the effects of that pain—and it's often the toxin handler who steps in to serve as a buffer, act as a peacekeeper, or play any number of other roles that will help restore equilibrium to the organization. Without anyone formally realizing it, the job of dissipating the toxins of everyday work life falls to those who have the skill and motivation to engage with the pain they encounter and neutralize it.

By taking on this difficult work, unbidden and unsupported, handlers can in turn become wounded healers. Furthermore, the fact that most organizational leaders lack awareness and appreciation of the handler's role magnifies the toxin handler's already hefty burden: the sheer volume of pain that organizations generate on a regular basis. Inevitably, toxin handlers eventually feel overwhelmed by their heroic role and they burn out. Organizations pay the price as well, of course, as the handlers lose their effectiveness or even leave their jobs or the organization altogether.

For example, Pamela, a senior manager in a major manufacturing organization, acted as one of the few pain handlers in a very toxic organizational environment. "Our budget process was always a 'gotcha' exercise," said Pamela. "The company officers would drastically reduce the budget you had proposed, knowing full well that with those resources, you couldn't possibly make the targets." The targets would inevitably be raised yet again, or the criteria on which projects were assessed would change. "It was a no-win game and it drove the managers nuts," she said. Although Pamela, through her toxin-handling skills, managed to turn around the fortunes of a large unit, her own fortune turned sour in the process. By the end of her tenure in the job, she was overweight, depressed, and had seen her relationship with her partner unravel. She could not go near a work challenge for over a year and needed professional help to heal.

Clearly, life in organizations is not benign. These are settings in which people strive, often with varying agendas and expectations, to accomplish organizational goals. And as people are increasingly invested in their work rather than in their personal lives or communities, organizations more and more become the stages where people's hopes and expectations play out.

Indeed, the modern work organization has become a zone where life is increasingly lived for full meaning—encompassing the full spectrum of human emotions and experiences.[17] Ilene Philipson, a psychologist in northern California, has seen the truth of that statement in her work at her group practice, Pathmakers Inc. In her early work with five women patients, she found them profoundly depressed about their jobs. They were hard-working and had dealt successfully with many other crises in their lives. "Yet being demoted or passed over for a promotion or just having an unsympathetic supervisor had devastated them." One client had anxiety attacks and uncontrollable crying bouts. The reason: "As an administrative manager in a small investment company, she had been lavished with praise and perks—until, that is, she asked for a raise. Then her bosses turned against her . . . she told Philipson how she had been stripped of her privileges, how she no longer receives invitations to client dinners, how she was no longer trusted to do million-dollar trades for clients."

Initially, Philipson could not make sense of these responses from her clients. The administrative manager, for example, had dealt very well with many other stresses in her life, including being a child of an alcoholic parent. To explore the issue further, in February 1993 Philipson sent out flyers announcing a therapy group for those "unable to work because of problems with supervisors or coworkers." She was quickly besieged with new patients—and found herself in the middle of a phenomenon that she believes is a disturbing by-product of the "new economy" touted in the 1990s: people who feel betrayed by their work. Her patients were women with ordinary jobs, such as police officers, bankers, office managers, and secretaries. For the 150 women in Philipson's therapy groups, work has become very personal, and the expectations have become very high. Although almost half of them have spouses or live-in partners at home, "work has become their passion . . . their primary source of self-esteem, recognition, respect—their only path to interconnectedness."[18]

Regardless of the evidence confirming how important it is to pay attention to people's emotions, however, most organizations and their leaders continue to disregard the feelings (particularly negative ones) that their own policies and attitudes trigger in employees. But anger, sadness, and disappointment don't go away. Into this unacknowledged and tricky world steps the toxin handler: the peacekeeper, the emotional firefighter, the lay therapist. Unlike the fighters of real fires, however, she has no admired and official status, nor has she the tools and training for the job.

The anguish of many toxin handlers is captured in the words of this manager in an international high-tech company: "I can help others but I can't seem to help myself. I keep seeing people suffering from the cruelty and indifference of their bosses, from stupid rules and decisions. I'm tired of being the one that people turn to when the 'shit hits the fan.' Whom do *I* turn to?"

BOX 4-2 SENT INTO BATTLE WITH A PLASTIC FORK

In the box "Buffers between Nations" in chapter 3 we looked at the work of peacekeepers—sanctioned intermediaries in international conflicts—and how that work holds lessons for organizational toxin handlers. It turns out that peacekeeping, like toxin handling, often exacts heavy tolls on the people in those positions. The high stress of their work is becoming increasingly well documented and includes evidence of emotional breakdowns and long-term illness among individuals returning from tours of peacekeeping duty.[19] In fact, like civilian managers, the leaders of peacekeeping forces often find themselves dealing with toxicity generated by the very organizations they serve—whose purpose is to keep the peace in volatile situations!

One high-profile example of a such a leader is documented in the book *The Lion, the Fox, and the Eagle,* which recounts the experiences of General Roméo Dallaire in Rwanda.[20] Dallaire, a Canadian who led a peacekeeping mission intended to monitor a fragile truce between the ruling Hutus and minority Tutsis, returned to Canada suicidal, his equilibrium apparently destroyed by the horrors he had witnessed and his inability to lead his mission to deal effectively with the situation. He attributed to his leaders much of the failure (later corroborated by the enquiry) of the United Nations initiative. (Indeed, as one observer characterized Dallaire's efforts, "He was sent into battle with a plastic fork!") For one thing, they were unwilling to heed his warnings of major arms buildup by the Hutus (who subsequently waged a genocide in which some eight hundred thousand civilians were murdered). But more directly applicable to the toxin handler at the organizational level is Dallaire's view that his leaders lacked the courage to confront the operational difficulties of the mission; they refused to alter policies and procedures to allow him and his peacekeepers to intervene to save people from dying. "They put on a good show, but they didn't give a rat's ass," said Dallaire of his bosses. "My tattered and logistically depleted force knew that no reinforcement or supplies would be forthcoming."[21]

Handling pain in such a toxic wasteland as Rwanda is obviously an extreme example, but it does point to the dangers of being in emotionally intense situations for too long, especially in an organization whose policies and practices don't support the handlers' work. The costs to Dallaire have proven high. Professional help has not yet healed him from his post-traumatic stress disorder, a severe psychological syndrome associated with the experiences of war. He's had several bouts of depression, including suicide attempts. Though extreme, the negative effects on peacekeepers such as Dallaire are also found in the ranks of handlers in business organizations, in not-for-profit operations, in health care systems—in any kind of human system.

As we've seen in this chapter, doing the work of the toxin handler is not in the manager's job description. It's rarely seen as real work and it gets bootlegged into the manager's workday. This alone is a stressor that contributes to the wear and tear of the manager-as-handler. But there is more. Handlers burn out because the work of handling emotional toxins is dangerous. Handlers don't have the training, equipment, or support to help them safely process all the pain of others that comes their way. They carry it home, they fret about it. It wakes them up in the middle of the night. It seeps into their bodies and their minds, and they get sick. They suffer from headaches, sleeplessness, bouts of depression; even physical ailments of one kind or another result, some of them life-threatening. The medical evidence on stress and the human condition confirms these dangers and outcomes.

Handlers, for their part, bring some of this suffering on themselves. They get careless about their own well-being. They pay more attention to others than to themselves. They can become consumed with worry about whether they are doing the right thing. They become addicted to the "fix" that helping people can deliver. These tendencies will feed any predisposition to aid others in exchange for gratitude or friendship. The handler can be lured into a seductive spiral from providing balanced and clear-headed support to feeding the handler's personal need to be a "savior."

Organizations, of course, contribute to the toll on these crucial contributors to well-being in the workplace when they create conditions of toxicity. They enact policies and practices that manufacture toxicity, a point we have made before. "Gotcha" games and other practices that put people in double binds create emotional stresses that can swallow up the efforts of even the most competent handlers, leaving them feeling that they're "damned if they do and damned if they don't." Moreover, organizations rarely recognize or support the efforts that handlers make. On occasion, they will recognize the handler and his role, but as a result organizations will often put the "squeeze" on the handler to do even more than they have the capacity to deliver.

Finally, like others in their organizations, toxin handlers have to cope with the stresses and strains of their personal lives while attending to the pain and suffering of others in the workplace. This too can add toxins to their load. In the time I felt I was most heavily involved as a handler in my organization, I was coping with the unexpected death of my mother and, fourteen months later, with the passing of my father, who had been ill for years. Other managers I interviewed had similar experiences, dealing with aged parents, deaths in the family, troubled offspring, or other significant strains in their personal lives. This is not to say that handlers burn out because of their own personal circumstances. Rather, organizations need to be aware that these people do their handling work *on top of* the normal personal strains that everyone else feels when pain strikes on the home front.

In this chapter we've seen how, as much as toxin handling keeps the wheels of organizations turning smoothly, the people who do that work can easily become stuck themselves. While acting as a healing force in human systems, therefore, handlers need to find ways to also salve their own wounds and gain protection from their organizations—as we will see in chapters 5 and 6.

CHAPTER FIVE

Healing the Handlers

Dadi Janki, a woman in her eighties from India, was named as one of ten "wisdom keepers" at the Earth Summit in Rio de Janeiro in 1992. It's easy to understand why. In a San Francisco University study of the brainwaves of yogis renowned for their positive influence on others, she was assessed as having the calmest brainwaves of all her peers, prompting the media to describe her as "the most peaceful woman on earth." "She can transform the atmosphere of a room simply by her presence," says David Cooperrider, a Case Western University professor of organizational behavior who met her at a conference.

Her stated goal in life is to be of benefit to each person she meets and to turn her thoughts to help lift them into happiness. Cooperrider recalls: "When asked how she stays in such a state of joy and happiness in the face of the suffering of others, she said: 'I do not identify with the pain of the other person. I don't take it on!'" When pressed for an explanation, she replied: "To take on their suffering would be to double the amount of pain in the world!" "How then do you help?" was the next question. "I try to wrap the other person's suffering in love," she replied.

When toxin handlers help others, they often do wrap the other person's suffering in love, though they might not characterize it quite this way. To respond constructively to someone else in pain is an act of compassion, a way of reaching out to a person who is alone and suffering. Efforts to reconnect people to their competence and sense of self-worth are expressions of love. The fact that this is done in business organizations and that it often also has an instrumental purpose doesn't change the caring nature of the intervention.

Of course, as we have seen, there is considerable personal risk in reaching out to help others who are hurting, and it can rarely, if ever, be done with detachment.[1] At the very least, handlers need to understand clearly what the other person is feeling so that their support can be informed and authentic.

There is a difference, however, between showing compassion when helping others and taking on their pain. As we discussed in chapter 4, when handlers (for any number of reasons) fall into this trap, they become contaminated by the experience and are liable to fall ill. They ingest toxins that damage them, and they gradually lose the power to help others or to feel a sense of personal gratification from this role.

Staying out of the danger zone requires, first, a clear recognition of its possibility and, second, a conscious intention not to get overinvolved emotionally with people in pain. Essentially, handlers need a personal vision of why they are helping someone else, along with some practical tools and skills to strengthen their ability to protect themselves. Like people who handle toxic waste in radioactive sites, handlers need a kind of "protective garb" to keep them safe from harm.

Healthy handlers choose to help and heal others and feel engaged and nourished by what they do. Rachel Naomi Remen, M.D., author and founder of the Commonweal Cancer Help Clinic, puts this view of toxin handling eloquently into perspective: "Healing is natural. It's not something I do to you, but something that is mutual, that comes from the integrity of the relationship between us. So both of us will be healed in that process."[2]

In this chapter we will look at ways that handlers can build caring connections to coworkers who are in pain without taking on the toxicity in the situation or risking burnout. To better withstand the effects of their work, then, handlers need to craft a plan of action they can tap into regularly.

Creating a Game Plan

> *The key [to sustained health and performance] is to establish rituals that promote oscillation and recovery.*
>
> —Jim Loehr and Tony Schwartz, *Harvard Business Review*

HAVING A GAME PLAN for self-protection is most powerful when it is established within a strategic framework of options for action. Handlers need to be able to access a set of attitudes and routines that keep them emotionally healthy even as they deal with unhealthy situations. They need practices that provide breaks that allow them time to catch their breath physically, emotionally, mentally, and spiritually and to recover the vision of what they're trying to do as healers and as managers. They need to have healthy connections with their organization, ones that sustain and support them in this difficult work. Actions to build and maintain such critical relationships are the main theme of the next chapter. In this chapter I will focus on what handlers can do to help themselves.

Above all, handlers need a kind of tempered optimism for the task at hand and a degree of self-compassion in their efforts to heal themselves. Attempts to achieve a perfect balance of activism and protection will likely lead to frustration, and are probably unrealistic in a world of constant change and intensity. Perhaps by accepting a more dynamic experience of moving in and out of balance over time, handlers can lead healthier lives. The trick is to redress the untenable condition of feeling overwhelmed and emotionally imbalanced, while keeping in mind that self-recovery and emotional well-being are ongoing processes that one works through over a lifetime. Similarly, attending to the relationships and connections that sustain emotional health is a continuing endeavor. As handlers, we will win some of the time and be less successful at others. But as long as we have a plan of action and work with it conscientiously, we will have a good chance of safely helping others as well as ourselves.

One way to create such a plan of action comes from a model that Jim Loehr and Tony Schwartz developed for enhancing executive performance.[3] Based on twenty years of work with world-class athletes, Loehr and Schwartz's model for sustained high performance in the face of escalating pressure and change contains two key components: the need to build in breaks and the need to build up one's reserves.

From the perspective of the toxin handler, building in breaks or "the rhythmic movement between energy expenditure (stress) and energy renewal (recovery) which we term 'oscillation,'" means that it's important to take time to breathe, to reconnect with one's own sense of comfort or calm before reentering the fray. "The real enemy of high performance," write Loehr and Schwartz, "is not stress . . . rather, the problem is the absence of disciplined, intermittent recovery."[4] One of the hazards of handling toxins is that this role can consume vast amounts of time, energy, and mental and emotional resources. When the problems to be solved are intense or enduring (or both), as they usually are, there's little or no opportunity for the "disciplined, intermittent recovery" that these authors (and others) argue is key to healthy and sustained performance. Like managers performing technical work (and unlike the successful athletes whom Loehr and Schwartz studied), handlers "spend too much energy without recovery."[5]

In their work, Loehr and Schwartz describe the biological changes that occur when people engage in prolonged challenging activity. Since the body's hormone, glucose, and blood pressure levels drop every ninety minutes or so, they write, "by failing to seek recovery and overriding the body's natural stress-rest cycles, overall capacity is compromised. As we have learned for athletes, even short, focused breaks can promote significant recovery." They go on to suggest five sources of restoring capacity: eat something, hydrate, move physically, change channels mentally, and change channels emotionally.[6] Mantras such as "don't take this personally" or simply "breathe deeply" remind handlers to remember the importance to their health and effectiveness of stepping back from the action occasionally. The image of handlers as having a body, a heart, a mind, and a spirit also can be a useful shorthand to remind them that their safety and health requires conscious attention to all these aspects of their being. Throughout this chapter, we'll continue to explore additional ways to build in breaks from the work of toxin handling.

Loehr and Schwartz's second component to effective energy management is what I would call the need to build up your reserves. Health and durability in the face of stressful situations is enhanced when individuals are physically fit, emotionally positive, intellectually sharp, and can tap into their deepest values. These authors argue that sustained high performance, then, requires athletes and managers—and for our purposes, toxin handlers—to develop practices that will strengthen four main areas of their lives: the physical, the emotional, the mental, and the spiritual. Each of these capacities in turn draws on rituals or practices that promote oscillation, or the rhythmic expenditure and recovery of energy. The four capacities also work in tandem; when you strengthen one capacity, all of the others benefit. Thus, for example, "vigorous exercise can produce a sense of emotional well-being, clearing the way for peak mental performance," write Loehr and Schwartz.[7]

Let's now explore the elements of a game plan for helping handlers to protect themselves or to recover from the ill-effects of working with emotional toxins. The plan draws on each of the four capacities—physical, emotional, mental, and spiritual—as they apply to the need for toxin handlers to

- strengthen their physical capacity
- boost their emotional capacity
- regenerate their mental capacity
- build their spiritual capacity

Strengthening Your Physical Capacity

You are what you repeatedly do.

—Aristotle

PHYSICAL CAPACITY develops through activities that involve exertion, making the body stronger and fitter, and through mechanisms that release muscular tensions, relaxing the body before or after stressful emotional work. Handlers need to build stamina through regular exercise to become more resilient to the demands of the emotional work they do. But they also need to engage in focused relaxation through practices such as massage or meditation to release tension and to build routines in the body and mind that help inoculate them from toxins.

Keep Fit

Exercise is an effective way for many managers who are toxin handlers to dissipate stress. "I don't feel thrashed if I do some physical activity," commented one toxin handler, who frequently takes a twenty-minute brisk walk along a river path to get rid of her stress.[8] Others take up sports such as softball or tennis, which helps to ensure that at least one day a week they'll focus on play and social connections rather than work pressures.

Loehr and Schwartz remind us of several obvious routines to build and sustain physical capacity, including eating a balanced diet, having five or six small meals a day (rather than three heavy ones, which tend to deplete rather than restore energy), and ensuring enough intake of water daily. ("As much as half the population walks around with mild chronic dehydration," they write.[9]) Loehr and Schwartz also point to the importance of getting enough rest as an antidote to emotional burnout: "Regular sleep cycles help regulate your biological clocks and increase the likelihood that the sleep you get will be deep and restful."[10]

The catch-22, of course, is that sleeping can be especially difficult for toxin handlers, since they often wake up in the early morning hours and relive the pain they're trying to relieve during the day. Restoring regular sleep patterns might require special medical attention, but physical exercise can also help. Moreover, people who exercise regularly need less sleep because the quality of their sleep is better: They sleep more soundly and reach deep sleep cycles much faster than people who don't exercise.

Physical activity can also contribute to sound mental capacity, another factor that we'll examine in more detail in this chapter. In a study of older women that spanned several years, women who consistently took walks showed less decline of their thinking abilities than those who did little or no exercise.[11] Certainly a toxin handler benefits from clear thinking when it comes to decisions about what to manage—and what to avoid—when dealing with toxic situations. Loehr and Schwartz advocate two weight-training workouts a week to increase physical resistance to stress. (They write, "It increases strength, retards osteoporosis, speeds up metabolism, enhances mobility, improves posture, and dramatically increases energy."[12]) Coupled with some form of regular aerobic activity, such as brisk walks, exercise can be an effective way to dissipate the toxins that handlers manage.

Get a Massage

Regularly scheduled massages can release tensions caused by both physical and emotional demands. They also have the added benefit of forcing handlers to step out of the workplace and take time for themselves. "Massage," write Andrew Vickers and Catherine Zollman in *British Medical Journal*, brings about "generalized improvements in health, such as relaxation or improved sleep, or specific physical benefits, such as relief of muscular aches and pains."[13] Indeed, the Touch Research Institute

(TRI) at the University of Miami has documented the positive effects of massage therapy on job performance and stress reduction. A basic fifteen-minute chair massage provided twice weekly, TRI found, results in decreased job stress and a significant increase in productivity.[14]

Maybe that's why massage therapy is becoming more mainstream. More than eighty companies, including many Fortune 500 companies, are using massage therapy to counter such ills as musculoskeletal problems, stress, and poor ergonomic design of furniture.[15] So far, the benefits are proving positive, at least in companies such as Reebok, where headaches, back strain, and fatigue have all fallen since the firm started bringing in massage therapists.[16]

Other techniques designed to reduce pressure in the body caused by stress include acupuncture and reflexology, which also can improve breathing. Stress almost always creates poor breathing habits, so toxin handlers need to pay particular attention to this area, taking regular time-outs to breathe and relax, whether through exercise or some other technique. Since the way people feel emotionally often stems from how they feel physically, relaxation techniques and exercise, which loosen tension in the body, help generate calmer emotions.

Boosting Your Emotional Capacity

In the midst of winter, I finally learned there was in me an invincible summer.

—Albert Camus, *Actuelles*

EMOTIONAL CAPACITY is "the internal climate that supports peak performance," say Loehr and Schwartz, who interviewed hundreds of athletes about how they felt when they were performing at their best. Their answers? "Calm," "challenged," "engaged," "focused," "optimistic," and "confident."[17] Handlers of toxins need to draw on similar emotions to both do their work and stay healthy.

Stay Positive

Managers who adopt positive attitudes toward the toxic situations they face say this helps them keep the pain and suffering in perspective. Looking at situations as learning opportunities, not taking things personally, being patient when emotions are turbulent, accepting that some situations cannot be resolved to everyone's satisfaction, and maintaining a sense of humor are all tactics that have worked for durable toxin handlers.[18]

To keep unhealthy stress levels at bay, it's important for handlers to feel good about the work they're doing. Even in chronically painful situations, positive thinking helps. One toxin handler helped a worker whose husband had committed suicide.[19] Because the work site was so emotionally toxic, rather than support the bereaved woman, her coworkers actually shunned her. The handler alone reached out to the woman, doing things like taking her to lunch or just providing a listening ear. Even though the workplace was dysfunctional, this handler found a way to feel some satisfaction by doing what was right for the widow. Other pain managers I've interviewed echoed this sentiment, expressing pride that their help was appreciated and led someone to recover their confidence and productivity. (Rarely if ever was the organization officially aware of these interventions.)

How does staying positive help inoculate the toxin handler against corrosion? In 1983, Norman Cousins wrote a best-selling book, *The Healing Heart,* in which he movingly described how he used laughter, among other tools, to overcome a life-threatening illness that doctors believed was irreversible. He used the same processes years later to help him recover from an acute heart attack. Although the media "made it appear that I laughed my way out of a serious illness," he wrote, careful readers of his book knew that laughter was just a metaphor. "Hope, faith, love, will to live, cheerfulness, humor, creativity, playfulness and confidence, *great expectations*—all these, I believed, had therapeutic value."[20]

Another way to put this might be that optimists "resist helplessness."[21] Staying positive acts as a barrier to depression when things go wrong, and those who exhibit optimism rarely give up easily. Researchers who have looked at the immune systems of caged rats found that the experience of inescapable shock—helplessness—weakens the immune system. "T-cells from the blood of rats that become helpless no longer multiply rapidly when they come across the invaders they are supposed to destroy."[22] Martin Seligman, in his book *Learned Optimism,* uses the term "learned helplessness" as the "giving-up reaction, the quitting response that follows the belief that whatever you do doesn't matter."[23] Not surprisingly, this is a response that handlers who have burned out, even those who were previously optimistic, recognize. It happens less for some than for others, but it surfaces when handlers no longer feel they can cope with the toxicity they're witnessing—and as a result, feel powerless.

To fight the impulse to give up, Cousins used positive imagery to put an optimistic frame on an otherwise painful picture. Similarly, Seligman refers to optimism as "changing the non-negative destructive things you say to yourself when you experience the setbacks that life deals all of us."[24] We already know that toxin handlers do this for other people, helping them to exercise optimism in order to heal. But handlers who can make otherwise destructive situations more positive or hopeful for *themselves* (like the handler did when helping the widowed employee) keep themselves healthy and resilient.

There's a wide body of evidence to support this notion that optimism actually makes you feel better. For example, it's been known for years that in some circumstances when people want to get better, they do feel better, even though they've had no real medical treatment.[25] This connection between beliefs and feelings is known as the "placebo effect." Placebos, of course, are "prescriptions" or treatments that contain no real drug and are given to some patients in controlled situations instead of an actual medicine.

Recent research led by Jon Stoessl at the University of British Columbia's Neurodegenerative Disorders Centre has again confirmed the placebo effect.[26] In a study on Parkinson's patients, some patients got real drug injections and others got salt water. What is intriguing about their findings is that the researchers detected an actual *chemical* change in patients after the placebo treatment, exactly the same one in Parkinson's patients receiving apomorphine, a common Parkinson's drug. In response to the placebo, the patients' brains actually released dopamine—the neurochemical that the brain releases in response to real Parkinson's drugs. "In other words," said Dr. Stoessl, "the expectation of benefits is enough to make them release dopamine even though they don't have a lot to start with."

The placebo effect, then, can go beyond a "simple" psychological reaction ("feeling good because I want to feel good") to translate into actual changes in the chemistry of the brain. This is good news for toxin handlers, who can use the "placebo" of optimism to protect their own emotional health by retaining an expectation of personal benefit from the work they do and believing that things will work out well, despite the pain involved.[27]

Don't Take Things Personally

Another valuable tool in the toxin handler's toolbox is the ability to separate oneself from the situation at hand. Ronald Heifetz, author of *Leadership Without Easy Answers,* knows this. In an interview in which he was asked, "How do leaders stay alive?" he responded: "To sustain yourself over the long term, you must learn how to distinguish role from self."[28] Dadi Janki, the woman in the example with which I began this chapter, also knows not to personalize other people's painful emotions—and expressions thereof ("I don't take it on!" she said).

Handlers get hooked on other people's pain when they get overinvolved in the emotions and the experiences of those they're helping. They lose sight of the fact that what they're doing to help others is a *role*—not their personal reality. They let their own emotions and sense of worth become part of the equation. Instead of helping others from a position of neutrality, that is, with no vested interest in a particular outcome, they want their own script for a result to take place—whether they are conscious of it or not. They want someone to be cured, and usually they want the workplace to be more productive as a result of their efforts. Or, they want to be liked for their kindness.

When the handler's motives are so connected to the results *he* wants for a situation, he easily becomes a target for the sufferer to unload his or her frustrations and pain. When the sufferer doesn't respond as hoped, the handler becomes defensive and broods over the way things are turning out. He blames himself for the lack of resolution and organizational progress—and thus the suffering of someone else transforms into that of the handler. On the other hand, it can be equally dangerous if the handler does win his hoped-for results, especially if he gets sucked in by the praise he receives from the victim (or others) for being such a "good-hearted" person. Becoming a slave to outcomes—whatever they may be—keeps the handler overly invested in toxicity and therefore in harm's way.

Connecting to the suffering of others while deflecting its impact is the primary emotional challenge of the toxin handler. Even when deeply concerned about the pain of a colleague, handlers need to remember that it is not *their* suffering (and healing) that's in question.

Not taking things personally isn't the same as being detached or unmoved by the conditions of others. But the healthiest handlers help others without taking responsibility for what people in pain *do* with the help they offer. They provide resources, opportunities, space, and counsel—but they leave it to the sufferer to work with these gifts to end their pain. (In chapter 7 we will discuss this notion again when we examine how leaders who act as toxin handlers behave with "professional intimacy" toward others.)

Consider this old Zen story. Two monks were traveling together in a heavy downpour when they came upon a woman who was having trouble crossing a river. "Come on," said the first monk to the woman, and he carried her in his arms across a shallow part of the river. The monks then continued their journey. The second monk didn't say anything until much later. Then he couldn't contain himself anymore. "We monks don't go near females," he said. "Why did you do that?" "I left the woman back there," the first monk replied. "Are you still carrying her?"[29]

This story reminds us of the power that emotional attachment to an idea or a judgment has to weigh us down—and the value of letting go. A useful mantra for the toxin handler, then, especially after intense involvement with the emotional pain of others, would be: "Let it go! Let it go! Let it go!"

Accept What You Can't Change

Calmness comes also from knowing the nature of a situation as accurately and honestly as one can, and then accepting the limits of what can be done about it. Sometimes emotional pain is simply out of anyone's control. David Crisp, former senior vice president of human resources for the Hudson Bay Company in Canada, speaks eloquently on this point:

> *One aspect of managing your own feelings is equanimity: the ability to face reality, which inevitably has some warts with it. You have to be able to say: "OK, I can live with the total truth, because I have a strategy. I can develop the habits to cope and I have the confidence to move forward. I have the tools to help me with that fundamental problem that we all have, which is that reality isn't as nice as we'd like it to be."*[30]

Toxin handlers can take a similar approach to problems, and ultimately protect themselves a little better than they otherwise might. For example, they can recognize that getting bent out of shape about things out of their control doesn't help. They can say to themselves (and those they help): "OK, this is a toxic situation and we can't change it. What constructive things can we do to help ourselves get through it?" At the same time, they can encourage people in a bad situation to stay balanced and to "take care of yourself as well as the business."

Another Zen story illustrates well the concept of equanimity. A man returned to his village one day with a horse. "How lucky you are," said the other villagers. "Perhaps so. Perhaps not," said the man. "We shall see." His son rode the horse out into the fields one day, fell off it, and broke his leg. "How unfortunate you are," said the villagers. "Perhaps so. Perhaps not," said the man. A week later, several soldiers came to the village to draft all the young men of age into battle. They left behind the man's son, because of his broken leg. "How lucky you are," said the villagers. "Perhaps so. Perhaps not," said the man.[31] The story can of course continue, but one lesson here is that the man accepts his fate without judging it. He faces each incident with equanimity—a useful posture for hard-pressed handlers.

Regenerating Your Mental Capacity

> *Argue for your limitations, and sure enough, they are yours!*
>
> —Richard Bach, *Illusions: The Adventures of a Reluctant Messiah*

HEALTHY TOXIN HANDLING means staying mentally focused on the issue at hand and not getting distracted by peripheral dramas. Loehr and Schwartz describe that kind of mental focus as "energy concentrated in the service of a particular goal."[32] In the case of handlers, focus helps to create a healthy space between themselves and toxic situations. Thus they can remain effective helpers without having their own emotions invaded.

Refocus the Mind

Mental activities such as meditation and breathing exercises (or other relaxation strategies) release stress, prevent handlers from absorbing negative energy, and refocus the mind to create more resilience. (As I mentioned earlier in this chapter, many of my recommendations cross over among the four categories of physical, emotional, mental, and spiritual strengthening. Meditation is a perfect example, applying equally to the mental and spiritual realms, a topic we'll examine later in this chapter.)

For example, one manager in a highly toxic work environment practiced transcendental meditation for almost thirty years. "I get up and shower and I meditate for twenty minutes in the morning. It makes a noticeable difference to my day. When I occasionally skip it for some reason or other, I have a more difficult time keeping myself emotionally clear when things heat up at the office."[33]

Michael Lerner, founder and president of Commonweal, a health and environmental center in Bolinas, California, has also spoken of the benefits of meditation. It "quiets your mind. It is a way of simply sitting quietly and allowing your mind to empty of all content, either by focusing on something, such as a sound or breathing or an idea, or by just emptying the mind and allowing things to come in and go back out again."[34]

There are many techniques for meditating, but most involve focusing on the breath or an object such as a candle flame while either sitting or walking quietly, and noting and then letting go of whatever comes to mind. These practices have been developed and used over hundreds of years, and variations are found in every spiritual tradition. When practiced diligently, meditation can help toxin handlers settle the constant chatter of thoughts, emotions, and anticipations that frequently assail them and then let go of toxins. It effectively injects a pause between the handler's actions and reactions to others' pain, and it can help loosen any growing attachments to the toxic situation itself. One handler, a senior manager from a large service organization, described his experience of meditation practice as follows:

> *I have practiced a form of meditation that has taught me to focus on my breathing and to simply let any thoughts that arise while doing this to float away like clouds across the sky. I like the quietness, the silence that it provides in my otherwise very hectic existence. I really saw the benefits of this practice when I did it consistently a few years ago. I was very burned out after a long period of dealing with very emotional situations at work. I took a few days of my vacation to attend a residential meditation retreat. I came out of it substantially refreshed. I felt as if I had dumped a whole load of emotional baggage at this site. I returned to work with much more enthusiasm than when I had left.*

Other relaxation techniques, such as yoga exercises that emphasize stretching and breathing, can enhance the capacity of the mind to focus.

As Lerner observes: "If you do gentle stretches, or progressive relaxation (tensing muscles and sequentially relaxing them), or if you just sit quietly and look inward, that's the equivalent of yoga."[35] The important point for toxin handlers is not to get stuck on a particular technique, but rather to look at these and related practices as ways that can help them calm their minds and build resilience to emotional toxicity.[36]

Another way to refocus the mind is through recreational reading, which, among other benefits, reminds the toxin handler that there's a world beyond the firing line of work. Phil Jackson, coach of two National Basketball Championship teams, describes how he challenged the minds of his Chicago Bulls players by giving them books to read on road trips. He's handed out titles such as *Fever: Twelve Stories* by John Wideman; *Ways of the White Folk* by Langston Hughes; *Zen Mind, Beginner's Mind* by Shunryu Suzuki and Trudy Dixon; and *The Way of the Peaceful Warrior* by Dan Millman, among others.[37]

For the toxin handler, reading provides an important break from too intense a focus on work issues. And as an added benefit, the right book can even stimulate a new perspective on a toxic situation.

Create Personal Space

Taking on the role of toxin handler in addition to his or her "real" work often consumes the handler's personal life. Handlers who are burning out begin to talk of their lives as an endless round of supporting others, leaving them little or no time to attend to their own needs. "I never get anything done for me," lamented one tired manager at a financial company. "My weeks and weekends fly by and I have no sense that I have a life!"

Certainly many books can provide handlers with ways to manage their time and life to have more personal space.[38] But toxin handling, by its very nature, prevents what these books often recommend: avoiding contact with others in order to attend to one's own work. Handlers do need opportunities to breathe, of course, but it is precisely their ability to notice and attend to others' emotional distress that makes them so effective.

The key is to find some balance, possibly by stepping back from particular situations or by leaving the work site completely from time to time to gain perspective. On a day-to-day basis, however, handlers at the very least need to track the time they spend doing their work (both technical and emotional) against their personal time. That way they can see where their personal lives get brushed aside and begin to incorporate those needs on their daily and weekly agendas in a realistic way. Too ambitious a game plan will likely collapse in the face of the high demands on handlers. But handlers with no strategy at all (and no mechanisms to evaluate it) will likely see their personal space vanish.

David Crisp recognized this dilemma from the demands and stresses of his busy life, and he recommends that people create a priority list such as Stephen Covey's four-quadrant model: activities that are urgent versus not-urgent; activities that are important versus not-important. In this model, work activities such as crises, pressing problems, deadline-driven projects, and so forth are found in the "urgent-and-important" quadrant (#1). Strategic issues around the organization's goals and objectives are found in the "important-but-not-urgent" quadrant (#2). Such activities focus on planning and preparation, values clarification, and so on. It is the most difficult arena of work for toxin handlers to get to, given the pressing need to help employees in pain. The "urgent-and-unimportant" quadrant (#3) is filled with interruptions, some phone calls, routine reports, and meetings that seem to flow endlessly from one to the next. The world of busywork and trivia characterizes the "unimportant-and-not-urgent quadrant" (#4).[39]

Crisp himself creates one list for work and one for personal issues on a single page. "One of my work priorities is to find, from my list, something every day to do for *me,*" he said. "I actively build that into my schedule. As a result, then, I don't let days and days, and then weeks and weeks go by feeling put upon." Then, each weekend he evaluates how he did the previous week and sets his priorities for the coming week. "Even though I get to the end of the week and feel that I didn't do a lot, I still feel that I have a plan and that I am in charge. It helps me maintain a sense of control even when the work situation might be out of my control."[40]

Create Mental Sanctuaries

As Crisp points out, creating personal space is inherently about taking charge of some part of one's life and safeguarding it from all intrusions. Phil Jackson describes a visualization exercise he calls the *safe spot*. He taught this to his Chicago Bulls players to help them concentrate on the things he needed to tell them during intense game situations. "During the fifteen or thirty seconds they have to grab a drink and towel off, I encourage them to picture someplace where they feel secure. It's a way for them to take a short mental vacation before addressing the problem at hand."[41]

Ronald Heifetz describes a similar technique that he developed for himself, which he calls "sanctuary." For example, he creates a daily sanctuary by reading an e-mail that a friend, who's a mystic and a biblical scholar, sends out each day. "Every day, he sends out an interpretation of one word from the Bible. It's just a few screens long, but as I am going through my email every day, I take a few minutes to read this thing, and it roots me in a different reality, a different source of meaning."[42]

Another way to provide that kind of quick respite is the "Freeze-Frame" technique developed by the HeartMath LLC (the consulting organization described in chapter 1 that deals with problems of stress in companies and individuals). Freeze-Frame teaches employees to recognize a stressful feeling, then freeze it—that is, take a time-out and breathe more slowly and deeply. It concludes with steps based on the biomedical theory of improving balance in the autonomic nervous system, brain, and heart to help employees react differently to stress. Instead of impulsively acting to share another person's pain, for example, Freeze-Frame teaches employees to stop, collect their thoughts, connect with their emotions, and then ask the other person to analyze his or her own unhappiness. Returning a problem to its sender in this way may seem like a minor change, but for toxin handlers, it's a radical departure from standard operating procedure. This technique thus serves two useful purposes for the toxin handler: recovering personal space in the heat of managing others' pain, and preventing the handler from taking on the sufferer's distress. Both outcomes help pain managers to prevent stressful situations from intruding on their personal space.[43]

Sanctuary as a state of mind and as a place of privacy is critical to regenerating mental capacity, and it can be done in short breaks or more extended ones. For example, André Delbecq and Frank Friedlander describe executives in very stressful environments who do not work on weekends.[44] They create a space between Friday night and Monday morning where they retreat to their homes, engage in personal hobbies or family events, and cut themselves off from the pressures of their roles. They will work as many hours as it takes during the week, but "walk away" when they enter their sanctuaries.

One manager told me of an effective image she uses to create a sanctuary and remind her to maintain personal space. Deciding that she wanted more balance in her life, she "also decided at that point that I was going to keep my head where my feet were. If I was at home, then that's where my head was going to be, and if I was at work, that's where my head was going to be. And I was not going to cross over. That took a fair amount of work, but I can honestly tell you I am 100 percent there."

Learn to Say No!

Maintaining mental focus also means being able to say no at times. One manager I spoke with found professional counseling helpful in this regard. He recalled: "I learned that it was possible to say no with options." Until that point, the manager had had a lot of trouble turning away people who needed to vent their emotions and, as a result, he was drowning under the combined workload of his real job and his toxic handling role. "I learned that 'no' doesn't mean 'I don't care,' and it doesn't mean 'not ever.' It can mean, 'No, I can't do this, but I could do this.' Or, 'No, I can't help you now, but how about tomorrow.' Or, 'No, I can't help you but let me find someone who can.'" That insight, the manager says, made work manageable again.

Do Reality Checks

Working intensively or over protracted periods of time with the pain of others can make the handler lose perspective on what's real and what she's imagining about the situation. One of the handlers interviewed during Laura Lee MacLean's research at the University of British Columbia said how important it was to have people around him to offer an objective perspective: "There are times when you get so buried in what you are doing that it's easy to go offside," he said. Having support from those who aren't caught up in the problem can help the handler retain her emotional distance from the situation. At other times, it can be refreshing to get confirmation from others in the same situation who are not as stressed at that moment. One handler put it this way: "There is so much angst and bad morale with the staff that we all lean on each other."[45]

Another form of reality check is for the handler to develop cues that tell him that he's getting trapped in the toxicity of his workplace. For example, I cited in the last chapter the case of Paul, the human resources manager in an educational institution who often felt "trapped like a deer in the headlights of an oncoming vehicle," unable to leave his office because he was so hooked to his work. He learned with practice to notice this trapped feeling and to recognize its meaning for him, thus using the cues of encroaching toxicity to stimulate him to act in self defense. In his own words: "Now when I feel like I'm under pressure, I say to myself: 'Uh-oh! I am getting hooked. It's time to take a break!' I'll typically book a day off or I'll make sure the next weekend is really work-free." The change in his stress level is almost immediate. "I become much calmer. I get things done more quickly. People's issues don't seem to hang around me so much after someone leaves my office . . . and I can get out of my office without difficulty at the end of the day!"

Leave the Site

There's an old song made famous by Kenny Rogers that goes, "You got to know when to hold 'em, know when to fold 'em, know when to walk away . . . and know when to run."[46] Indeed, there might come a time in the life of a toxin handler when she finds herself overwhelmed by the toxicity in her organization and sees no hope for improvement. The general conditions of suffering in her workplace are so great that whatever she does is only a Band-Aid solution to a more deeply rooted set of organizational problems. The trouble is that handlers who are burning out are usually too worn down to recognize when they need to walk away from a toxic site altogether. This is where the honest counsel of others (who become toxin handlers to the handler) can help handlers regain their mental capacity to rethink their commitment—and perhaps find the courage to leave a toxic organization.

One longtime toxin handler, revisiting his time at a major brewing company, described to me how a mentor in his organization advised him to get out while he could:

> *He told me, "There are wars going on here that are not going to end anytime soon, and you are just getting chewed up in the process. If I was your age I wouldn't hesitate. I'd be gone as soon as I could find another job." His advice was sobering and I took it to heart. I quit a couple of months later and it was probably one of the best decisions I ever made. I would not have had the guts or even the inkling to do it, if he had not said those words to me.*

Another source of insight and courage for the beleaguered toxin handler are workshops or projects that take her away from the immediate toxic site and give her time to think and regain perspective. Seminars with a focus on personal leadership or on work/life balance can be triggers for change of employment. Whether company-sponsored (which adds a touch of irony) or chosen and financed by the handler, such programs offer valuable breathing space and can challenge the handler to confront her values and how they fit with her current job. Of course, handlers in less ill fitting situations might well return from such a seminar with renewed energy for their jobs. But those for whom the situation is beyond recovery find resources and connections that can help them move to a healthier workplace.

Building Your Spiritual Capacity

How shall I live, knowing I will die?

—Wayne Muller, *How Then Shall We Live?*

LOEHR AND SCHWARTZ define spiritual capacity as "the energy that is unleashed by tapping into one's deepest values and defining a strong sense of purpose." This energy, they point out, provides support and nourishment in the face of adversity—something that toxin handlers often experience—and is a "powerful source of motivation, focus, determination, and resilience."[47] Let's look now at some ways that handlers can develop their spiritual muscles.

Be Clear on Values

Toxin handlers can sustain themselves through much organizational toxicity by simply defining for themselves *why* they are doing the work of handling other people's suffering. There are many tools and methods for clarifying values, including meditation and keeping a journal of daily experiences. Working with a professional such as a counselor can help as well. As a result, the handler might discover that she does this work, for example, out of a strong sense of compassion for others, or a highly developed sense of fairness or justice, or because of a belief in the value of accomplishing things by treating people with dignity. Or she might have a deep-seated understanding of the value of healing itself, since healing others often helps the healer as well.

Author Rachel Naomi Remen, who works with at least thirty cancer patients every week as well as codirecting retreats for cancer sufferers in Bolinas, California, speaks to this issue:

People sometimes say to me, "How do you stand this? How come you're not eaten alive?" But I am not eaten alive at all. As a matter of fact, at the end of the week I feel fed and strengthened. Healing is natural . . . [it] comes out of the integrity of the relationship between us. So both of us have been healed in that process.[48]

These are strong words, but they ring true for many professionals who have worked with people suffering from an illness or some other trauma. Still, toxin handlers in organizations are different from healers like Remen in that they don't choose to be handlers as their primary source of work and meaning. Even those within specialties such as human resource management handle the pain of organizational members as only a part of their function—and many HR specialists don't work as handlers at all. Furthermore, the work of toxin handlers is not celebrated or admired, perhaps not even by those they help, since often this role is played out "behind the scenes."

Therefore, unless the handler recognizes the origins of her intentions, values this way of responding to others, and is comfortable with why they "make sense" to her personally, she risks feeling discounted or otherwise let down by the organization's indifference. And because of the invisibility of this work, many handlers describe their confusion and guilt about the legitimacy of what they are doing—at least as far as the organization is concerned. Having a strong sense that their helping actions reflect deeply held values can sustain the handler through the hard times.

On the other hand, doing the work of toxin handling so as to be liked, to "look good," or to control others' emotional states in order to accomplish work goals are values that can quickly trap the handler. For example, the handler can easily become someone who "over-cares" for others, which will soon pull him into a cycle of burnout as he seeks more and more ways to meet such personal needs. Overinvolvement in other people's suffering can leave the handler unable to let it go at the end of each day, neglecting personal routines that could help keep him healthy, as we discussed in chapter 4.

Revere Life Balance

On September 11, 2001, passengers on flights who faced certain death as their planes were hijacked by terrorists used their cell phones to call home. Their message to family or close friends had nothing to do with work. Instead, every one of them said: "I love you!" This speaks to another key spiritual tool for pain managers to develop: values that emphasize the importance of life balance. Without this value, the toxic nature of their work will draw them inevitably into burnout and ineffectiveness.

This is so even for those with such lofty values as compassion, dignity, and humanity. In fact, valuing compassionate actions for others without also valuing them for oneself is the most dangerous state of all: Any intervention becomes tainted because the handler will continue to help a sufferer again and again, without regard to his own safety.

The mythology of healing tends to overlook this condition, focusing instead on the "goodness" of the healer. Even psychotherapists, who have extensive training in handling the suffering of others, aren't immune to losing a sense of balance in their lives. William Grosch and David Olsen describe the case of Robert, a social worker in a psychotherapy group. At the beginning of the first counseling session, Robert is described as slumped dejectedly in an easy chair and announcing in a lifeless tone that he is burned out.

> *He described how his initial enthusiastic idealism had turned into boredom and apathy. . . . Where once he had been passionately committed to his career [of helping others] he now found himself watching the clock and daydreaming of bass fishing in Maine. He spoke of the dread of taking on a new client, feeling he had heard it all before. He was tired of hearing about all the tragedy and sorrow in people's lives and losing confidence in his ability to help them.*[49]

These authors, examining the lives and the burnout of trained toxin handlers, point out that the causes are both individual and organizational, as are the remedies. They note also that handlers like Robert are experiencing a "painful erosion of the spirit," which is the response to workload and "*an insufficiently sustaining personal life*" (my emphasis).[50]

Others who study and teach healing work are also bringing this aspect of handling pain out of the closet. Jack Kornfield, a Buddhist monk and Western clinical psychologist, points out the growing acknowledgment of the costs to healers of ignoring their own life balance. Quoting a Western Tibetan lama, he notes:

> *I've seen a lot of pathological detachment in myself and others . . . I don't know how many meditation teachers . . . I have met who are having trouble with their health. . . . Most of these teachers haven't taken care of their bodies for years. . . . Now, twenty five years later, I'm starting to respect my body, my need for rest, for exercise, to find physical wisdom I lost for so long.*[51]

Toxin handlers in organizations are not psychotherapists, meditation teachers, or respected religious teachers. Nevertheless, they deal with suffering and help others just as these professionals do. They too tend to sacrifice their own personal lives to this work and to neglect their physical, emotional, mental, and spiritual well-being along the way. And although the ideas discussed in this chapter are meant to help address this imbalance, toxin handlers must acknowledge in the first place that life balance matters—and must vigilantly ensure that they maintain balance. Otherwise, toxin handlers in the workplace, like their counterparts in therapy, counseling, and spiritual practice, will burn out and lose their health, vitality, and influence.

The plan of action to heal and protect ourselves as toxin handlers calls for two key components: building in breaks and building up reserves. These are designed to provide a perspective on emotional safety and well-being that encompasses the physical, emotional, mental, and spiritual capacities. When we take breaks on a regular basis from the intense work of helping others, we give our bodies, our minds, and our spirits an opportunity to recover their own rhythms. We take time to breathe, to eat, to rest, to take a physical "energy break," to get some immediate perspective so that we can reduce the insistent pressure that builds up from the contagions of the emotional front line. By doing so, we're more likely to let go of the toxins we are dealing with, and we will be able to identify and to extricate ourselves from the situation's emotional hooks.

When we invest time and effort into building up our reserves of energy, we will be more compassionate handlers of other people's suffering—without being drawn into the emotionality of the situation. We can achieve this by making our bodies stronger and more resilient. Or, we can learn to put the emotional issues we are handling into a healthier perspective, by not taking them personally, for example. We can also become systematically more mindful, through meditation or other practices, of the situations we find ourselves in—including being more aware of when our own responses to someone else's pain lead down the slippery path to burnout. We can protect our peace of mind (and our other capacities) by establishing a personal space or sanctuary to which we retreat. We can practice saying no! We can seek feedback from others to help us sort out reality from delusion. We can even walk away.

We can create time to examine the spirit of our endeavors. What are our values in the role of toxin handler? Why are we doing this work? For others or for ourselves? Undoubtedly for both reasons. But are we doing this only to be liked? If so, we need to examine this tendency and find ways to neutralize the dangers to ourselves that this orientation brings. We can reexamine the notion of life balance knowing that it is a dynamic through which we move in and out—even with the best of action plans. Nevertheless, we can tilt the odds toward more resilience in our lives if we remember to keep one eye continually on our own well-being.

As valuable as I hope the tools in this chapter will be for toxin handlers, because of the high levels of toxicity in many organizations today, it's critical that the people who help heal emotional pain receive additional support. After all, dealing with toxicity always takes place in a context.[52] Handlers' health, therefore, depends on assistance from the organization itself. The cultural beliefs, practices, and norms in a workplace, as well as its leadership, can either help sustain handlers or add to their difficulties. And as we have seen, the pain that handlers experience when they take on toxicity comes from a combination of their own actions *and* the organization's attitudes.

In chapter 6, we will explore the various ways that interactions between the organization and the toxin handler help and hinder the handler's well-being.

CHAPTER SIX

At the Interface

What Handlers and Their Organizations Can Do

In the investment firm they named the work that wasn't getting recognized or rewarded as "invisible work.". . . Naming the problem had a striking effect. For senior managers who saw the link between invisible work and their goal of moving to a team-based structure, the challenge was to find ways to make invisible work visible—and to ensure it was valued and more widely shared by men and women.[1]

—Debra Meyerson and Joyce Fletcher, *Harvard Business Review*

While it *is* ultimately up to the toxin handler to take care of himself, toxin-handling actions are relational. They involve the handler and the person in pain; they involve the handler and others in the organization. Thus, part of handlers' protection from the kinds of physical and emotional distress that can accompany the work of managing pain lies in how well *connections* are built between them and their organization. Handlers need to find opportunities to educate their organizations about the value of what they do and to create mechanisms at work to make their jobs safer. For their part, organizations and their leadership must also play a role in nurturing and protecting these people.

This chapter will explore the ways that handlers and their organizations can work in tandem to reduce the hardships that result from handling everyday toxicity. Let's begin with a look at what handlers can do to increase the organization's understanding of their work.

What Handlers Can Do: Creating Understanding and Respect

PROBABLY the first and biggest hurdle handlers must leap is garnering organizational understanding of—and respect for—the work of toxin handling. Indeed, most handlers feel as if they toil alone, without an organizationally meaningful reference frame to nurture them. Then, as handlers begin to wear down, their work increasingly isolates them from others. And, in fact, they usually have few outlets where they can let off steam or "dissipate the toxins." Typically, neither they nor their colleagues have a way to talk about their work in ways that help them heal.

But handlers need to know they are doing worthwhile work, and that others appreciate their efforts. Without addressing this condition of isolation and confusion ("Should I be taking valuable time to do this work?") and resolving it in systemically supportive ways, handlers can't hope to create conditions that will help them maintain a healthy work/life balance. That's why it's crucial to develop a language that helps the handler and the organization to grasp and celebrate the contributions that pain managers make to the whole working community. What follows are a few ways to begin crafting just such a language, specifically by

- naming the experience and
- managing the message (by using the language of competence and by building and maintaining connections).

Naming the Experience

The handlers' sense of disconnection from the workplace begins with the fact that their work isn't discussed. We saw in chapter 4 that managers, not surprisingly, feel awkward and even guilty about describing the emotional work they do for others. But without ways to talk about this work—in language that feels credible to them and to others in the company—how can handlers hope to communicate how they spend their time? The question, "What did you do at the office today, dear?" is hard for the toxin handler to answer in terms that sound as if any real work was done. She might say, quite honestly, "Well, I had a succession of unhappy staff come through my office to tell me their woes." But while a handler's spouse might well understand what such an answer means, the handler would be hard put to give the same reply to her boss. Indeed, in the bottom-line-oriented organization of today, somehow that reply doesn't carry the same weight as something like, "We met a very challenging sales target today."

On the other hand, if the manager has a legitimate label and a language for doing work to resolve others' pain, he can more easily reply to a boss: "I spent quite a bit of time working with emotional issues in the group this morning. There's a lot of pain in the office from the recent layoffs, and we can't move forward until I've dealt with it. I think I'm making progress. People are beginning to pay more attention to targets again!" This response references the constructive contribution of this work to the company's goals, allowing the handler to feel much better about himself and what he's doing. The language effectively communicates that the manager is taking care of some dysfunction or poison in the system, and as a result the system as well as the individual in pain benefits.

First, then, handlers need to find ways to identify their work, creating a frame of reference and a language for communicating within the organization the value, importance, and nature of that work. By thus "naming their experience," handlers begin to build bridges of communication to other organizational members.

When I started investigating the notion of toxicity in organizations, I was struck by the visceral responses of the managers I interviewed when I named their experience as "toxin handling." One manager said, with much feeling: "Thinking of it as a *task,* as handling toxins, has 'connected the dots' for me," he said. "All these years I have been doing this sort of thing and thinking it was just 'touchy feely' stuff that somebody had to do but wasn't really what managers do. I couldn't really justify it to myself or to anyone else."

Another common response that I heard time and again went something like this: "I've never been able to tell this story to anyone before, and it feels so much better to have a way to explain it so it doesn't sound so soft." It is as if the phenomenon of toxin handling was always there, hidden behind a perceptual or a cultural barrier that prevented it from being seen. There's just never been a clear way for handlers in organizations to understand this work in a way that would allow them the satisfaction that can come from helping others to heal. That "aha!" response that I heard again and again was a first step for those managers to begin helping others in the organization understand the experience as well. It begins to "connect the dots" of what otherwise appear to be random, spontaneous, work-distracting, and individualistic sets of behaviors.

Once the handler himself grasps the full meaning of his work, then, the next step is to begin discussing the subject with his supervisor. For example, in a performance review session, the handler might show his boss—through specific examples—the ways that he, the handler, has consistently provided emotional support to his own staff and peers, and how that has made a difference to both the individuals and to the organization's goals. It's also effective, if not overdone, to communicate such actions and results in more informal settings. One toxin handler from a retail company told me how he does this occasionally when traveling on business with his CEO. "When the mood is mellow and the conversation is flowing freely, I'll take the opportunity to tell him about some of the traumas that we're dealing with and how I and others are successfully handling them. The CEO doesn't like a lot of 'I' stuff, as in 'I did this or that' (and I agree with him), so I am careful to phrase this in terms of 'we.' But he gets the point that I'm doing things to help the organization that involve working with the emotions of others."

Handling issues, crises, problems, and the like is simply what people do in organizations to keep them running smoothly. Giving these activities a name, particularly one that signifies "real work," provides individuals and their organization with the beginnings of an organizationally relevant role and agenda.

Managing the Message

It's one thing for handlers to show people with influence in the organization the reality of the work handlers do; it's quite another to build widespread support for their role. To do so, handlers and their supporters need to take creative initiatives and use political skills to shift their organizations from indifference (or disdain) for this work to a fuller appreciation of its value. Specifically, they need to position the toxin handler's work as a set of competencies that are crucial to the organization's success.

Using the Language of Competence

Joyce Fletcher, in her study of the experiences of female engineers, found their work discounted in many of the ways that toxin handlers report (e.g., the attention they gave to building and maintaining relationships with staff wasn't valued by their superiors).[2] She describes the initiative that one engineer took when she became aware that her efforts to help her team were discounted by management:

> *Rather than simply working behind the scenes to make sure key people outside the team were doing their jobs and not feeling exploited, she started to talk of her role as "interfacing." At team meetings she reported regularly on the status of these interfacing efforts, and eventually the practice became so routine that others adopted the term, and it was put on the agenda. In this way she rescued the term from obscurity and put it on the organizational screen.*[3]

Fortunately, the language of competence for the toxin handler is already gaining a degree of acceptance in organizations, since it relates to "emotional intelligence" (EI), which is an increasingly recognizable term in today's organizational lexicon. As noted earlier, there's a growing body of empirical evidence that correlates the actions of managers who exercise high emotional intelligence with positive organizational outcomes such as increased sales, lowered turnover, and reduced levels of grievances.[4] Handlers can take advantage of this growing respectability of EI in management circles and of the organizational perspective that views it as contributing to the success of the organization. In particular, the EI competence of responding compassionately to the feelings of others applies directly to toxin handlers. The emotionally intelligent manager listens carefully to her staff, harnessing what she learns about other people's feelings to make good decisions for the organization. Similarly, the manager with toxin-handling skills makes decisions based on empathy: The person in pain benefits, yes, but so does the organization.

The key, then, is for handlers to communicate throughout the company that their work enables them to head off or help heal a painful condition that, untended, would hurt the individual's performance and ultimately the company. Like the "interfacing" of the engineer, the listening and even the buffering activities of the handler need to get on the agenda as contributing to the organization's progress.

Part of the challenge for handlers is to raise the issue of competence without undermining anyone's abilities. For example, the handler wouldn't tell a superior simply that she's "lightening Jeffrey's load for a while"—as if it's a matter of technical incompetence. Rather, she would say "I'm shifting Jeffrey's responsibilities to help him cope with his recent stress [or loss in his family, or whatever]. I want him to be able to come back and work harder, not burn out on us." In this way, the toxin handler rallies the support of others around Jeffrey as well. Accordingly, sometimes the decision to help an employee needs support from higher-ups in the organization. For example, the manager who argues for a day off for his staff to grieve the death of a supervisor needs to remember to make the competency case to his bosses. By listening to his staff and by giving them space to mourn, he is recognizing that the funeral day is in effect a "write-off" in terms of attentive work by staff. He also sees that the time together in mourning will hasten the healing and cohesion of the group as well as their return to a strong work focus and good customer service.

In other words, as a toxin handler, the manager essentially performs two key tasks: He makes decisions to help staff members in pain, but he also must convince his superiors and the organization at large of the value of those decisions. By using the language of competence, he ensures he gets the necessary relief for his staff *and* he registers the value of what he's doing on the corporate scoreboard.

Handlers also need to remember to take an extra step: to look for indicators of how well their intervention worked and to communicate any positive outcomes tactfully to the organization's leaders. They can also look for ways to recognize the efforts of other handlers in the workplace—especially since handlers aren't always the best at blowing their own horns. (After all, compassionate actions tend to be made by people who do not like to draw attention to themselves.) Naming the emotional work of others thus adds to the overall awareness of this important work, and carries the added benefit of connecting handlers to a network of like-minded individuals.

Most helpful of all is when toxin handlers can garner a champion—someone with power, influence, or access who communicates to others how the handler's actions serve the goals of the organization. These naming strategies can be "as simple as substituting the word 'effective' when someone else notes the 'nice' or 'sensitive' attributes [of a toxin handler] . . . or, it can mean suggesting more formal ways to document or make visible the invisible contributions others have made."[5]

Most important, handlers need to be diligent about introducing into work conversations the listening or buffering roles they undertake for others, so that such handling activities and their productive links to performance are continually reinforced. Introducing toxin handling as a competency into the discussion of work goals and outcomes provides many organizations a new way of thinking about what counts toward the successes they achieve. It surfaces, for example, as an important aspect of conducting team-based projects (handling emotional pain within the team well) that is typically overlooked but critical to a team's success.

Over time, handlers' skillful communication of the work they do and what it accomplishes for staff and for the organization will help other managers appreciate what actually goes into a successful project—and how that outcome might be repeated. Otherwise, without the benefit of knowing toxin handlers' contributions to results, organizations are blind to the full picture. They become like the person who, in trying to understand the functioning of a fish, looks only at the bones and misses the skin, the color, and the movement of this animal swimming in the water.[6] They miss the full complexity and richness of the phenomenon.

An executive in the publishing industry commented that it was only after one of the editors left the company that management and others realized just how many relationships the editor had held together and how much of the pain in the company she had contained. "We saw her only for her editing skills," he said. "We never recognized all the work she was doing to sort out the tensions and hurts in the group. She kept people together and made the department functional. We just didn't notice until it was too late."

When handlers communicate the organizational relevance of what they are doing, or if someone else who champions their work does so, they educate others in a constructive way. They also ensure that their supportive actions aren't interpreted as something without organizational value. Whether this message is couched in terms of "listening" and "buffering," or is framed in other words more congruent with the culture and day-to-day language of the organization, depends on the judgment of the handler about what works in her situation.

Using the language of competence, however, carries one caveat: The integrity of the toxin-handling work, like any act of compassion, rests on *the purity of the intention to help*. When managers or other organizational members take steps to help others only to smooth the path of a project, or when communicating these competencies is solely self-serving, the handler's contribution is degraded. Promoting the value of toxin handling soon becomes viewed as just another management manipulation for profit or for the handler's own career enhancement. People begin to distrust the handler's actions, and the handler loses the power to help.

Similarly, if managed poorly, communication about toxin handling could be seen as "grandstanding" rather than a valid activity—and thus something to be dismissed. That's why toxin handling should always be a "technique of authenticity"; that is, the authentic work of handling toxins is first of all concerned with the person in emotional difficulty—organizational concerns are secondary.[7] Authentic handling, then, is neither purely selfless, nor instrumental. It is an activity that connects the handler to the person in pain because the handler *wants* to be of assistance in a compassionate way. The actions link handlers to the system because they *intend* their actions also to help the organization. Handlers, of course, do benefit from their actions: A project succeeds, or they gain the loyalty and commitment of their staff. But in a truly authentic intervention, these outcomes are secondary to the concern for the suffering and recovery of the person in pain.

Building and Maintaining Connections

Let's go back to the female engineers that Joyce Fletcher researched in her book. She found that these women—like many toxin handlers—often find it difficult to know what they know and what they feel. "Trusting their instincts, when the organizational system is giving them error messages for doing so, is tough," Fletcher writes.[8]

A good way to counteract that isolation is for toxin handlers to create support networks or groups where they can talk about the work they do and how they feel about it. Being in such a setting often restores the handler's confidence and sense of empowerment. They hear the stories of other handlers and they see the connections between their own experiences, dilemmas, and difficult decisions and those of others. Simply relating to a supportive group their actions, the outcomes, their doubts, and the personal costs of their work can serve as a release from pent-up stress and discouragement. Support networks thereby provide a highly effective mechanism for dissipating the emotional toxins that handlers invariably accumulate over time.

One manager in a government organization I spoke with described how her network has kept her "sane and willing to continue to work for this organization"—something she believed was true for others in the group as well. After years of dealing with the varieties of toxicity that can accompany government bureaucracies, the manager attended a workshop, sponsored by the organization, in which she met several other managers who had experiences similar to hers. "That really opened my eyes," she said. The workshop facilitator encouraged the group to meet regularly to share their concerns, and she offered guidelines and structures for the meetings.

> *We were to create time for each member to share whatever was on their minds and hearts, and our role was simply to listen and to witness. We weren't required to provide solutions for any problems the person identified. Each person had a fixed amount of time "on stage," then someone else had a turn.*
>
> *I was ready to quit. I was so burned out and disillusioned. The group changed that. It has been the most amazingly helpful experience for each of us. I walk away from each session feeling lighter and ready to deal with the pain in my unit.*

In this case, a group grew out of an organizational initiative to provide training and education for its managers. Management may not have intended this particular outcome; it seems to have been a product of the participant's experience and the facilitator's intervention. But such an "organizationally aided" creation is perhaps more likely to be the norm for the development of support networks for handlers, since their very isolation and "invisibility" make it difficult for them to initiate such a network. This is especially true when handlers have reached the point of burnout and are thus unable to see that they need help, much less find the energy to create such a group. Furthermore, most toxin handlers, focused as they are on others, pride themselves on a high tolerance for personal pain. As one CEO I interviewed noted: "These folks don't know when to ask for help; they're too busy giving it. And it would kill them to let others down by breaking down themselves."

Even so, toxin handlers can and often do create support groups themselves, especially as they come to realize the importance of having systemic mechanisms of self-healing. At one company in the oil industry, toxin handlers spontaneously formed a support group when the company began downsizing rapidly and the burden of assuaging widespread sadness, fear, and anger fell largely to five managers. After a month of going it alone, the group started to meet for dinner once a week to "let off steam," as one manager puts it. Another recalls:

> *One of the worst parts of the downsizing was that there was no quick bang of departures, just a slow, painful bleed. We were helping individuals to leave the organization on a nonstop basis. We were the ones who helped the managers prepare for the termination discussions and supported the employees when they received the news. Needless to say, it was a heavy emotional burden. The only way we got through it was to support one another. It was like a bereavement group, to tell you the truth—the thing that helped the most was just knowing I wasn't alone.*[9]

The question remains, should support groups be formed solely of members in a particular organization, or should they expand to comprise handlers from other companies as well? There's no obvious answer. On the one hand, groups formed within a particular workplace have the advantage of a common frame of reference; handlers can identify sources of toxins and possible resources that everyone quickly recognizes. Of course, such internal groups also risk being stigmatized by others in the organization as "weak," or as a group of "soft managers" or "whiners" (or even as a "women's group," if they're mostly female). Senior managers who've been instrumental in forming the network can help. For example, they can provide a name and a structure that project an "official" image to others in the organization—thus protecting the network's healing power even further.

On the other hand, networks formed outside of the handler's workplace have the advantage of providing a setting that is more protective of the handler's anonymity. His stories and concerns are less likely to leak back into his workplace. His support from others remains hidden from the view of his organization. The added diversity of an external network increases the range of shared experiences available for learning and expands the base of healing alternatives. Handlers have a

BOX 6-1 HEALING CONNECTIONS

The healing power of support groups is illustrated quite dramatically in settings designed for individuals with serious illness. For example, the Commonweal Cancer Help Program, cofounded by Michael Lerner and Rachel Naomi Remen, runs a group in which eight people with cancer, previously strangers, spend a week together at the center. There, they learn to name their condition out loud, and they listen to one another's stories, fears, and concerns. They spend time together doing yoga and exploring their feelings through talking and writing poetry, which they share.

Most important, the participants learn from one another and begin to recognize that they must heal internal and psychic wounds and come to terms with their lives, "which they may soon be leaving," Remen observes. Bill Moyers, who interviewed Lerner and Remen for his TV series *Healing and the Mind,* describes this group of former strangers at the end of their week: "As they shake hands, embrace, mug for one another's cameras, make small talk and joke, it is hard for me to imagine them as they were a week ago: strangers, arriving here tense and fearful."[10]

Indeed, recent research confirms the value of such support groups. David Spiegel's research on women with recurrent breast cancer revealed that the average life span for women who had a support group was *double* that of women who simply got mainstream medical treatment. Measures on patients' quality of life significantly favored those with group support.[11] The lesson for toxin handlers, of course, is that people who are seriously hurt emotionally or physically benefit significantly from being in a supportive space where they can recognize and work through their fears, their sense of isolation, and their sheer exhaustion. And, like the Commonweal program, rather than operating with a specific agenda to "cure" the participants or "do something to them," such a space operates simply to help people to calm their minds and their bodies. It allows them to recover their vitality and their ability to participate more confidently in the work of healing.

chance to debrief and to revitalize themselves from ideas and insights derived in novel settings.

To recap, then, handlers can help themselves in a variety of ways, including forming support networks (in which they can release built-up toxins) and finding ways to name the work they do (so that they and others can better understand their contributions). But since toxin handling takes place *in a context*—specifically, in the framework of workplaces—organizations, too, need to take responsibility for the health and well-being of the handler.

What Organizations Can Do to Help Their Handlers

ENLIGHTENED ORGANIZATIONS are learning that, to continue reaping the benefits of the work toxin handlers do, they must find ways to recognize and support this valuable function. Some companies are already beginning to take the following positive actions to systematically manage and diffuse the emotional pain that comes with everyday organizational life:

- Acknowledge the dynamic
- Offer support
- Assign handlers to safe zones
- Model healthy handling
- Create a supportive culture

Acknowledge the Dynamic

Just as handlers themselves need to name their work, thereby giving it focus and legitimacy, leaders of organizations need to acknowledge that toxin handlers exist—and that they play a critical role.

Of course, there's nothing simple about such a public admission from top management, especially in cultures that tend to value technical competence above all else. But another aspect of corporate life often makes organizational pain a difficult, even dangerous, topic to bring to the table. Middle and senior managers are usually expected to "tough it out" during hard times. As one manager in a communications company recalls, "After a particularly bitter strike that churned up a lot of agony and anger, the company provided counseling for the workers. There was nothing for any managers. We were expected to suck in our emotions, stay quiet, and cope alone." Indeed, managers at the company felt, perhaps rightly, that to talk about their feelings would have hurt their careers.[12]

And yet, despite the strong corporate ethic not to discuss organizational pain—let alone to thank toxin handlers—when executives do so, the effects are likely to be immediate and positive. For example, one team leader at a media company played the toxin-handling role during a difficult six-month merger in which many employees lost their jobs. The team leader had managed to hit all of her financial goals during the upheaval, and she expected that would be the main focus of her performance review—which it was. However, this woman had also managed to save the emotional health of the merger's survivors. Had her boss only recognized this crucial aspect of her performance, the toxin handler might have gained a renewed sense of energy, along with the sense of relief that comes when one's efforts are recognized.[13]

To raise consciousness about the toxin handler's role, companies need a forum to discuss the topic in the first place. The nature and importance of this work needs to be on the agenda of management meetings or retreats, and it needs a champion to ensure that it gets sufficient time and attention in these settings. Of course, when the source of a particular organizational toxin is a toxic boss, open discussion is unlikely. Such circumstances may require a more neutral setting, such as a conference of senior managers from several organizations.

Ultimately, however, any successful consciousness-raising about toxin handling requires that everyone recognize that effective pain management can and does contribute to the bottom line. No company can afford to let talented employees burn out, nor can it afford to have a reputation as an unhappy place to work. Many good people simply won't join. Therefore, it is up to senior management—people with visibility and influence—to make the business case for recognizing the work of toxin handlers. In chapter 7, we will see some specific examples of how this has been done in organizations.

Offer Support for Toxin Handlers

Enlightened company leaders can minimize the toll on toxin handlers by bringing them together in support groups or by arranging for them to meet periodically with professionals who are trained to help them decompress and rejuvenate. One manager in my study who had been a toxin handler for two years during a company restructuring said: "It took a therapist to help me to recognize that I was taking [the toxicity] into my gut. I was ignoring all the signs my body was sending me. I was taking things very personally. The therapist allowed me to hear myself in denial."

Of course, the process of raising consciousness about the work of toxin handlers is an important precondition to setting up the necessary support for them. (Remember, this work is often done by individuals who do not see it as legitimate. Therefore, it isn't something that's easily discussed.) One relatively straightforward way for organizational leaders to broach the subject is to provide opportunities for managers to come together to discuss concerns about the health and productivity of their units, or to attend a workshop on "conflict management" or "emotional intelligence" (both terms with credibility today in many organizations). The agenda of such meetings can include discussion of toxin handling or managing emotions in the workplace or some other relevant term. At such meetings, it becomes quickly apparent who is tuned into the issues and challenges of the toxin handler. Then, if the setting feels "safe" (often that means if the meeting is run by some kind of outside professional or consultant), people will likely begin to discuss the issue.

Alternatively, companies can bring in experts who can guide handlers through conversations that allow them to see, understand, and appreciate the pressures of what they do. Experts can also help toxin handlers recognize if they are dangerously close to burnout or presenting worrisome physical symptoms. The point, however, remains the same: for organizations to play an active role in the process of supporting the people who manage the emotional pain of their coworkers.

Assign the Toxin Handler to a Safe Zone

Even when other actions, such as counseling, can help toxin handlers deal with stress, it also makes sense on occasion to move them out of a particularly stressful situation. These moves need not be long-term. One company, for instance, sent a toxin handler who was showing signs of burnout to a two-week conference in Florida. The conference was work-related—there were at least three hours of meetings a day—but also included heavy doses of rest and relaxation. It was, in essence, a forced vacation. (Of course, for a solution like this to work requires a high level of trust, openness, and cultural support in the organization; otherwise, the toxin handler might feel threatened by the assignment—that she's done something wrong and that her career is in jeopardy.)

Research confirms the healing power of taking breaks or retreating to some form of "safe zone." André Delbecq of the Leavey Business School at Santa Clara University and Frank Friedlander of the Fielding Institute in Santa Barbara studied the habits of 166 business leaders in the computer and health care industries. All participants were known to be happy, healthy, and well balanced, and all worked in companies undergoing rapid change—and therefore managed considerable organizational pain. One thing they had in common was that they frequently took short (two- to five-day) vacations, typically with their families. "The breaks allowed the leaders to step back, regain a fresh perspective on themselves and their situations," Delbecq observed. "Each time, they returned to work like new people."[14]

Organizations obviously can do much to encourage such breaks by enacting policies that make vacations a legitimate and even expected form of replenishment. In one department I observed at a management training company, the staff was often called upon to handle the emotional outbursts of customers and of members from other units. When a policy institutionalized days off for staff after intensely emotional projects, morale rose markedly—and the staff members lost their signature "tired and frazzled" look.

In cases of extreme organizational distress, however, a short break is not enough to restore toxin handlers, and they should probably be reassigned to less emotionally strenuous areas of the company. Naturally, most toxin handlers will resist such a move, especially if they've come to value what they do (as they should) and to understand its importance to the organization's well-being. In such an instance, then, an organization's leaders should use extreme care and discuss the move thoroughly with the handler, rather than making a unilateral decision to transfer her. Later, the employee may well come to see the wisdom of such an intervention and may even appreciate the spirit with which it was done.

Model Healthy Toxin Handling

If handling organizational pain becomes an open topic in a company, then managers can feel comfortable demonstrating how to do it right. For example, following his heart attack, Intel's Dave Marsing (whose story appeared at the beginning of chapter 4) made it a point to show other managers how to stay calm at work, even under intense pressure. He said in an interview:

> *I try, to the greatest extent possible, to maintain a level of calmness in the face of frantic issues. I try to be as objective as possible in discussions, and if I'm in a face-to-face meeting with someone who has a short fuse, I'll sit right next to that person to make sure the fuse is never lit. I do that by being calm, even overly calm. When things get heated, I even change my voice. I will consciously take a deeper breath, or two deep breaths, in front of everybody to get them to calm down a little bit and talk about the specifics, about solutions.*[15]

Marsing also encourages his staff to keep their work and personal lives in balance. He reminds his direct reports, for example, to spend more time with their families, to exercise, and to delegate work rather than putting in overly long days. Teaching toxin handlers how to stay healthy, in what is inherently an unhealthy role, is something Marsing says is one of his most important jobs as an executive.

BOX 6-2 PROTECTING TOXIN HANDLERS: LESSONS FROM THE HAZARDOUS WASTE INDUSTRY

Toxicity can make a workplace feel as lethal as a hazardous waste zone. So what do you do when the toxin your organization handles is hazardous waste? Safety managers at Roy F. Weston, Inc. in West Chester, Pennsylvania, who worked on the anthrax cleanup at the U.S. Capitol and U.S. Post Offices in the fall of 2001, offered the following advice for protecting handlers. Whether the toxin is anthrax or an overbearing boss, three main rules of thumb can prevent toxicity from putting workers out of commission.

1. Use the Buddy System

"The first rule of working in hazardous waste is that you always go in with a buddy," said George Crawford, a twenty-year Weston veteran. The idea is to pair newer hires with more experienced people. But the system also ensures that no one feels they have to "go it alone"—or absorb, if you will, all the toxicity by themselves.

Similarly, toxin handlers in the business world could benefit from organizational structures that ensure such support. This could mean making counseling available for people who handle organizational toxins as part of their jobs or creating support groups for toxin handlers that meet regularly onsite.

2. Shield Workers from Harm

In the hazardous waste industry, "shielding" means anything from wearing protective suits with respirators to working behind dense barriers made of concrete or lead, depending on the hazard. In organizational life, top management can effectively shield its toxin handlers—first, by acknowledging their contributions, and second, by actively protecting them from burnout. For example, handlers could be granted flexible work deadlines to accommodate the "double duty" they perform because of their roles.

Of course, the reality is that toxin handlers themselves often act as human shields for coworkers and the organization. But doing that work without respite can be dangerous. As Weston safety managers point out, even the best shields are designed for only short periods of use. "No protective suit is good indefinitely," said Greg Janiec of Weston's environmental health and safety group. "If you're exposed continually and if the toxin is aggressive enough, you will still be susceptible."

Likewise, repeated or prolonged exposure to organizational pain will soon wear down a toxin handler's defenses. "In the corporate world, you can't wear an actual lead suit," said Bob McGlade, a site safety manager. "But you can limit your time exposure to the toxin, and periodically create distance between you and it." This points to the Weston team's third recommendation.

3. Mandate Regular Breaks

Every Weston project has an onsite health and safety coordinator who looks for signs of fatigue and makes sure that people are prepared to do the work, emotionally and physically. "You want your safety managers to be your most level-headed people in the organization," said Peter Ciotoli, Weston's vice president. "They're the people I trust to make the right assessment—to tell someone to leave a site, or to stop the job entirely if there's a safety problem."

The key learning points for the corporate world? People are monitored and breaks away from the toxic site—be it an hour or weeks, depending on need—are standard operating procedure. "Everybody understands, from the top down, that breaks are required," said McGlade. "There's no stigma attached."

Such regular retreats to a safety zone proved crucial when the group worked on the anthrax cleanup at the U.S. Capitol. "We had people working fourteen, sixteen hours a day, seven days a week," McGlade said. "You can do that for only so long." What happens when toxic waste handlers don't take time away from a hazardous site? Effectiveness decreases, accident rates go up, and people become ill, the managers said—all of which have costs to the company's bottom line.

The safety managers drew one final parallel between handling toxins in the world of work and working in the world of toxins: "Recognize the relationship between cause and effect," said McGlade. "The longer you leave a toxin out there, unidentified and uncontrolled, the more people it's going to affect."

Create a Supportive Culture

Think about the following two comments for a moment. They were made by social workers in two very different work cultures who were part of a study of stress conducted by Debra Meyerson of the Stanford University School of Engineering.

> *Social Worker #1:* "That's my professional job—to fight off burnout. If [another social worker] said to me, 'I'm burned out' then I would call them a very nonprofessional person. I wouldn't deal any more with them because they should just quit."
>
> *Social Worker #2:* "[Burnout] means that what we do here is stressful, that we are asked always to give and sometimes there simply isn't anything left to give. So we take a break and then we are okay."[16]

In the first example the social worker was in a predominantly medical culture in which workers viewed burnout as something one controls, and as a weakness to be avoided. The second worker's culture was more attuned to psychological views of behavior. Burnout was discussed as a normal experience of working with others as a caregiver. It was considered normal for people to talk openly about their feelings of being worn down by their work; in fact, the group had developed ways to look after each other and to cover for one another. Not only was strong emotional control not considered desirable or even possible given the nature of their work, but the belief and practice was that the workplace community was responsible for coping with the difficulties of handling clients' suffering.

Unfortunately, many toxin handlers I've interviewed find themselves in cultures resembling the one in the first example—in which technical skills are valued, and emotions are excluded from the work-to-productivity equation. Think how different handlers' experiences could be in a supportive culture, where people are respected for skills other than purely technical and economic ones; where emotional and social competencies are valued and rewarded.

Context and culture *do* matter to how toxin handlers fare in organized settings. Accordingly, an organization's leaders can do much to protect and heal handlers by instituting and modeling practices that allow more open acknowledgment of the handling role. They can also communicate to handlers themselves that the work they do to help people cope with the inevitable toxins in the workplace largely determines the organization's overall effectiveness.

Routines of support, opportunities for handlers to share and talk about their own pressures (as handlers), modeling of healthy behaviors for dealing with emotions by leaders—all the practices noted above—apply. But from a cultural perspective, they need to be built into the "way we do things around here," into the very culture of the organization. This makes the task of working with toxins a much safer and more sustainable activity.

I have outlined in this chapter the importance of healthy connections between handlers and their organizations in providing protection against the ravages of toxicity. Handlers have a part to play in creating these connections. They need to consistently look for opportunities to educate others in their organization about the value of the work they do and its contributions to the success of the system. They need to build bridges of understanding by ensuring that this work of handling toxic emotions is recognized for what it is, that it is named so that they and others can learn to value its importance. Handlers can shape the meaning of the work they do so others begin to hear and acknowledge it and so that it becomes part of the day-to-day language of work, something that competent managers use when they talk about emotional issues in need of attention.

Organizations can do a number of things to make the handler's life safer and more rewarding. Treating the existence of emotional toxicity in the workplace as real and worthy of attention is a useful start. Better still, organizations can recognize that some managers do work to contain or dissipate pain, and that this work is important to organizational performance and resilience. Organizations can provide handlers with resources—financial, technical, moral, or emotional—to help them perform their jobs well and to maintain their own equilibrium. They need to step in when handlers are in danger of burning out and exercise their own brand of compassionate action. At a more strategic level, organizations that develop cultures of support for the activities and the emotional ups and downs of handling toxins—and managers who model healthy handling behavior for their staff and peers—will greatly diminish the dangers of this important activity in their workplaces. In the long run, these cultures generate the preferred solutions, values, practices, and actions that convey to everyone in the organization that toxicity exists, that it needs to be handled in healthy ways, and that when the burden of doing this work becomes onerous, there are accepted and supported ways to help handlers heal.

Of course, the implications of validating the toxin-handling function in the ways we've examined in this chapter stretch far beyond what I've covered here. It could mean a shift in the very things that are given prestige in organizations as well as what's typically devalued. If, as HR specialist and University of British Columbia professor Daniel Skarlicki (among others) has written, "what gets rewarded gets done," then the prestige so often awarded—consciously or not—to tough-minded and performance-driven managers might shift to people and policies that take into account human emotions and their wider implications for organizations' success.

To that end, chapters 7 and 8 will examine more fully how organizational culture and practice can encourage the healthy management of toxicity. Let's begin with a look at what a company's leaders, in particular, can do.

CHAPTER SEVEN

Leaders Handling Pain

We were going full tilt on a new project that I was leading, when we had one of our late afternoon meetings to review where we were. I was feeling the pressure of our deadline, which was coming up fast. I'm usually quite patient in these meetings and try to listen for mistakes and things we might have missed along the way. But this time I found myself butting in and pushing one team member for explanations—really being curt with him. After that, he didn't say much for the rest of the meeting.

That night, I woke up with the meeting playing over in my mind and thinking, "Oh shit! I really blew it with Mark." Like me, he was under a lot of pressure, and I really needed to have him fully on board if we're to meet

---

I gratefully acknowledge the contributions of my colleagues in the CompassionLab team at the University of Michigan: Jane Dutton, Monica Worline, Jacoba Lilius, and Jason Kanov. They include access to our pool of interviews, including those at *Newsweek,* Cisco, and the Benjamin Group; the benefits of the research process that informed our January 2002 *Harvard Business Review* article "Leading in Times of Trauma"; and the insights and support the team provided me that helped shape ideas in this chapter and in chapter 8.

our deadline. In my replay of the meeting, I could see his face and I sensed the anger and hurt he was feeling. I'd made an example of him, something I rarely do, and I'm sure he lost face with the others. I wished I'd not been so darn testy. The next evening, before we got down to the business of the meeting, I told the team: "I was out of line in my criticism of Mark last night. He is doing his best, as we all are, and his suggestions were constructive. I'm feeling the heat of this project, and I let my emotions get in the way." I then apologized to Mark. Boy! You could have heard a pin drop in the room. Then Mark smiled and said, "That's OK Pat, I probably deserved it. I wasn't that careful in the way I gave my answers." I'm not sure he really believed that, but he was offering peace. Almost immediately, the energy of the group picked up and we had a very productive session.

—Pat, a project manager in a high-tech firm

PAT is a good leader with a strong technical background who gets results. His team is loyal and committed to him and to the organization. Like all of us, he has his "off days" and he makes mistakes, but what makes him effective with people and high-pressure situations is that he not only knows how the organization works, he also reads emotional situations well. He usually anticipates when there's going to be a painful response to something he or the organization demands of his staff, and he knows how to cushion it or to discuss it with the team as a message hits home. He sometimes misses a key cue, however, as he did in the opening example, adding to the frustration in the team. But as we saw, he does eventually "get it," in the same way that other compassionate leaders do—often in the small hours of the morning, when the rhythm of sleep typically shifts out of deep REM sleep mode, and things that are nagging at us float to the surface.[1]

Leaders who easily connect with others' pain often get these belated "hits" of awareness some time after the event, particularly if the situation is complex, if they have a lot on their plate, or if, like Pat, they become emotionally involved in the process and temporarily miss the plot. But in general, these kinds of leaders make excellent toxin handlers, understanding what is going on around them in work or social situations and well attuned to their own and others' emotional states.

In this chapter, we'll explore the role of formal organizational leaders in handling toxins and how, in the process, these leaders also effectively acknowledge and support other toxin handlers throughout the organization. Indeed, paying attention to emotional pain can serve leaders well: It prompts them to do something constructive with the insights and information they perceive. For example, Pat waited until the next team meeting and made his apology in public, which was probably the right time and place to do so, since he had criticized Mark in front of these same people. He set the scene for his apology, sharing his feelings and his views on the pressures surrounding the project with the team, thereby naming the issue that had triggered his initial critical response to Mark. It isn't surprising that his leadership initiative worked here.

Pat's intervention might not always work so well, however, and Mark might not always be so gracious: Emotional issues are often more complex or protracted than this one and require a more involved response. Unlike managers who are cruel or vindictive, who are ignorant of or indifferent to their effect on others, or who just don't know what to do, leaders who are attuned to people's feelings strive for more compassionate answers to the emotional dilemmas they create or encounter. They are quick to recognize the pain a situation might cause.

Leaders like Pat recognize—sometimes in advance, sometimes later—that pain happens for a variety of reasons and needs to be resolved. Otherwise, both suffering *and* performance will worsen.

Placing Responsibility Where It Belongs

> *Being responsible sometimes means pissing people off.*[2]
>
> —Colin Powell

LEADERS and their organizations create toxins. It goes with the territory. But these toxins—the pain and suffering that occurs in the workplace—can be dealt with more effectively when leaders in organizations consciously assume the work of the toxin handler. Better still is when they do this as a formal part of their responsibility, sanctioned and supported by the firm. The load thereby shifts from the few to the many, and this work is no longer relegated to a back burner.

Distributing the work of managing toxicity among multiple leaders accomplishes at least three things. First, it lifts some of the relentless burden of dealing with organizational toxins from those who have stepped in simply because no one else would do so. Second, it puts the responsibility for managing the toxins with those who have power, resources, visibility, and connections—enabling real and effective interventions when necessary, and rooting out toxicity where it has taken hold. Third, an organization that expects and reinforces toxin handling in its leaders creates a force for positive experiences. It naturally engenders a more healthy work environment than one that ignores or blocks this competency. A crucial contribution to developing support and understanding for the toxin handling activities of leaders is that they be seen and supported as *part* of a leader's normal work—*not* as an "added extra" or an activity that is "bootlegged" into the daily agenda.

The following story illustrates eloquently the importance of leaders recognizing that they or their organization have triggered suffering and then taking responsibility for fixing the ensuing pain. A decade ago, Steve Snyder was running GE's Canadian appliance subsidiary when tragedy struck. His wife died, leaving him a single parent with two children, aged five and two. At the time, Snyder was about to be transferred to a new job in Europe. As he was preparing to move, however, he realized the mistake he would make if he uprooted his children from their Toronto home.

Wanting to be fair to his employer, he resigned from GE, which drew an invitation from then-CEO Jack Welch to fly immediately to his Fairfield, Connecticut, headquarters. Snyder, now president of TransAlta Corp. of Calgary, remembers the gist of his boss's remarks: "He said, 'Well, we screwed up, didn't we? We should never have planned to move you, given that situation. Will you stay with us in

Canada and we'll sort this out later?'" Mr. Snyder was promptly appointed chairman and CEO of General Electric Canada Inc., a job that kept him from having to shake up his family's lives any more than they already had been.[3]

When leaders are willing to deal with toxicity, even cleaning up their own mess as Welch did in this situation—there is a marked increase in people's responsiveness to issues of morale, creativity, and performance. Listening, creating breathing space, buffering toxins, and preventing or dispersing pain are some ways of handling toxins, as we described in chapter 3. But there are other aspects of this competency that are particularly relevant to people in leadership positions, and that should become part of the repertoire of the compassionate leader. These skills are

- paying attention
- putting people first
- practicing professional intimacy
- planting seeds
- pushing back

Paying Attention

There is always grief somewhere in the room!

—Birgitt Williams, Dalar International Consultancy

RECENTLY, while walking from an international flight to the customs and baggage collection section of Vancouver Airport, I found myself behind a couple in their thirties who were playfully discussing their plans for the next couple of days in the city. As we progressed toward the escalators to the main hall, in the middle of this animated exchange, the woman literally stopped in her tracks, spun around, and walked over to an older man sitting slumped and gasping for breath. "Are you OK?" she asked. "I am just getting my breath back," he replied, gray-faced. He'd been sitting there for a few minutes, and we'd all walked by without noticing him—but *she* had noticed. She and her partner stayed with the man. Later, as we waited in line at the customs counters they reappeared, pushing the man in a wheelchair. They went through together and I saw them help him with his luggage on the other side.

The scene made me think about how some people really know how to pay attention, and are willing to stop their own progress to help another person in distress. This is exactly what leaders who are adept at handling toxins do well.

Phil Jackson, in his book about the Chicago Bulls' journey to greatness during the 1990s, gives us another angle on paying attention. He says: "Awareness is everything."[4] He means that having an open mind to whatever one sees or encounters increases the capacity of an individual to respond appropriately to a situation. Jackson gives the example of what happens when one is *not* aware and is not open-minded to what is happening:

> *When I was a player, not surprisingly, my biggest obstacle was my hyperactive critical mind. I'd been trained by my Pentecostal parents to stand guard over my thoughts, meticulously sorting out the "pure" from the "impure." That kind of intense judgmental thinking—that is good, that's bad—is not unlike the mental process most professional athletes go through every day. . . . By the time they reach the pros, the inner critic rules. With the precision of a cuckoo clock, he crops up whenever they make a mistake. How did that guy beat me? Where did that shot come from? What a stupid pass! The incessant accusations of the judging mind block vital energy and sabotage concentration.*[5]

Jackson is talking about the way preoccupation with ourselves and our inner voice of self-criticism and defensiveness takes our "eye off the ball." This applies to managers in organizations as well as to athletes. Instead of being able to observe what is actually going on and listening to what others are saying and feeling, we're busy processing, often defensively, only what we think *we're* doing wrong.

Leaders who pay attention to toxicity become aware of unfolding situations by being alert to the presence and signals of others around them and by being open-minded, rather than prejudicial or defensive, to emotional "data" they experience. They're also open-hearted in their responses to the situation. There is an interplay between paying attention to emotional conditions and being more sensitized to its nature. Being alert to the condition of others increases the likelihood that leaders will pay attention to what is going on around them. Paying attention increases the likelihood that leaders will be alert to the condition of others. The capacity of leaders to step into toxic situations and help resolve them is enhanced by their alertness and their openness to what they encounter. Being open-minded enables leaders to discover workable responses to a situation. Being open-hearted encourages compassionate and caring behavior. Troubled employees don't always present the real source or depth of their pain to their leaders. Nor do they signal clearly that they are suffering in some way. Yet those who engage in leadership can be assured that in most situations involving people, there will be pain somewhere in the room, as Birgitt Williams says, and it will be evident in generally subtle ways. The task for the leader is to look for cues and symptoms of pain, and to respond to that distress with empathy and without judgment.

Attentive leaders know they need to be alert to all the emotional clues, no matter how subtle, that occur in their interactions with others. The root of an emotional response from a staff member or a colleague often lies in how that person is feeling about something in his life, whether work-related or not. He might be worried over a sick child or the breakup of a relationship. He might feel betrayed or undervalued, at work or at home. He might have financial concerns, or be depressed, feeling that life has passed him by. Paying attention to emotional clues and being alert to what happens in subsequent conversations opens the possibility that the source of the pain will be revealed. Leaders attuned to the emotional condition of their staff tend to make better-informed decisions with longer-lasting effects than if they respond impulsively or judgmentally.

It isn't easy, however, to fully pay attention in this way. The press of deadlines, the demands of multitasking, the emotional equilibrium of the leader, the time of day, and even the time of year in the organizational calendar—all of these things can interfere with the ability to focus clearly. By the end of a busy day, leaders often have little patience for anything emotional and are more inclined to miss important details in a situation or to rush to judgment. Budget times, for example, are notoriously stressful periods for everyone.

How clearly other people signal their pain is also a factor. Carter, an administrator in a legal firm, recalls a time when he was rushing to his fourth meeting of the morning, papers tucked under his arm, and his mind filled with how he would respond to questions from the finance manager on his latest proposal. He met a staff member in the corridor, and they exchanged quick hellos in which the staff member commented that she was feeling some anxiety over a family matter. Carter heard the comment, but was in such a hurry that it vanished quickly from his mind. A few days later, as he was driving to work, he recalled the exchange. He told me:

> *I went to the staff member and asked how things were going. She said she was reasonably well and then said how upset she felt about all the infighting in her family over the settling of her mother's will. I offered words of condolence and she said she was feeling better about it, but that earlier in the week it had really been demoralizing for her. I know that it was not a situation for me to resolve but I recalled our earlier meeting in the hallway and realized now that she'd been in pain. If I'd not been so preoccupied with the upcoming meeting—and perhaps had she made her feelings more clear—I'd have taken the extra few minutes to comfort her. It might have helped her personally and I suspect she would have been able to focus more easily on the work she was doing.*

Carter does not deserve censure for his omission, of course. He was caught up in the flow of a busy day. He heard, however fleetingly, a call for some connection to the staff member's pain and judged it unworthy of attention, at least not at that moment. We know it registered, because as is often the case when there are too many "messages" to process at once, he recalled it later. And, as is often the case when personal issues interfere with work, the staff member was reticent about what she was feeling and sent only a muted distress signal. Granted, the woman's pain and the leader's reaction in this story represent relatively minor issues. But this scenario illustrates how paying attention could in fact have made a difference to how the staff member felt at the time.

The trouble is that these opportunities for connection around pain often open up for only short periods of time, creating a "reachable moment" and then closing, sometimes almost irretrievably. The emotional component that is so important to establishing a healing connection often disappears with minimal trace. It is hard to rekindle, requiring more time and effort than when it is presented in the first place. Carter's response, which was as helpful as it could have been at the time, would have been more effective as a toxin intervention had he made it in the first instance. He then could have signaled his support and helped shift the staff member from a preoccupation with her personal concerns to a focus on her work.

When it comes right down to it, the quality of paying attention often translates to simply acting like a compassionate human being. And often it's an organization's top leaders who are in the best position to shape how attentively their people act toward one another. John Chambers, CEO of Cisco Systems, is a good example of such a leader. For example, he doesn't accept e-mails from his managers on customer accounts that are considered critical; instead, he asks them to leave him voicemails. His intent is to capture the emotion, the frustration, or concern expressed by the caller, and he wants his managers to do the same with their staff so that they understand what's really being said. In other words, he lets staff know that emotions are valuable, and that messages contain more than mere words.[6] The tone, speed, and cadence of a message can convey how the person is feeling about what they are saying. Ronald Heifetz calls this the "musicality" of communications between people in organizations.[7] Over time, this kind of attention and feedback can lift an organization's level of emotional intelligence as people become more aware of and responsive to what their colleagues are feeling.

Finally, a significant aspect of paying attention is being aware of the cultural influences. Cultures are "infused with emotions."[8] People often feel deeply attached to the values and norms of their culture, even if they are harmful or could be replaced with healthier ones. Emotional attachments to a culture affect how the leader, the sufferer, and other members of the organization respond to change or to efforts to deal with sources of pain. Leaders need to factor in the values and norms of the organization as they assess and respond to painful situations.

For example, a seasoned manager who had worked for the same company for many years told me that he'd come to understand that there was a particular way to talk about pain in the company. For one thing, he said, the word "pain" is not to be mentioned. Instead, when he sees that one of his staff is having trouble, he'll sit with them to talk out what is happening. If the person needs time to recover, he'll schedule some slack for her and position it to appear that she's helping out with some development work that takes her out of the line of fire for awhile. "If I said she was going on 'stress leave' or something," the manager told me, "she'd be punished by the company for being weak. If I said we were confronting an emotional situation in the group, my boss would flip, because we don't use 'emotional terms' around here."

Thus, leaders need to pay attention to what words and actions are seen as acceptable expressions of how people feel. For example, is it OK to talk about stress or about problems at home? Is it customary to use direct language, such as, "There's a conflict here that is burning everyone up and needs to be confronted"? As the manager in the previous example illustrated, what may be an acceptable response in one organization may be inappropriate in another, even a company in the same industry.

Putting People First

Strong leaders have to care about people; it has to be part of their DNA.

—Bob DeRodes, president and CEO of Delta Technology, Delta Airlines

EMOTIONALLY responsive leaders enhance their competence by putting people first. Jeffrey Pfeffer, author of *The Human Equation: Building Profits by Putting People First,* says: "People are looking for the opportunity to have variety in their work and to tackle challenging assignments. The best companies are figuring out how their employees can have both opportunities—without leaving."[9] I would add that they are also looking for workplaces where their feelings are treated with dignity and respect. As we have seen elsewhere in this book, people in pain aren't usually working at their best. They lose focus; they withdraw commitment to their organization by giving less effort or simply by leaving. They behave with less concern for organizational goals and objectives. Leaders lower these propensities for poor performance by treating their people well and handling toxic situations as they arise.

Like paying attention, the practice of putting people first ensures that for any decision and course of action, the leader recognizes that employees make a key difference to the result; they are assets, not expenses. Thus, good leaders ask questions such as: "How might this change affect those who must carry it out or be on the receiving end?" and "How are things going for them now?" Or, as Pfeffer suggests, they ask, not "Is this the way we did it before?" and simply follow precedent, but rather, "Is this a sensible thing to do?" And, given the frame of reference of this book, leaders should ask, "Is it sensible emotionally for those who must carry out whatever we do?"

In the context of toxicity, leaders do best when they keep the feelings and well-being of staff or of other colleagues centrally in mind—an encouragement to consider the emotional costs and benefits of any initiative. Patricia Benner and her coauthors capture this tone as they discuss working with people in the arena of pain and suffering. In their book about expertise in nursing practice, they describe the orientation that expert nurses have to their patients, which is not unlike the way leaders might view staff. Nurses who have achieved a high level of expertise and leadership respond to their patients "as persons, respecting their dignity, caring for them in ways that preserve their personhood, protecting them in their vulnerability, helping them to feel safe in a somewhat alien environment (and comforting their family), striving to preserve the integrity of close relationships."[10] Viewing people in this way reminds leaders of the need for dialogue before, during, and after any organizational initiative. When leaders put people first, the intellectual and emotional communication between leaders and their people becomes a central feature of effective action.

These leaders know that things such as a planned change will typically trigger unhappiness among those affected by it. Some staff may have to give up work habits that have been comfortable and emotionally sustaining; others might have to break up teams or move from cherished work spaces. Unanticipated stress and strains might grip people as a change takes hold. For example, a CEO may order a reappraisal of the way a particular system such as distribution should be organized, and those who have been working extremely hard and apparently successfully in the current arrangement are thrown into disarray and defensiveness.[11] As a toxin handler, the leader will have the emotional well-being of her staff in mind and build in ways to prevent anticipated effects, or to address and minimize them when they happen. Also, leaders may increase their vigilance for early signs of distress and develop ways to cope with it at all stages.

Consider the case of Clark Elliott, who managed the Space Planning Department at the European headquarters of Digital Equipment Corporation, International in Geneva from 1984 through 1998. He describes a change process he managed in Digital Switzerland in the 1990s, when he worked with a sales force of 150 people who were demoralized from five years of downsizing and rightsizing. His challenge was to get the salespeople to buy into a radically new work arrangement that required employees to leave their territorial work spaces. They would move into a new business center designed to offer a mixed-use office environment, supporting the diverse activities of mobile and desk-based employees. In addition to the turbulence following the downsizing experiences, these new work arrangements seemed revolutionary to conservative Swiss employees.

Nevertheless, the change succeeded—something that Elliott attributes to the attention he gave to listening to the concerns and tapping the ideas of the salespeople. He says: "I was a 'Big Ear.' I listened to people's complaints and helped provide solutions. I talked to everyone on the staff for between forty-five minutes and an hour and a half. We provided lots and lots of feedback along the way." At the end of the project, Elliott was elated at the outcome. "Two weeks after the move, the biggest complaints were 'the printer isn't working,' and 'there aren't enough trash baskets.'"[12]

Understanding the value and importance of placing people at the center of decisions and actions isn't easy for many leaders, especially if they've spent their careers in organizations that put profit or competitive dominance at the forefront of their priorities. One leader, a manager of a team of specialists in a highly competitive service industry, told me how she ultimately had to learn to put people first and appreciate their value. She believes that attitude enables her team members to help each other get through difficult times. She said:

> *We see more of the person and understand her better, so when she is hurting—and therefore work is suffering—we can support her through difficult times. I've known this, more or less, in my head but never really felt it like I do now. We miss the boat if we don't take the time to see and listen to the person we are working with. And we need to ensure that people we hire get good skills training and that the team works well together. When it does, I don't have to do all the work showing people that I value them—the team does this for me—and for themselves.*

Making people the center point of any leader's thinking and actions is not about making it "easy" for others or being "soft" on moving the organization and its projects forward. Leadership includes making tough decisions that sometimes set very tight performance deadlines, push people beyond their comfort zones, or involve letting staff go. The leader in the previous example told me about how she recently accepted the resignation of a staff member—and felt it was the best thing for everyone. "We had explored several options for her to contribute to the organization," she said. "But in the end, it became clear to everyone that while she was a good worker, no amount of money or discussion was going to make her career with us work. She wanted something different, and our conversations helped her figure this out. She left feeling good about her treatment here."

By thinking first about the person and her feelings and then assessing her performance, a leader can create a culture in which compassionate responses to pain become a natural part of doing business. Handling toxins becomes more naturally one of the things that leaders, formal and informal, do for one another. The residues of toxic actions or events become more rapidly absorbed, and their levels in the workplace are lower—and therefore people can get on with doing their jobs well.

Practicing Professional Intimacy

> *There is no formula for the practice of compassion. Like all great spiritual arts, it requires that we listen and attend, understand our motivation, and then ask ourselves, what action can be really helpful.*[13]
>
> —Jack Kornfield, *A Path with Heart*

LEADERS INHERIT a complex relationship with their followers—those "in their care." They are the recipients of a whole range of emotions from others as they go about their work—from love, adulation, or respect to anger, fear, and distrust to indifference and disrespect, among other responses. What emotions are prevalent at a particular time and place depend on the work and personal circumstances that are in play and the actions and personalities of the leaders and their staffs.

Emotionally charged situations are inherently toxic. When leaders step in to defuse them, they must strike a tricky balance between detachment from the pain of those they're helping and an excessive emotional involvement with the situation. They are most effective when they use their emotions as a guide to responding to what has transpired and its effect on others. But managers are most helpful when they can do this with "professional intimacy"—without clouding their judgment by over-identifying with the sufferer.[14]

This quality of professional intimacy relates directly to emotional intelligence as interpreted by researcher Jennifer George. Emotional intelligence, she writes, "describes the ability to effectively join emotions and reasoning, using emotions to facilitate reasoning and reasoning intelligently about emotions."[15]

A good example of this leadership dichotomy that is both professional and intimate comes from Richard Smith, chairman and editor-in-chief of *Newsweek,* who described to us his actions during a crisis at the magazine in the 1990s. One of the magazine's longtime editors, Maynard Parker, was diagnosed with leukemia—an illness that he fought bravely but would ultimately succumb to. Once the diagnosis was made, Smith, who'd worked closely with Parker for thirty years and considered him a close personal friend, brought his leadership to bear on the crisis. He immediately let the staff know what was going on, and told them that he and the magazine were doing everything they possibly could to help Parker. "I wanted to make it absolutely clear to the staff what the situation was," Smith said. "This was a shock because he was an extremely energetic and vigorous person . . . he would have been the last one you would have picked [to have health problems]."

Leaders who have high emotional intelligence know that the source of people's pain can come from almost anywhere in their lives. The capacity to read emotions well and attune to the person and the situation are skills that enable leaders to help sufferers address their situation and then move on.[16] Although Richard Smith clearly had his

BOX 7-1 PRACTICING PROFESSIONAL INTIMACY

The notion of professional intimacy is perhaps best conveyed through an example of a nurse, since nurses' work almost by definition involves large doses of such delicate handling. One nurse in a general medical unit described her care of a man in his mid-sixties who was admitted with liver failure. When, after a night of treatment and then several hours of dialysis the next day, it became clear that the man would not improve, the physicians recommended to the family that the dialysis be stopped and that they "let him go." At that point the nurse, who had stayed with the man throughout most of his treatment and knew that he could hear her, felt it was important to tell the man what was happening to him.

"You're going to be taken off the dialysis," she told him, "and you're probably going to die in the next couple of hours." Hearing this, his eyes suddenly opened, and a peaceful look came over his face. "It was an amazing transition," said the nurse, who felt that the news helped the man to begin to let go.

The nurse displayed professional intimacy in her interactions with the family as well. She talked with them often, especially when the direction of the illness became clearer. Later, she made sure the man's room reflected the kind of intimacy that she felt the family needed to say their good-byes. She brought in extra chairs and water glasses and boxes of Kleenex. "I felt a great urgency to get all the peripheral junk out of the room," she said, so she removed as many machines as possible. She then left the family alone, returning about every half-hour to "keep an ear out for what was going on and keep an eye on the monitor . . . and see how everybody was doing."[17]

This is a good example of someone practicing professional intimacy. While offering all of her technical skills, as well as her compassion, the nurse nevertheless didn't get overly involved in the man's or his family's pain—thereby allowing her to be truly helpful. An overly emotional response, or one that overtaxed her own physical resources, wouldn't have helped the man—and would certainly have harmed the nurse herself.

own feelings about his friend's illness, he knew that he needed to step outside of his own grief and reach out to his staff, who were also grieving. And though he couldn't have been absolutely certain of the correctness of his intervention, he nevertheless acted from both his heart *and* his intellect, keeping everyone's best interests in mind. By meeting the shock of his staff with a flow of communication that both kept people informed and signaled his own concern for his fallen colleague, Smith exercised his power with thoughtfulness and care in a situation fraught with pain.

Describing the effect that his policy of open communication had on the staff, Smith said: "The more you're there to answer questions or to make comments, the more they feel included in the organization's response to the problem." He also heard from staff that his response made them feel good about their organization since "the people at the top are clearly active and engaged and doing everything they can to help."

The benefits of offering this kind of professional intimacy ripple throughout an organization. Mark Whitaker, a *Newsweek* editor, commented, "Everybody really rallied around in a very impressive and moving way to help [Parker]. . . . Dozens if not scores of people from the office and the organization pitched in to give blood." Whitaker said that even people who had left the magazine but had heard about Parker's illness went to the hospital and donated blood and platelets. Staff stepped up in other ways as well. The four or five editors working with Richard Smith began to play a "broader leadership role," Smith said. They and their staff wanted to honor Parker's style and standards for excellence in journalism. "The efforts of everyone involved were aimed at putting out the best possible magazine each week," observed Smith. "We won a National Magazine Award for the reporting that we did in that period."

Leaders who are effective handlers of pain draw on their own emotional competence, that is, their self-awareness of what they are feeling in a given circumstance; their self-management skills, or their ability to manage those feelings; their social awareness, or sensitivity to what others are feeling; and their relationship management, or their ability to work through emotional issues with others.[18]

BOX 7-2 ASSESSING PERSONAL CAPACITY FOR COMPASSIONATE RESPONDING

At some point, most leaders will have to intervene in a toxic situation. But how can leaders be sure they're prepared for such intervention? One way to start this process is for leaders to seek honest answers to questions such as the following, which focus around four competencies: silence, support, sympathy, and speed.[19]

- **Silence** Can you listen and be aware of grief and, quite separately, of your own and other's intuitive responses to it?
- **Support** Do you know how to support initiatives that come from subordinates and may be well outside the corporate norms? Can you see yourself using company infrastructure to help in an intervention? Can you provide personal support to people in grief? Whom can you turn to for support, advice, and inspiration?
- **Sympathy** How have you expressed sympathy to others in the past? How have others expressed sympathy to you? Can you imagine this happening in the context of your work life?
- **Speed** Can you personally deal with fast-moving changes in circumstances that have an emotional focus? Trauma rarely strikes slowly—can you keep up with it? Leaders must be able to manage immediate traumatic situations even as they plan their next responses. Can you keep both plates spinning?

Paying attention to these kinds of questions and pondering how one might answer them, at least in the abstract, begins to give the leader a role in the story of trauma and suffering. Inevitably, it is the people who see pain and trauma who start the systemic response to the situation. By thinking through scenarios for response, leaders can begin to develop a critical competency in themselves and their organizations: attending to compassion.

In this role, leaders resemble counselors or therapists, and like these professionals, they bring a degree of disciplined compassion and intimacy to their work. They take into account the situation that presents itself, "responding to the vulnerability, needs, and possibilities at hand." They connect to people in pain with "an emotional involvement that varies considerably in terms of the needs of [the other person]."[20]

Planting Seeds

To everything there is a season.

—Ecclesiastes 3 v.1

LEADERS deal with longer-term issues of pain as well as those that present themselves in the moment. Part of their competency as toxin handlers is their ability to anticipate what might become painful for employees or for the organization itself at some later point. This is especially important given the reality of organizations today, where rapid change often takes them into uncharted territories, with unknown effects. Moreover, there will always be people in organizations whose personal lives are falling apart for some reason. There will always be "grief in the room," be it in the office or at home or in a hospital.

Handling pain is something leaders need to anticipate. Thus the ground must be prepared and the seeds of a healthy response planted. Leadership when people are hurting requires some luck (for example, being in the right place at the right time, or getting a "heads up" from someone else about a troubled situation that is unfolding) as well as thoughtful planning that anticipates the emotional reactions that accompany change. Sam, a leader at a marketing firm, told me of his efforts to plant seeds of leadership in his organization, which is run by a command-and-control type of CEO adept at producing toxicity. Said Sam:

Since the CEO is a one-man-band type leader, we all fall into the trap of going to him to get answers. It's a lot quicker to just do what he wants than to try your own idea and fail. That may be okay for now, but if and when he leaves, we'll be rudderless. I knew I couldn't change the boss, but what I could do was to get some really good leadership training into the organization. We've done that for four or five years now, and that's helped us to move more toward what I'd call self-responsibility training. We're encouraging people to take charge of themselves and their situation to a greater extent.

Sam also saw that customer focus was one particular area of weakness that he knew the company would need to address at some point in the future. Predictably, the CEO resisted Sam's ideas and "just humored me when I spoke to him about them." Nevertheless, Sam was able to seed the ground. He constantly raised the issue at management meetings, he said, and "through the leadership of others coming through our training program who have caught fire on this issue, the groundwork was laid."

Sam saw his efforts pay off when the CEO returned from a business conference and announced to the group: "I heard this wonderful speaker, and we've got to get him here." It turned out that the speaker had been talking about making the very same changes in customer service that Sam had been pressing for the last five or six years—but that the CEO had ignored until now. "We were all sitting in the room thinking, 'Hallelujah. It's about time,'" Sam said. "But the best part was that the organization was ready for him. The groundwork had been laid. We created a scenario in which we decided that's where the troops were going to be, and now we've finally arrived, thanks to that groundwork."

Leaders "plant seeds" because they know that pain always accompanies some organizational actions, whether from the boss or elsewhere, and that measures to restore equilibrium need to be in place. They also do so if they believe implicitly that part of their job is to make their workplace more humane. That requires getting the organization to invest in processes that prepare people to respond to each other and to difficult situations in caring, attentive, and respectful ways. They plant seeds when they know that it takes time, patience, and sustained effort to bring about significant changes to the nature of toxicity in their organization.

Leaders with this mind-set also prepare for opportunity and sheer luck—such as the fortuitous events in the previous example, where the CEO finally came around on Sam's pet issue. In that case, Sam had prepared the ground for a good harvest of outcomes. He knew he couldn't directly change a boss who was both commanding and successful, yet he was still committed to growing a workforce that would have important competencies for the next phase of the organization's life. That phase could have been signaled by the departure of the boss—or, as in this case, by a surprising change of mind (and heart).

All of this amounts to "preventative toxin handling" and requires the leader to stand firm without knowing when or if his strategy will take hold. The break can come as it did here because the CEO saw a better path to profits. It can come because the seeds planted produce a product or service that can solve pain-filled problems. Sometimes, however, leaders plant seeds by transforming a local issue into a general one so that a force and an urgency for change emerge. Ronald Heifetz talks about this as "ripening an unripe issue." It is dangerous work that takes courage, emotional sensitivity, and much effort. Heifetz uses the example of Lyndon Johnson's leadership in bringing the civil rights issue to a head. He writes:

> *Six weeks after Kennedy's assassination, [Johnson] called Roy Wilkins, executive secretary of the NAACP, and said, "When are you going to get down here and start civil rights?" Then he gave Wilkins counsel on how to lobby Everett Dirksen, the senate minority leader. Johnson was ripening an unripe issue: He couldn't get out front on the Civil Rights Act of 1964 [because it was too emotional an issue], but as an authority figure, he could provide counsel and cover for leaders without authority—leaders who could then disseminate a sense of urgency.*[21]

One final example of how leaders can plant seeds in an organization is by modeling caring and respectful behavior. In chapter 5 I mentioned the story of a woman who inherited a toxic organization when she began work as VP of operations in a retail chain. She described her modeling of healthy behavior this way:

> *Right from the start, I was incredibly vocal about work/life balance. I am at work for as long as I need to be to get the job done. My balance comes from making sure that I am at work because I am adding value and not to fill hours or be "seen." In addition, I live by the rule of keeping my head where my feet are. In other words when at home I do not think about work and visa versa. This strategy keeps me sharp, focused, interested and loving my job.*

Because this VP chose to be at home with her children on her days off, she expected everyone else to follow her example. "Anybody who thought otherwise, that they were going to gain brownie points by doing something different, was in for a shock," she said. "Too often I have seen staff members racing to be at their desk before the boss arrived and stay until the boss left. I expected everybody around me to have balance in their lives, because that would then allow me more balance in mine."

People in the VP's organization eventually came around to this new behavior, and the quality of life at work improved dramatically—as did performance. However, modeling a better balance in life was not all that this executive did to transform the organization she inherited into a healthy one. She devoted a great deal of energy and time to pushing back against the extremely negative experience staff had had of past leadership in this 35,000-strong workforce. We'll follow this story further in the next section.

Pushing Back

> *Gary had walked into the meeting with a baseball bat, and he asked the employees, "Tell me everything you hate." . . . They pointed at the*

cameras. And Gary took a swing with the baseball bat. Knocked the camera off the wall. . . . Then he says, "Does anyone else want the bat?" And they threw blankets over the cameras and they destroyed all of them. And that started the whole conversation about cultural change. Now they haven't had any turnover . . . in six months.[22]

—Charles O'Reilly and Jeffrey Pfeffer, *Hidden Value*

OCCASIONALLY, leaders must take bold steps to eradicate emotional pain in their workplaces. They need to push back on the sources of the pain to eliminate their effects.

The Benjamin Group, a Silicon Valley–based public relations firm, demonstrates its values by taking a stand on how employees are treated, not only by their colleagues and managers, but also by their customers, suppliers, and other business partners. These values are represented in a code of principles established by Sherie Benjamin that includes the statement "We're all in this together." One message implicit in this slogan is that the company is prepared to cancel an account if the client develops a track record of being abusive to Benjamin Group staff:

A few years ago, the firm dropped a million-dollar account—at that time, worth fully 20% of its annual business. Employees were startled that the firm would go so far, but they were energized, too: Inspired by the knowledge that their company cared about their well-being, staff worked extra hard to bring in new clients.[23]

Benjamin's action of surgically eradicating the toxin by cutting a customer out of the system no doubt engendered considerable anxiety at the time. Organizations eliminating 20 percent of their business run the risk of losing momentum, given the drop in revenue. On the other hand, when surgery eliminates toxicity from a body that is basically healthy, the patient draws on their inner resources to rally and heal. The analogy is apt for the Benjamin Group and for other organizations that have inherent resilience and the courage to act on undesirable pain.

Pushing back on a toxic source, however, can take more time and energy than a quick intervention. Dissipating the toxins that have built up and permeated the system and its people can take intensive effort over a prolonged period—and not a little courage and determination. For example, the VP of operations we met in the previous section at one point worked under a toxic boss in that same company. "His attitude was that the only way you get anybody to work is by beating them down, making them feel small, and controlling them," she told me. As a result, she experienced a period of depression and a severe loss of confidence—something that took a lot of "pushing back" for her to overcome.

When the toxic boss eventually left the organization, the new CEO expressed confidence in the VP, helping to restore the damage done by her previous supervisor and giving her the task of rebuilding the morale of the staff in the company's stores. "Even though he was a CEO, he had so much humility, so much concern for the individual, that he became a real inspiration for me," she told me. "That's when I realized that I wasn't going to be driven blindly by work anymore." In fact, the burden of trying to please her previous toxic boss had affected her health, her home life, and her children to the point that she felt she'd hit rock bottom.

So, spurred by her new CEO's injunction that she rebuild morale, she went on the road to visit as many of the stores in the operation as she could. "As much as the head office was feeling low morale as a result of the old CEO's style," she said, "the stores were feeling even more crushed by that whole period of mismanagement." Her approach was to take her newfound confidence and begin pushing back against the old toxic mores that had become ingrained throughout the company. She told me:

> *My mission was to show these store managers that I didn't have any airs about me—that I can be wrong and I can be corrected. That I can have my mind changed. I wanted to give them a very different flavor of what a leader can be in this company, versus what their experience had been in the past. My object was to go into stores and not look for the bad, which was what the former boss had always done. I'd been on the road with him, and I'd seen him do it. So I chose the exact oppo-*

site approach. The object of my visits was to meet everybody in the store and talk to them. To let them know that they had a voice, and that I was going to listen to what they had to say.

As positive as all of this change sounds, however, this VP did not emerge from her experience without enemies. Pushing back, like planting seeds and ripening issues, can provoke strong resistance. "There were a lot of people who saw no value in the work I was doing in the stores," she told me. "They thought it was all fluff, especially since the numbers were not initially there." Eventually, though, the tide started to turn. "It took a long time," she said, "but it's like a wheel you start to push downhill. Suddenly there were more people behind this kind of change. And because I gave the people in the field a lifeline—showing them that there could be another way to act, poor behavior became unacceptable. People just didn't allow it anymore." As a result of that momentum, the organization eventually went from being an extremely toxic environment to one that was very healthy. In a national survey of workplaces, over 95 percent of the employee base responded, and this company was voted the best in its industry.

When leaders push back in the way that this VP of store operations did, they turn their talents for handling toxins toward changing the very source of the pain, be it a boss, a colleague or staff member, or an organizational policy or practice. At times their actions are radical, such as firing a customer or taking a baseball bat to a hated management control tool. At other times, pushing back is more measured and low-key. With the help of the new CEO, the VP changed the health of her organization over a long period of time, during which she demonstrated and reinforced new behaviors and expectations about performance.

Leaders who act in this more evolutionary way might be called "tempered radicals." This term, used by authors Debra Meyerson and Maureen Scully, describes individuals in organizations who believe in the value of contributing in constructive ways to the organization's success but who have key values and beliefs that may not (yet) reflect those of the cultures they work in or of the occupations they represent.[24] These leaders are tempered in their assumptions about how to change the way things are done in an organization (to heal the organization rather than to destroy it) and also in the steeliness of their resolve to intervene when they see evidence of unfairness and pain in the workplace. They target their efforts toward specific as well as institutionalized incidences of suffering experienced by those they consider discriminated against or in some way disadvantaged by the system. They lead with courage and by example, demonstrating thoughtful and compassionate strategies. After all, to push back in ways that we have seen in this section is to put one's own career on the line.

Meyerson describes one such case from her research, about a black executive who started out as one of the only people of color in the bank where he worked. He began by hiring another highly qualified member of a minority, and encouraged him to hire in the same way—who then encouraged his hires to do the same, and so on. All the while, the executive comforted and counseled those minority employees to stay the course, even when they were frustrated and angry about their treatment in the company. This continued over a thirty-year period, so that by the time the executive retired, he left behind a legacy of "more than 3,500 talented minority and female employees [who] had joined the bank."[25]

While not every leader is a natural toxin handler or has the inclination to be one, there are practices that leaders can implement to handle employee pain in constructive ways. When leaders implement such practices, they can attend to their employees' suffering in a timely way, and in some cases even prevent it. The compassionate actions of leaders can contribute significantly to an emotionally healthy and energized workforce.

First, leaders must be willing to place responsibility where it belongs, that is, with whoever in the organization is accountable for the toxicity or in whose territory the suffering occurs. Of course, other managers in the organization must play this role as well. Leaving it all to the CEO restricts solutions to the actions of a few toxin handlers and undermines the principle of leaders taking responsibility for the pain created in a situation.

Second, leaders need to adopt a set of practices for responding to toxicity in the workplace that are particularly relevant to people in their role. They need to "put people first," to remember the value of employees and how corporate decisions will affect them emotionally. They need to pay attention to what is going on emotionally with others. They must acquire the skill of professional intimacy, in which they address the pain in their workplace, drawing on their own emotional responses to the situation as well as those of the sufferer without crossing the line and becoming too personal or intrusive. They need to plant the seeds of strategies and systems in their organizations to head off unnecessary toxicity and prevent later harm. And finally, compassionate leaders must learn to push back against the sources of emotional toxicity. Like many other toxin-handling practices and like much of leadership activity in general, these practices require conviction and courage.

In all of these ways and more, leaders who are responsive to the pain they create or encounter in their organizations draw on the skills of the toxin handler. Their ability to develop and sustain the loyalty, commitment, and effort of those they lead is more enduring, and their workplace is healthier, when leaders incorporate attention to pain into their repertoire. Even so, leaders work in a larger context—that of the organization—and they need support and understanding from the organization at large if they are to be successful toxin handlers. We turn to this issue in chapter 8.

CHAPTER EIGHT

The Compassionate Company

Architecting Responses to Pain

Those companies that have developed positive and constructive, as opposed to toxic, workplaces won't ever notice a talent drought because they currently enjoy, and will continue to enjoy, a surfeit of applicants and loyal employees.[1]

—Charles O'Reilly and Jeffrey Pfeffer, *Hidden Value*

WE CANNOT LEAVE all the handling of emotional pain solely to the leaders of organizations, anymore than we can leave it to the few gifted handlers who excel in highly toxic situations. Rather, organizations themselves must play a key role, and this chapter will examine the institutional venues in which organizations can architect responses to pain to create healthy and productive workplaces.

Think again of biological systems. The toxins they produce in the natural course of their functioning are flushed out through their own internal mechanisms and subsystems, effectively eliminating viruses and other threats to their existence (see chapter 7). However, when they cannot cope with these toxic invasions and events, for whatever reason, outside help may be needed. When the biological system is a human being, help may mean medical intervention (possibly surgery) to remove the source of the pain, a regimen of antibiotics, or even the introduction of toxin-reducing repertoires from alternative sources of healing. Following such outside intervention, the body normally redresses its balance and eliminates the toxins, or at least restores them to manageable levels. Then, during recovery, the body and its systems rehabilitate, and the stability of the system is restored or otherwise reconfigured to maintain the gains triggered by the healing interventions.

If we translate this process practically and metaphorically to the challenge of managing toxicity in the workplace and creating healthy organizational systems, we can use the following strategies.

- *Prevention strategies,* such as:
  - Choosing employees for attitude and competence
  - Developing people and helping them shine
  - Building fair-minded workplaces
  - Creating a healthy atmosphere by allowing spaces for healing
- *Intervention strategies,* such as:
  - Dealing with downturns by building bridges for people to leave with hope and opportunity
  - Dealing with people's personal pain by creating policies that are compassionate and systematic
  - Dealing with trauma by helping people find meaning in the midst of tragedy

  - Maintaining a presence in the face of great suffering
  - Providing a context for meaning
  - Providing a context for action
- *Restoration and recovery strategies,* including:
  - Showing patience and trust in the belief that time heals
  - Providing process: letting people talk
  - Providing guidance: helping people see positive options
  - Exhibiting confidence: treating people as if they can cope
  - Providing hope and inspiration
  - Providing focus: restoring active routines
  - Fostering rituals and symbols for "letting go"
  - Providing a basis for renewed trust
  - Helping people focus on constructive action

Preventing the Toxicity of Emotional Pain

We're in the people business, not the suit business.

—George Zimmer, founder, The Men's Wearhouse

THERE WILL ALWAYS BE PAIN in the lives of people in organizations. We cannot prevent all of it, but organizations can create the conditions that keep many kinds of toxicity at bay and maintain healthy workplaces. Such a result depends in part on the willingness of top management to take seriously and embed deep within the organization's culture

- the value that people matter in and of themselves;
- the belief, often expressed but infrequently honored, that people are essential to the success of the organization; and
- practices that address people's needs and expectations so as to realize their contributions to the organization's bottom line.

In other words, preventing toxicity in organizations means creating and sustaining a culture that screens out the toxins most damaging to the human spirit. Such organizational cultures are built on the recognition that what their employees feel and think matters—and affects, for better or worse, the emotional tone and level of toxicity in the workplace.

The institutional tools for crafting workplaces that put people first and prevent toxins from intruding, that nurture the creativity and commitment of employees at all levels, are readily available. Let's look now at how the practices of recruiting, developing, rewarding, and engaging employees, integrated with an organization's overall strategy, can prevent toxicity from rearing its head.[2]

Choosing New Members

Organizations that are aware of the damage that can come from high levels of toxicity take seriously the emotional climate of their operations. They devote considerable time and attention to whom they hire, whom they keep, how they develop staff and enable people to be their best, whom they promote to positions of authority, and what they emphasize to ensure good connections between employee and company goals. Such organizations hire for attitude over technical and other skills—a wise approach when you consider the evidence offered earlier in this book of the damage people can do when they're emotionally incompetent. Techniques and skills can be taught and improved on the job, but it's very difficult to change people's attitudes.

One way to ensure that you hire for attitude is to involve employees in the recruiting of their peers. At Southwest Airlines, pilots hire other pilots, baggage handlers hire baggage handlers, and so forth. In one case, a top pilot working for another airline was turned down because pilots involved in recruiting him observed his rudeness to a Southwest receptionist.[3]

The concern with attitudinal fit in creating a healthy workplace helps limit toxicity to manageable levels. Picking up on the pilot's approach to receptionists and then keeping him out of the organization was a systemic way to prevent emotional pain in the workplace. No recruiting system is foolproof, of course: Neither Southwest nor any of us would want incompetent pilots to fly our planes, no matter how respectful of others they are. But making emotional attitude a key factor in hiring can significantly influence a company's overall emotional tone.

Strategies to keep "toxin carriers" out of an organization are part of the process of creating health. Making sure that those who are invited in (even those who aren't) feel good about themselves is also important. When people are turned down with dignity, the impact on their self-confidence as well as their attitude to the company can actually be positive. (In many cases applicants are also current or prospective customers, and a "turned-off" customer typically influences the opinions of others who weren't even in the recruiting exercise.) Those who are hired also benefit by seeing the process as responsive to the emotions people have regarding acceptance and rejection.

Of course, this kind of careful selection takes time and attention. Companies like Southwest will often take a prospective hire through several single-interviewer sessions, at least one group interview, some tests that allow observation of the applicant's behavior in a work-simulated situation, and an opportunity for interviewers to vote and seek consensus.

Screening for attitude, however, does carry a danger: Companies may in the process screen out toxins that could stimulate the corporate immune system to exercise and improve its defense responses. Systems that do not embrace diversity of all kinds can also reduce the kinds of innovation needed to survive. If there is only one model of performing and it fails, the entire system will likely perish. Dependence on a single or limited variety of a crop, for example, can wipe out the species in times of adversity, leaving no safety net for recovery.

However, the high levels of pain in so many workplaces suggest that organizations would have to clean up a vast amount of toxins before they would create an unhealthy homogeneity. The best solution to minimizing pathological toxicity in organizations is still to keep it out of the system in the first place, in part by hiring for attitudes that embrace dignity and respect.

Hiring for attitude carries an added benefit: It injects a system with health and vitality. Organizations that have this quality have toxin "antibodies" that can carry them through inevitable times of fierce competition and uncertainty.

Developing People

An organization sustains its resiliency and health in part through the ways it revitalizes its members. A key to this resiliency is the extent to which members feel connected to the organization, see that what they do is valued, and believe that the company is willing to invest in them as people. Innovation, loyalty, and commitment to excellence flow in no small measure from staff who trust their organizations and who feel valued as members of the corporate team. Not surprisingly, they have very different experiences than do the people I have described throughout this book, who worked in highly toxic organizations. Just as toxin-conscious companies hire for attitude, those same hires perform in response to the attitude of their employer.

Consider the likely emotional atmosphere in a company that encourages risk and innovation compared with one that punishes honest efforts to do things in new and better ways. George Zimmer, founder of the Men's Wearhouse, says: "I take the position that the best way to grow a business is to encourage people to make mistakes and learn from them. In fact, our corporate mission statement says that we're a company that wants to admit to their mistakes."[4]

Moreover, rather than keeping to a strict budget for training, the Men's Wearhouse spends "whatever senior leaders think is necessary to keep the culture vital and people energized."[5] In addition to providing selling skills and product and market knowledge, the high investment in training tells people in the company that they're valuable and that they're taken seriously. These are healthy investments in the battle to keep pathological toxicity out of the organization.

Developing such a robust organization can also mean allowing people to learn from their own mistakes or offering them training in skills that reinforce a culture of respect. Another important element, however, is to provide flexibility in the way people grow and progress. Not everyone can be a good manager or someone who can provide the kind of leadership I'm advocating in this book. People can be trained, yes; but too often leadership development focuses on competencies that do little to enhance people's toxin-handling capabilities. Even training to develop emotional intelligence, though it may improve the sensitivities of managers to pain in others, can fall short for people who "don't really get it." Some managers simply aren't interested in the hard emotional work of sorting out toxic situations in their departments; others channel all their passion into the technical aspects of their work.

Why, then, do we so often take talented operators away from what they do best and try to turn them into managers, especially when the move isn't in their or the organization's best interests? One argument is that there is a shortage of managers in any organization, and we need to make do with whomever we can persuade to step up to the plate. More frequently, though, we promote people to managers because of their technical skills in finance or information technology or marketing, and we fail to factor in what it really takes to manage people well. Such logic and practice produce high doses of debilitating toxicity.

Creating parallel tracks in organizations that allow technically gifted staff to keep doing what they do best, and encourage those who demonstrate high toxin-handling skills to step into management roles, can help maintain a healthy workplace. So, too, can systems that allow people to move between management and technical roles in ways that energize them and the people they work with. Both employees and organizations thereby adjust their contributions to minimize the levels of toxicity and accomplish other key tasks as well.[6]

Another version of this strategy is for organizations to move people out of jobs they are not good at (repositioning them inside the company) and then reach into the workforce to find talented employees who show facility for this work. It takes courage to make these kinds of moves, and they need to be done with care and compassion. However, they are a healthy response to stagnation, as they address the frustration of those who are misfits and provide inspiration and incentive to those who have potential.

Building a Fair-Minded Workplace

PERHAPS NOTHING creates or exacerbates people's emotional pain more surely than feeling that the psychological and emotional contracts they have with the organization have been betrayed.[7] We've all seen cases where people who've been treated unfairly withdraw their effort, refusing to do work beyond their job descriptions or assist coworkers. On the other hand, organizations that promote trust and a sense of fair play reduce the likelihood of emotional toxicity among their employees.

How can organizations craft such fair-minded workplaces? For one thing, they must begin by treating everyone, regardless of position or level in the hierarchy, with respect and dignity. People must feel that they're considered in actions and events that affect their well-being in the organization, and they must feel equitably acknowledged, celebrated, and compensated for their work. Regardless of the specifics of reward and compensation practices—which vary widely from company to company—what's important is that employees experience those practices as consistent and fair, and that they enhance employees' feelings of trust.

For example, Southwest Airlines tends to reward people collectively (through profit sharing and stock options) rather than paying people individually for particular levels of performance. The company also keeps executive pay relatively low and treats people equally across the board (i.e., executives won't get big raises if employees are suffering through a wage freeze).[8] Moreover, Southwest's executive response to the post-9/11 dramatic drop in air travel was consistent with this philosophy: Executives took no salary for the duration of the year 2001 as one way to avoid staff layoffs and to signal their solidarity with their staff.

HeartMath LLC, the California training and consulting organization, promotes trust among staff by ensuring an open flow of communication. Executives share information with employees about the financial health of the company and take time to involve staff in decisions that affect them. Similarly, VeriFone, a global company providing electronic payment systems, considers sharing information essential to maintaining a sense of fair play in the organization. To ensure that all employees understand that information, VeriFone publishes its company philosophy in seven languages and makes it available to staff as a pocket-sized book. That way, everyone can reference this guide in his or her own cultural terms. Moreover, the principles of its philosophy make clear the importance the company places on respect for employees; for example, viewing each individual in the organization as important and as part of a team in which trust and cooperation are touchstones.[9]

In these ways and others, companies such as VeriFone, HeartMath, and Southwest clearly demonstrate that people come first. They understand that when people feel fairly treated, there's a lot less pain and a great deal more vitality, productivity, loyalty, and commitment throughout the workplace.

Creating a Healthy Tone

David Russo, head of human resources at the SAS Institute, a worldwide software company headquartered in Cary, North Carolina, observes:

> *The best way to produce the best results is to behave as if the people who are creating those things for you are important to you individually. Every night at six o'clock, all our assets walk out the door. . . . We just hope they come back at nine the next morning. . . . If you believe that, then it's just a waterfall of common sense. It means that you take care of the folks who are taking care of you.*[10]

An important part of taking care of one's people is through strategies that, in effect, boost the corporate immune system and make it more resistant to the emotional toxins that come its way. Earlier in this book, we looked at Normal Cousins's theories and practices on the healing effects of humor and a positive attitude. Robust organizations know how to apply this wisdom to the workplace, creating a healthy tone by giving serious attention to fun. They also emphasize work/life balance, and they invest in policies and activities that create in their employees a sense of belonging, of connection and of community. In all these ways they contribute to a healthy organizational system, one that helps keep toxins at bay—or at least dissipates them quickly.

For example, SAS company policy encourages employees to work no more than thirty-five hours per week. Southwest Airlines, on the other hand, boosts its immune system by encouraging groups of employees to acknowledge and celebrate the contributions of their peers. Similarly, at PSS World Medical, leaders know that attention to relaxation and community building will not take place unless it is built into the routines of their employees. They therefore hold annual sales meetings in resorts and make sure the meetings themselves include healthy doses of celebration and humor.[11]

Intervention Strategies

> *No one can possibly know what is about to happen. It is happening each time, for the first time, for the only time.*
>
> —James Baldwin, *The Devil Finds Work*

DESPITE THE BEST prevention strategies, leaders inevitably have to cope with emotional pain that undermines organizational systems. It comes from an accumulation of unresolved tensions and disappointments at work or at home, from the fraying of tempers and the loss of humor that result from working under deadline pressure. It comes from the challenges of change that demand new responses not yet in the repertoire, understanding, or hearts of those affected. However natural the source, emotional pain can verge on pathological and can undermine the spirit of both individuals and the workplace.

Abusive bosses, destructive policies and practices, and the unexpected onset of traumas all demand significant skill and attention to handle the toxins produced. The problem, however, is that they're also conditions that create the most wear and tear on a company's toxin handlers, and therefore require the intervention of the organization itself. Large problems need large doses of institutional attention. The decision to downsize is one such situation, where both those being laid off and those left behind feel significant pain.

Unfortunately, we have also learned that pain can come to employees, organizations, and indeed a whole nation in tragic and unspeakable forms, such as the September 11, 2001, attacks on the World Trade Center and the Pentagon. But even less dramatic events can also affect people deeply, such as the unexpected death or firing of a key leader or a natural disaster that upends the organization.

Sometimes emotional pain affects just one or a few individuals, such as in a death in the family or the onset of a serious illness. The point is that healthy organizations recognize that extremely painful experiences can happen to any staff member or to the organization as a whole—and they implement policies and practices to deal with them on a systematic basis. Such interventions will inevitably require skilled and empathetic people to make them work. It is *always* action or intervention by someone that triggers the organizational response to pain. We can therefore expect to see, directly or indirectly, the presence of toxin handling in the initiation and implementation of an organizational stratagem. The key to consistent success, however, is that handlers' responses are underpinned by *developed policy* designed to meet predictable recurring sources of organizational pain.

Typically, organizations learn to be compassionate by dealing empathetically with situations and events as they arise. They also draw from the values in their culture. Organizational interventions to deal well with pain are much more likely in those systems that treat people with respect and dignity and see them as an investment rather than a cost, as part of a community or family rather than as "hired hands." Compassionate responses are more likely when the leaders tap into that culture and into their own humanity to create contexts that give constructive meaning to the pain and that enable actions to address the pain.[12]

Every painful situation that an organization faces is in some sense unique, requiring leaders to fine-tune their responses accordingly. Nevertheless, there are some forms of pain that are bound to arise in every organization at one time or another, and that leaders can address in a somewhat systemic way. In the following sections we will examine such common situations as coping with downturns, addressing personal pain, and dealing with trauma. We will also look at intervention strategies—such as maintaining a presence in the face of suffering, providing a context for meaning, and providing a context for action—that organizations can apply in almost any painful circumstance.

Dealing with Downturns

Large numbers of employees were laid off during the economic downturn that started at the turn of this twenty-first century. And as we are well aware, the acute pain that resulted was quickly multiplied by the trauma that occurred on September 11, 2001, which led to (among other things) loss of consumer confidence and a shrinkage of workforces in many industries.

Some organizations took steps to deal compassionately with the human predicaments posed by layoffs. Cisco Systems, for example, arranged that laid-off workers would receive one-third of their salary, keep their stock investments, and continue to receive their benefits. Siemens, the German electronics giant, introduced a similar scheme in 2001 when it lost $446 million in a three-month period in its Information and Communication Mobile Group (IC Mobile). It offered employees the opportunity to apply for a leave of absence while still earning a percentage of their regular pay, depending on the length of the leave.[13] Because of employees' positive response to the time-out offer, the pilot project (involving around a hundred employees), originally planned only for Munich, was extended to cover the whole of ICM throughout Germany.[14]

Such interventions ease the burden of redundancy and signal the employees who remain that they "matter," that the company cares about the emotional well-being of its staff and, in times of difficulty, will try to resolve problems in ways that consider employee concerns. Through their actions, however, Cisco and Siemens were also paying attention to the long-term relationship they have with the staff they value but had to let go. By finding innovative ways to act with compassion, they'll more likely keep an open connection to these employees that will benefit everyone involved when the economy eventually rebounds.

Dealing with Personal Pain

Life experiences, in all their forms, intrude upon people at work just as they do elsewhere. When suffering and pain surface, organizations can and do respond in practical ways. As we've seen in earlier chapters, a death in someone's family, the onset of illness, or even a major life change such as a divorce can draw a compassionate response from colleagues or from a supervisor. Of course, as we also saw in previous chapters, not all bosses respond well to such situations. That's why creating systematic, compassionate responses in organizations is so crucial, enabling single incidents of toxin handling to be transformed into corporate institutional practices.

At Cisco, such a policy was created after Barbara Beck, a VP of human resources, learned that an employee's illness was managed poorly during a business trip overseas. The employee had a medical emergency in Japan, where little English is spoken, and had difficulty getting help. That's when Beck realized that the company needed a special system for dealing with such situations. Cisco partnered with AEA, a group that connects foreigners with the doctor they need for their condition and will even double-check a diagnosis. Today, if an employee who isn't in her country of origin has a medical emergency, there's one number she can call to connect her with immediate help.

Such organizational practices and policies can be simple and even ritualistic. Yet they still reflect a caring response to personal pain, be it an illness or a death within the organization or in an employee's family. For example, a colleague of mine remarked that she was deeply touched when her dean's office sent her a huge bouquet of flowers and a "really compassionate note" when her father passed away.

Organizational responses to personal pain need come not only from the top, however. Often, momentum and initiative rise from the grass roots, especially in healthy organizations with cultures that value people. Still, while bottom-up responses to pain may occur spontaneously, it is often the compassionate example of the leader, reinforced by values and practices in the company culture, that emboldens others to acknowledge pain in their workplaces and act to address it.

Dealing with Trauma

September 11, 2001, was the first time for many people and organizations in North America and elsewhere to experience emotional pain on such a major scale. One brokerage firm, Cantor Fitzgerald, lost 658 people—about 70 percent of its staff, who had worked at the World Trade Center.[15] The immediate aftermath of the attacks froze many people in their tracks. Reports of people suffering from depression, nightmares, and loss of confidence in the future were widespread. For their part, organizations were confronted with a deepening of the existing economic downturn, and as a result of the additional drop in consumer confidence, laid off thousands of their workers, particularly in the airline and related travel industries.

Other kinds of trauma that produce emotional pain include a death in the organization, such as the story recounted in chapter 7 regarding *Newsweek*'s loss of its admired editor, Maynard Parker, to leukemia. Similarly, traumas such as a fire, like the one in December 1995 that destroyed the Malden Mills manufacturing plant in northeastern Massachusetts, can cause pain since employees lose their livelihood (in this case, affecting hundreds of workers). A natural disaster inflicts the same kind of pain—such as the 1994 Northridge, California, earthquake in which Macy's lost two stores, and many employees lost their places of work.

When people are thrust into traumatic situations, they tend to ask questions that go to the core of life's meaning: "Why did this happen? Could I have prevented it? How will we cope? Why me?" And, for employees who witness a tragic event but are not directly affected, "Why *not* me?" Leaders cannot be expected to answer such questions. At the same time, when staff and their families are feeling emotional turmoil as a result of a traumatic event, the role and skills of toxin handling become critical. Leaders can work as handlers by making themselves as available as possible for their people, by helping employees begin to make sense of what they are experiencing, and by assisting them in mobilizing their emotions and energy so that they can "fight back"—and start to heal.[16]

In general, though, when traumatic events occur, all the usual guidelines for managers go out the window. The impact of a trauma strips away, for a while, the mask of the rationality of organizational functioning. It reveals starkly that what goes on in organizations is not only about roles, routines, and tasks to achieve operational goals or to meet a "performance target." (In fact, perhaps those are never the most important organizational functions.) Tragedy reveals a different, more human face of the organization. Those experiencing or witnessing trauma see life and death, pain and loss, heart and courage as the real issues. "Next week's budget" or "today's meeting" or some complaint about the boss's work demands may not be such a big deal after all.

There simply are no prescriptions in any management rulebook for dealing with a traumatic situation. Even given the lessons that we can learn from other examples of traumatic episodes, organizations still need to improvise according to the mood and crisis of the moment. No two traumatic events are alike for those who experience them, and the same emotional event impacts people differently. That is the nature of trauma: The specific remedies for particular situations require responses that are custom-made for the moment. Organizations can, however, develop some standard practical responses that can be customized according to the situation.

The emotional strength and competency of an organization's leaders can be a critical resource for helping staff in their time of suffering, as we have seen. So are the values and practices of their organizations, which can be used to generate compassionate solutions. Equally important is the emotional and practical resilience that exists among the organization's community itself.

Whether responses are leader-initiated or emerge from within the organization's workforce, dealing with trauma as it unfolds is not an arm's-length undertaking. Although some strategic aspects of responding to trauma will come into play over time, the early visibility and actions of the organization's leaders are crucial for giving hope to those in pain and for helping to stabilize the situation. Recovery comes later. What the leader does in such instances becomes all-important.

Leaders of organizations can help shape the development of institutional responses in three ways. First, they can be present, physically and emotionally, for those who hurt. Second, they can provide a context for meaning by creating space for people where they can express and explore—without embarrassment or guilt—the way they feel, and where they can begin to visualize recovery. (This is the "holding space" of the toxin handler and the "being present" of the leader writ large.) And third, they can provide a context for action, a context in which people in pain can begin to respond constructively to their experience, to channel their grief and start to mobilize their resources to move on. (This is "pushing back" and "planting seeds" on a grand scale.)[17]

Leaders do some or all of these things in concert; there is no fixed formula or sequence. The efforts are inevitably improvised. Leaders can exhibit presence and signal sensitivity to the grieving process in themselves and others and create both contexts—of meaning and action—through the same sequence of interventions.

BOX 8-1 ASSESSING ORGANIZATIONAL CAPACITY FOR COMPASSIONATE RESPONSE

As with individual leadership, an organization's capability to deal with trauma can be assessed in terms of four competencies, albeit each with a different focus: scope, scale, speed, and specialization. Each indicator is a rough measure of the organization's compassion competence that, in turn, helps people to heal and to continue with the work of the organization.[18]

- The *scope* of compassionate response: What is the breadth of resources that can be provided to people in need, such as money, work flexibility, and physical aid, as well as other people's time and attention? If an employee falls ill, is time off the only support, or does the system provide a wide range of healing resources such as flexible hours, gestures of comfort (like food, flowers, and cards), financial support, and assistance with child care?

- The *scale* of compassionate response: What is the volume of resources, time, and attention that people who are suffering receive? Companies that are most effective at unleashing organizational compassion match the scale to the need. When a block of apartments was destroyed in a fire, for example, the people who lived in those apartments found a wide variation in how each of their different employers responded. Some received a routine distribution of insurance coverage, while others were astonished at the outpouring of help from both corporate channels and individual colleagues—money, housewares, furniture, and offers of places to stay. The compassion competence of the latter system is more likely to help employees heal faster, and at the same time strengthen employee loyalty to the firm.
- The *speed* of response: Companies with compassion competence extract and direct resources quickly, with little hesitation. Responding compassionately is a hardwired capability that is core, rather than peripheral, to the system. Even in highly regimented bureaucracies, compassion can be shown quite quickly. In one manufacturing organization, a manager suffered a severe head injury that required almost three months in recovery, just after he had been appointed to lead an important experimental project that removed him from his regular compensation scheme. His previous job had been filled and he was effectively stuck in no-man's land. A senior operations manager swiftly reinstated the man's previous compensation, obtaining the necessary sign-off without delay, an act that allayed the family's anxiety over their financial circumstances.
- The degree of *specialization* of response: To what degree does the system custom-fit resources to the particular needs of an individual or a group? If, for example, several employees' children are injured in a bus accident, some families will need close communication and hands-on comforting. Others will need to grieve privately and get back to work quickly.

Maintaining a Presence in the Face of Great Suffering

Being fully available to one's people means paying attention to how one's staff, colleagues, or bosses, are feeling, as discussed in chapter 7. In a traumatic situation, the intensity of the pain is much more widespread than in the usual instances of emotional pain; the pain runs deeper, and inevitably, the leaders themselves are caught up in the predominant emotions. Leaders can intervene by making themselves emotionally available—for example, by being open about the way they are feeling. Jane Dutton and her colleagues suggest that "openly expressing these feelings can be very powerful, especially in times of extreme pain. . . . When people know they can bring their pain to the office, they no longer have to expend energy trying to ignore or suppress it, and they can more easily and effectively get back to work. This may be a mutually reinforcing cycle, since getting back to routine can be in itself healing."[19]

The exact means of "being present" will differ according to the situation. Leaders need to be attentive to the cycle of grief, a process that accompanies experiences of significant pain. This means that they remind themselves that when people have been emotionally hurt (including themselves), they typically go into a sequence of emotional responses of shock. This cycle starts with denial ("This is not happening to me!"); shifts, often rapidly, to anger ("Why me?"); and then turns to despair ("There is nowhere to turn!") that needs to be acknowledged before the suffering person can begin to let go of past experiences and move on.[20]

Wherever staff are in this cycle, the key to this act of leadership is to take the time to call, visit the site of the trauma, or in some other way demonstrate visibly to those who are suffering that she is there for them and feels, even shares, the pain. For example, after the September 11 attacks, New York City's Mayor Rudolph Giuliani was widely praised for his perpetual presence—at Ground Zero and later at funerals—and for his sincere expressions of grief, all of which helped restore people's confidence and resolve to rebuild.[21]

Unfortunately, such compassionate responses to trauma don't always occur. As in other situations affecting staff, leaders and their organizations often leave people in pain to their own devices, or intervene in ways that make things worse. That was the case at one architectural firm when a visitor died suddenly in the hallway. Rather than acknowledging the event and offering mechanisms for staff to discuss their feelings, the firm's leaders effectively ignored it. According to one account of the incident:

> *Employees who tried to help the dying man felt guilty for having failed in their efforts. Others felt helpless because they could not speak about the feelings they had about seeing or hearing that someone had died in their midst. The company provided no leadership, no way for employees to find a healing meaning to their experience, no way to act, to move forward with some sense of consolation and peace.*[22]

Such an obvious lack of organizational intervention damages not only individual employees but also the entire social fabric of the company. When there is no organizational understanding of the cycle of grief, staff are left without a way to channel their feelings, and they will find it difficult to regain their focus on work.[23] In the case of the architectural firm, the rift that occurred between management and staff has yet to be repaired.

Providing a Context for Meaning

Leaders can use the resources and practices of their organizations to create space for those struggling with their pain. For example, when the daughter of an employee in a consulting firm was seriously injured in an automobile accident, firm managers rented an apartment close to the hospital so that the family could be near their daughter. This eliminated a source of stress and inconvenience for the family and allowed them to concentrate on their daughter's recovery.[24]

Such symbolic gestures provide a context for meaning at the moment of pain. They are important interventions, since they create an opportunity for those in pain to pause, to "regain their breath," and to begin to move on. They also become part of the "database" of compassionate responses by the organization that can be recalled as precedents when later traumas occur.

Providing a context for meaning also entails creating an environment or an emotional climate in which people feel it is safe to express their feelings (of shock, or fear, or anger, and so on) and discuss these reactions with others. Organizations can hire skilled facilitators and provide time out so that this process can take place. Some organizations that are in industries where physical danger is a significant factor in their work have external "SWAT" teams of therapists who are brought in to counsel staff when there is a fatal accident at a work site.

A context for meaning can also be accomplished when leaders tap into and reinforce important organizational values. In the process, leaders remind those suffering about a larger purpose in their work and reaffirm for them that they're part of a community, and not alone with their despair. For example, Richard Smith of *Newsweek* (whose leadership we discussed in chapter 7) provided just such a healing environment for his organization when he reminded his staff, faced with the illness and death of editor Maynard Parker, of the magazine's commitment to community and to being an outstanding publication. Staff, editors, and those in other roles responded with quality work as they put out the magazine. They felt secure in the knowledge that they had support and encouragement to talk about their feelings, that Parker was getting the best care available, that they would be kept apprised of his condition, and that one way to respond was to honor Parker's and the organization's drive for excellence.

Mark Whitaker, Parker's successor, observed that the interventions of Smith and others at the top of *Newsweek* gave staff a way to make sense of this tragic situation and to sustain them through the long months of Parker's illness. "I think it made people realize, 'Well, if I ever had a situation like that myself, God forbid, this is a company that will be there for me.' That is an intangible thing, but I think it's really powerful."[25]

Providing a Context for Action

A context for meaning helps stabilize the condition of people in pain, helping to stem the emotional hemorrhaging. Providing a context for action reorients people to reconnection and recovery. Leaders and their organizations can uncork and mobilize people's energy to heal through the example they provide in their actions. Such was the case when a fire destroyed student living quarters at the University of Michigan Business School. B. Joseph White, the dean at the time, interrupted his scripted annual "State of the School" speech with some moving personal remarks. He assured students that the school would house them, and he wrote a personal check on the spot to make sure that happened quickly. Word of White's actions spread fast, catalyzing a campuswide effort to tap into alumni, faculty, and staff networks to help find housing, financial support, and other resources for students affected by the fire.[26]

An organization's existing infrastructure can also be used to locate useful resources, generate ideas, and link disparate groups of employees who need to know what is happening and who might be able to provide assistance. Leaders and their organizations therefore provide contexts for action not only through their own acts of compassion or sensitive applications of their infrastructure, but also through the climate they set that inspires others to help as well. Bottom-up initiatives can be powerful and transforming. For example, at *Newsweek,* one employee organized a blood and platelet drive when Maynard Parker fell ill, another managed home chores for Parker's family, while another took on the job of babysitting his children.[27]

The key role for leaders in such cases is to be a resource and a supporter, not to take control of the efforts from the grass roots and so undermine their contribution. Managers can actually *create* pain by trying to take over employee-initiated projects. On the other hand, organizational compassion can be contagious, whether it originates from the leader or from others in the workplace, creating "positive spirals of compassion," where one act of compassion inspires another.[28]

Restoration and Recovery

Hope is the oxygen of the human spirit.

—Margaret Somerville, *The Ethical Canary*

WHEN INTERVENTIONS to handle trauma have begun to take hold, when people have passed the intensity of the toxic moment and begun life anew, another set of toxin-handling issues emerges. How do those who have suffered begin to function in a healthy way in the post-traumatic era of their lives? What does it take for them to return to confidence and vitality? How do we as leaders help sustain the recovery from pain? What can the organizational system do to help? This is the domain of recovery and restoration, of helping people "pick up the pieces" and move on.

Recovery from emotional pain requires that those who have suffered regain their confidence that they can cope well on their own; chart their courses of action; feel competent again in what they do; and feel comfortably connected to others, that they are no longer isolated from others in their families, at work, or in their communities.[29]

Recovery from pain takes time and requires safe emotional space and compassionate support from others. People also emerge from trauma at different rates and in different ways. A manager with colleagues in an organization affected by the September 11, 2001, attack observed: "Our staff in New York had a very difficult time when the dust settled and the obvious shock period had passed. They said that it was hard to know how to 'act'—when was it okay to tell a joke again or laugh in public? Some of them were irritated that others just were not starting to move on already."[30] When caught up in the day-to-day pressures of organizational life, it is easy for organizations and their leaders to overlook the fact that people heal at different rates. And even if we do recognize that fact, it is often difficult to know how to accommodate them.

Although specifics will vary for different people and organizational responses may vary according to the nature of the resources available, the cultural values in place, and the skills and temperaments of the leaders, some restorative processes and broad principles are transferable from one situation to another. Leaders serve well their organization and those suffering by taking the time "to stay attuned to what is happening and developing a deeper grasp of what is happening."[31] Through this close, empathic attention to the specifics of restoration, they observe that people respond to help in their own ways, that they recover at their own pace, and that true healing grows out of the application of hurt people's inner resources to the condition they are in.

Leaders help with recovery and restoration through attending thoughtfully to actions and practices that provide time and space for staff to begin to heal. In the sections that follow we will examine these healing practices, which include

- showing patience and trust in the belief that time heals
- providing process by allowing people to talk about their pain
- providing guidance by helping people see positive options
- exhibiting confidence by treating people as if they can cope
- providing hope and inspiration
- providing focus by working on restoring active routines
- fostering rituals and symbols for "letting go"
- providing a basis for renewed trust
- helping people focus on constructive action

Exhibiting Patience: The Belief That Time Heals

People who have been upended by pain need time to learn to trust again: to believe that the painful experience won't recur; that their boss or their organization will not hurt them this way again; that their ability to perform well at work will return; that they'll be able to laugh again and regain meaning in their lives; that they'll feel safe in their world; or that they'll stop feeling guilt and regret at the loss of a partner, a family member, a friend, or a way of being.

Emotional pain disconnects people from hope and self-confidence, and it takes awhile for the repair work to be completed. Leaders and their organizations therefore need to build patience into their strategies of assistance. This is not about enabling helplessness or reinforcing a person's endless preoccupation with their hurt. One might say that "time alone does not heal," but it *is* an important aspect of the recovery. Leaders and their organizations can do many things over time to help staff heal, but accepting that there is no "quick fix" to suffering and allowing the healing to emerge haltingly can help in the recovery phase. Pressuring those in recovery to return to normal is counterproductive, undermining recovery in the long run.

Providing Process: Talking Helps Release the Past

As Karl Weick of the University of Michigan has observed, people "don't discover sense, they create it, which means they need conversations with others to move toward some shared idea of what meaning is possible."[32] People in pain need a way to talk safely about their experiences with supportive others in order to begin letting go or to dissipate their toxins. Unless this happens, the emotionality of the experience remains, even if masked, and stifles the possibilities of a healthy reengagement with life and productivity.

In my own case, when I faced the trauma of cancer, I discovered that by talking about my condition with colleagues—explaining why I was disconnecting from some of my leadership roles—I began to create a coherent way of understanding and coping with my situation. It certainly helped me feel more confident about my prognosis. I believe that talking with others also helped many of them find a way to deal with the initial shock of my message and find ways to address their own concerns about illness. (People's own sense of mortality is often jolted when they learn that one of their own circle has cancer.) The dialogues we had most certainly gave me comfort, helped me see past the grimness of my diagnosis, and gave me a "storyline of hope" that stood me in good stead during my recovery period.

Such "story making" through retelling the painful event helps people acknowledge their experiences. It honors and validates the pain and it makes sense of the event in ways that feed their sense of purpose and significance. Though the healing effects of talking are often enhanced when those present simply listen without comment, there's a stage in this process where the nature of the story and the emotionality of its telling trigger sharing that contributes to release. People in pain are reminded through the responses of others that they are not alone in their grief, that others have felt this way too. Moreover, listeners can affirm that what the storyteller is saying has value.

In organizational settings, sharing one's story with supportive others requires careful facilitation. After the September 11 attacks, several companies brought in grief counselors for their staff. According to VP Kirk Warren, spokesperson for the Men's Wearhouse, the company provided a full-time mental health counselor for its employees in the aftermath, available through e-mail and an "800"number. This counselor also communicated with employees in the New York City stores, all of whom had to be relocated. Other organizations also used the accessibility of the Internet to create virtual town hall meetings, where staff from anywhere that the company operates could join in the dialogue, express their pain, and seek inspiration and solutions.

Thus, the immediate or inevitable use of grief counselors may be less important than ensuring that those in pain have a way of being heard and of working through their pain in doses that do not overwhelm them. In some cases, writing in a journal specifically about the trauma over several days may prove to be the "therapy" that is most helpful.[33]

Providing Guidance: Talking Helps Fashion the Future

Talking about experiences of pain can also help sufferers create a new beginning, a more hopeful future. Saying one's thoughts and fears aloud and reflecting on them moves the speaker toward possible explanations of what occurred. Though such insight is helpful, the initial conclusions that people reach about their identity are often limiting and may even be dysfunctional. "I must be useless or helpless," "I am a victim," "I am invincible and I'll beat this thing" are initial interpretations that may restrict the options for recovery.

By listening closely to the words they use to describe their feelings, leaders can help emotionally injured people find other terms that connect them to positive possibilities rather than to doom-and-gloom scenarios. Leaders can help their staff discover other identities—for instance, that they are "a sounding board, witness, source of resilience, information hub, storyteller, companion, caregiver, and historian, all of which are roles that help people build a context that aids explanation."[34]

Indeed, people can be helped to reinvent themselves as a contribution, rather than as a failure or a victim in their time of trauma. "Unlike success or failure, *contribution* has no other side. It is not arrived at by comparison. . . . Questions such as, 'Am I good enough? Will others only love me if I have been strong and successful? Will my expression of pain be seen as weakness?' which are all about winning and losing, can be replaced by the joyful question, 'How will I be a contribution today?'"[35]

Talking one's way into resilience takes time and attention. The sense that people make initially of their path to health rarely is the final answer, though the core of a recovery sometimes starts with a strong communication of support from a leader.

Exhibiting Confidence: Treat People as if They Can Cope

There is substantial research evidence of the so-called Pygmalion effect, or the "self-fulfilling prophecy," which shows that people, especially in learning situations (which is what recovering from pain is about), respond in the direction of the expectations of their teachers or leaders. Expecting high performance and coping behavior from a learner contributes to those outcomes—and expecting poor performance and inadequacy contributes to failure.

Leaders can harness the positive direction of these tendencies. They can signal to those who are struggling to see beyond their suffering; they can let people know that they as leaders have confidence in their staff members' ability to perform well. And that message is enhanced when leaders are viewed as supportive and concerned about the well-being of those employees.[36]

Providing Hope and Inspiration

Clearly, how an organization conducts itself and what it says to its people about the future can either help or hinder recovery. Companies help with recovery when they communicate their expectations with integrity, in a way that tells sufferers there's a path out of their sadness. In the aftermath of September 11, 2001, and massive layoffs in the airline industry, Southwest senior management provided hope and inspiration by sending a memo to all staff stating that board members had waived any director's fees for the remainder of 2001. The memo added that the three top executives of the company, Colleen Barrett (president and COO), Jim Parker (vice chairman and CEO), and Herb Kelleher (chairman) had terminated their salaries for the balance of the year. The memo concluded with a note of thanks for staff members' "superb *esprit de corps*" and for their efforts on behalf of the company.

Providing Focus: Restoring Active Routines

People who are recovering from an emotional episode remain numb to their surroundings for some time after their experiences. They can find it difficult to recall the energy they had for activities that they formerly did well. After being damaged by a traumatic experience, the way back to confidence can seem long indeed. Organizations can help by focusing staff to work on small things that they can do well, thereby rebuilding a structure of manageable routines and accomplishments that provides positive feedback and begins to restore their confidence.[37]

When, as recounted earlier, employees laid off by Cisco were offered nonpaying work with nonprofit organizations, the story of support had just begun. (Remember, they were still on the payroll at a reduced salary and full benefits.) Being laid off can be devastating to someone's confidence and capacity to cope, even if an opportunity to recover is provided. Cisco insisted that these employees follow a set of procedures and be accountable for their time. They were required to meet measurable objectives, goals, and milestones. They used offices at Cisco for meetings, and the whole project was treated as a Cisco-sponsored assignment.[38]

Such a process of recovery through structuring and facilitating active organizational routines works because it gives hurt people a taste of success. It keeps them moving. It turns their attention to the task at hand and to using their inner resources to cope with what needs to be done. They begin to make sense of themselves and their world in more constructive and positive ways, and this process allows them to share this with others.[39]

Providing Opportunities for Rituals and Symbols of Remembrance

People need ways to honor and then let go of the pain and loss they feel, and they often benefit from doing this in a shared public forum and through ritual. For example, when several years ago a Canadian insurance company was acquired and folded into a competitor in France, managers from the acquired business invited employees to a churchlike ceremony, where the company was eulogized by executives and by hourly workers alike. Afterward, people went outside and, one by one, threw their business cards into a coffin-shaped hole in the ground, which was covered by dirt as a funeral dirge was played on bagpipes. Employees reported later that they felt they "had buried their old company and were ready to embrace the new one."[40]

Such rituals allow people a way to let go of some of their grief. They are a form of collective storytelling and a shared enactment of pain, where the more typical censure of emotional display and the expectation that people will show restraint and keep their feelings to themselves are suspended. The rules and practices of the rituals prevail and usually borrow from those that people recognize from within their larger culture. Grief has a safe place to be displayed and shared. As part of the recovery process, people need to construct a symbol or a storied record to honor the memory of the event. War memorials, scholarships, photographic albums, and other creations can serve this purpose. For example, several years ago at the business school where I teach, the sudden illness and rapid passing of a much-loved secretary was marked by a moving memorial service and the placement of a bench with a plaque on it, paid for by contributions from staff, under trees on a boulevard outside the school.

Rituals and symbols offer a way for those who have survived a painful experience to remember those who still suffer, or who were lost in a traumatic event, while simultaneously providing a way for people to get on with their own lives. Such rituals and symbols of remembrance can also help assuage "survivor guilt," and they create a gesture of connection to a world that in some way has changed irrevocably.

Providing a Basis for Restoring Trust

Truth may be one of the first casualties of war, but trust is one of the first certainties to disappear when someone gets hurt. When we're in pain, it becomes harder for us to believe other people's intentions toward us are good—especially if they're the very people who caused the pain in the first place. We no longer take it for granted that the other person has our best interests in mind. Similarly, when an organization's practices and policies create pain, the afflicted employees will lose their confidence that the organization is safe or supportive, and they will withdraw their commitment to it.

Trust is also about having confidence in the effectiveness of our own intentions and actions, toward ourselves as well as others. Throughout this book we've illustrated how toxicity plays havoc with people's sense of order, security, fair play, and confidence—confidence in themselves, in their leaders, in their organizations. How can anyone move forward toward recovery if she doesn't trust herself and the world around her? Leaders and their organizations play a vital role in restoring links and rekindling expectations in those who've been hurt, reassuring them that they are worthy people—and that where they work is emotionally safe.

When the pain that destroys trust comes from the actions of a leader or from the organization itself, a crucial first step is acknowledgment and apology. Recall for example Pat, the project leader discussed in chapter 7, who apologized in front of the whole team the day after he had unfairly criticized a team member. Making an apology is difficult for many people, especially those who work in toxic environments where blaming others is the norm and when the transgression is serious. But it is essential to a restoration of trust. Apologies need to be specific and to incorporate acceptance of responsibility and to communicate what will be done to make amends.[41] As in other paths to recovery, people who have lost trust need time and opportunity to respond, to give their views on what has happened and how it affected them.

Leaders help rebuild trust when they communicate honestly to their staff mistakes that the company has made. Indeed, vulnerability is at the core of trust-building. Words are a start; actions that accompany descriptions of what will happen to redress the concern are an important part of moving back to a trusting relationship. Of course, such actions take time, perseverance, and consistency. They require close attention to creating actions and routines that are different from those that undermined or destroyed trust, and to replacing them with messages that are consistent across time, individuals, and audiences.[42] Trust begins to return when leaders make themselves vulnerable to others, and transparent in their handling of the processes that they are engaging in, to help repair the damage done.

Rebuilding trust occurs in work environments where information is shared openly, and where people know what the limits to sharing are and why they exist. Unfortunately, organizations tend to err on the side of secrecy, often because of legal advice and assumptions that their people are not smart enough or strong enough emotionally to handle bad news. But the experiences of organizations such as HeartMath, Southwest, Cisco, and the Men's Wearhouse show that trusting in employees' resourcefulness leads to trust and commitment from those same employees. Moreover, when properly supported, such employees will often contribute innovative solutions to problems, even when they lack the formal training to address them.

Helping People Focus on Constructive Action

When trust has been restored and people have come to understand that they are operating within a safe, fair, and responsive system, they can begin to bring their own resources to take action toward their own healing. For that healing response to occur, however, leaders and their organizations must recognize the systemic nature of recovery and the various ways it can affect people. The practices we have discussed above often need to be harnessed in concert to create effective momentum for recovery.

The thrust of this chapter has been to explore ways that organizations can deal systematically and effectively with emotional pain, even when its onset is dramatic and unexpected. Emotional toxins inevitably find their way into the day-to-day activities of the workplace. As we have seen, however, there are strategies that organizations can take to minimize toxicity. They rest on a fundamental appreciation of the importance of people to the health of the organization. In addition, they create work conditions that make it easy for people to be enthusiastic about the organization's vision and mission—and to respond openly and with resilience to pain-inducing challenges and threats when they do arise. The health of such organizations helps keep pain at bay.

But as most people who work in organizations recognize and as this chapter has emphasized, pain can't always be prevented. "Deep pain" happens, and when it does, the intervention of leaders and their companies becomes critical. Once again, the core of a health-giving response is to believe in the intrinsic worth of employees and to attend with compassion to the emotional needs of those who are hurting. There are no easily accessible strategies, however, for handling these kinds of emotional toxins. It's important, therefore, that the response is quick and the level of both leaders' sensitivity and the organization's improvisational skills is high.

Finally, effective organizational responses to emotional pain, once in the system, don't stop with the urgent, immediate response to a painful, traumatic experience. In too many aspects of organizational life, we tend to be short-term responders, jumping into action. Then, as soon as the problem has been examined, we move on to "fight fires" elsewhere in the system. It is an understandable strategy, but not very smart or compassionate when the issue is emotional pain. Such a "Band-Aid" mentality won't ensure the long-term health of the organization or of its members. As we've seen in this chapter, leaders and their organizations can play a key role in the recovery of those who have been hurt, speeding up the well-being of those who have suffered and facilitating a healthy workplace.

We've traversed here a terrain of organizational life, looking at the nature and causes of emotional pain, the important role of the toxin handler (and the challenges and pitfalls of that work), and the roles that leaders and their organizations can play in managing toxic emotions at work. In the following concluding chapter, we'll examine what's to be learned from considering pain in the workplace, not only as an inevitable part of organizational life, but also as a way to understand some of the most challenging and intractable aspects of getting work done through the efforts and interactions of people.

CHAPTER NINE

Looking through the Lens of Pain

The only things missing from the office memo were expletives. It had everything else. There were lines berating employees for not caring about the company. There were words in all capital letters like "SICK" and "NO LONGER." There were threats of layoffs and hiring freezes and a shutdown of the employee gym.

The memo was sent by e-mail on March 13 by the chief executive officer of Cerner Corp., which develops software for the health care industry and is based in Kansas City, Missouri, with 3,100 employees around the world. Originally intended for only 400 or so company managers, it quickly took on a life of its own. The e-mail was leaked and posted on Yahoo. Its belligerent tone surprised thousands of readers, including analysts and investors. In the stock market, the valuation of the company, which was $1.5 billion (U.S.) on March 20, plummeted 22 percent in three days.[1]

—Edward Wong, "A Stinging Office Memo Boomerangs," *New York Times*

MORE THAN ANYTHING ELSE, in this book I've tried to show the importance of recognizing and treating emotional pain—and its handlers—in organized settings. That pain can be intentionally inflicted through leaders' and organizations' emotionally ignorant actions and attitudes, which was clearly the case in the memo described above. Or pain can be simply a by-product of organizational life, as we've also seen, brought on by inevitable changes such as layoffs, mergers, shifts in leadership, outside economic conditions, and the like. Whether intentional or not, however, the toxicity that results from emotional pain can disrupt productive effort and cost the organization dearly. Cerner Corporations's loss of 22 percent of stock value in three days, for example, illustrates dramatically how leaders need to understand the connection between pain and people's response to the demands of their work.

Pain thus can provide a powerful lens into organizational life that leaders can use to tease out the roots of many kinds of vexing organizational problems. The CEO of Cerner Corp., Neal Patterson, intended with his memo to get his managers' attention, to crack the whip, and create discomfort that would spur them to productive action. But he hadn't thought through the way pain can confuse, demoralize, and anger those who experience it. (Nor had he considered the dangers of broadcasting his frustrations on the Internet!) "I was trying to light a fire," he said later about his memo. "I lit a match and I started a firestorm." Indeed, he "created an atmosphere of fear without specifying what, if anything, was actually going wrong at the company."[2] The people whom Patterson addressed, therefore (and those around them), tended to focus on their fears and their anger—one avenue of which was to leak the memo. Clearly, some sensitivity to the dysfunctional possibilities of inflicting pain (as well as the dangers of doing so electronically) could have led Patterson to consider other ways of creating renewed enthusiasm among his managers.

Recognizing that toxicity exists as a potentially debilitating ingredient in organizations and acknowledging the value of handling these toxins well are attitudes that offer leaders a glimpse into fresh ways of tackling difficult problems. Recognition allows for new kinds of conversations between managers and staff about painful issues in organizations. And it allows for creative solutions that can help dissolve the pain and thus contribute to more enduring solutions to problems.

The Case of the Deadlocked Staff

> *Life is pain, Highness. Anyone who says differently is selling something.*
>
> —Dread Pirate Roberts, *The Princess Bride*

As LEADERS and their people explore the potentially toxic situations in the workplace and find ways to resolve them, possibilities emerge for reengaging staff in their work and revitalizing their performance. Such leaders will find that those they lead become more committed to them and thus to the goals of the organization. The following story is an instructive case in point, illustrating the potential of using pain as a diagnostic, as a lens into the sources of a vexing staff problem.

George, a team manager at a nonprofit organization, returned from a three-week residential leadership-training program to find his staff in turmoil. One of his subordinates, a supervisor, was at loggerheads with a staff member. The staff member, who, in George's mind, did valuable work in the unit and would be hard to replace, was looking for another job. "She's a gem," George told me, "I cannot train anyone else to do what she does. She's not perfect, of course, but she's essential to our success." The supervisor, who was exceptionally efficient and carried a very heavy workload, thought the staff member needed too much reassurance and attention to be worth keeping. But George reported that the supervisor herself was often frustrated and therefore short-tempered. "Still, I need her to stay as well," said George. "She can be tough and blunt with people, but she is conscientious, carries a huge load well and I rely on her for her organizational skills and her energy."

The rest of the staff had become somewhat traumatized by the conflict and were taking sides. Work was suffering. The final straw for the staff member had been a performance review delivered bluntly by the supervisor. The staff member had refused to sign it. When she sought clarification of several points, the supervisor told her that she was much too emotional and demanding of attention—and that everyone on staff thought of her this way. This was when the staff member began to search for another job.

George listened to each person's side separately, and learned that they both seemed to know they needed to change. Even the supervisor eventually acknowledged that the loss of the staff member was undesirable. The problem was that when the supervisor and the staff member spoke to each other, neither one listened well to the other. "I proceeded then from the premise that the issue was around poor communication skills, particularly their listening skills," said George. "They were not hearing each other, nor did they seem to be aware of the impact each had on the other when they spoke."

George began to look into communication courses inside and outside his company, and both the supervisor and staff member agreed to attend. But the more he thought about it, the less confident George was that a course would resolve the problem. Around that time, he happened across the article in the *Harvard Business Review,* "The Toxic Handler: Organizational Hero—and Casualty," which I wrote with Sandra Robinson. "A light bulb went on!" George said later. "Perhaps the issue I was dealing with was fundamentally about two people who were in pain, and their relationship was damaged as a result. As soon as I took this view, I had a different way to talk to these people and to see what really might be going on."

What came out of these conversations was revealing. The supervisor told George she was very angry that she had so much of a load to carry. She was resentful that the organization, including George, seemed to just take this for granted. Dealing with the staff member only magnified these feelings, and that's why she reacted the way she had. In addition, she was trying to cope with feeling quite "devastated" by the feedback she was being given about her impact on the staff member (and on others). "I had no idea I came across as short-tempered," the supervisor said. In tears, she told George she hadn't slept well for days as a result of the feedback.

The staff member, also in tears, told George she felt she had next to no self-esteem left as a result of the experience with her supervisor. She admitted that she often felt undervalued and unappreciated by others she worked with, and that this had happened to her in previous jobs. She acknowledged too that she needed many positive strokes to keep her happy.

Having heard from each of them, George concluded that each person was in considerable pain and was now obsessing on it. "I realized that I would get nothing accomplished until I helped them each work through this condition. I also recognized that to some extent I was in over my head, and I sought out guidance from HR." The strategies that emerged were more complex than George's original "listening skills" formulation. He hired an expert in conflict resolution to work with him and the staff, and later with the whole team.

The two staff members in conflict met together with the consultant and they spent time together privately afterward. As a result of these meetings, they developed a set of signals that would cue them to the fact that one was triggering pain in the other. That way they could head off conflict or diffuse it quickly when it occurred. "I noticed a lot less animosity and tension between them after these sessions," said George.

George also had met with everyone on the team individually to discuss the situation and the impact on them. Not surprisingly, they'd been distracted by the conflict. It had made them unhappy and they were spending time talking about it endlessly, letting their work slip in the process. Their general consensus was that they were tired of the whole drama and just wanted everyone to get back to business. But George felt that sweeping the problem under the rug this way might be damaging in the long run. "Instead I decided that the consultant and I would design a planning seminar for all staff to attend," he said. "This was to be followed by everyone taking the workshop on giving and receiving feedback that I had originally contemplated for the two people in conflict."

The listening skills sessions turned out to be "the toughest workshop I've ever done," said George. "It is so hard to do it properly. We used real examples from our workplace. The hard part was to really *listen* to someone telling you that something you said had hurt him—rather than racing ahead with an explanation of why you had said what you said. It was an emotional session. We learned some skills but what we really learned was the importance of valuing each other first." As a result, the group started to act in ways that would put the value of a person at the center of any issue or conflict.

George reported that people have begun to share some of their personal experiences at meetings. "We learn from each other and we begin to see more of the 'person' in each of us," he said. "It helps us to adjust and to offer help when someone is hurting from overload or because of a family matter like a serious illness or a death." For example, staff members began to change the way they conducted group conversations. Said George:

> *We've now built into our weekly meetings some tactics for checking in with how everyone is feeling. We can do it so quickly now that it's part of our routine. We ask things like, "Who's feeling overloaded?" or we check in with others in the meeting and ask, "Where are you for load now on a scale of one to five?"—with five being the heaviest load. I'll often see two team members after a meeting talking, one whose load was two, with one whose load was five, and the "two" person is offering help to the "five" person.*
>
> *They've learned to take time during work, however simply, to celebrate when they've done things well. The staff has even instituted the concept of "quiet time," which allows for staff to get away by themselves when needed to recover from the hectic pace of the office.*

What difference have these changes made? "Morale has soared," George reports. "There is much more supportiveness within the team. There's lots of laughter and fun. At the same time, my staff are much more focused on their work. They get on with the job." Looking at problems through the lens of emotional pain in this way—and taking seriously its deleterious effects—can deepen people's understanding of what is happening in a conflicted situation, or when morale is down or productivity is slipping. Listening to the pain of those in his team helped George to gauge its depth and led him to widen the search for causes and solutions. "I think that recognizing and dealing with the pain in these two people was essential to any real resolution of the problem," said George.

A Search for Deeper Solutions

Every powerful idea is absolutely fascinating and absolutely useless until we choose to use it.

—Richard Bach, *One*

GEORGE'S EXPERIENCE encapsulates many of the hopes I have for people in organizations who are intrigued by the arguments in this book. He stumbles on a key insight about pain when he rethinks the conflict between his two staff members in terms of the pain they are feeling. That, in turn, triggers a deeper search for a resolution. Inevitably, the way to resolution of almost any problem is by first acknowledging, understanding, and dealing with the anger and hurt that any two protagonists feel, and then addressing the toxic effects of this conflict on other organizational members. They too are hurting, and an effective solution requires that they be involved in the healing process.

Clearly, George had a strong motivation to resolve the problem: He didn't want to lose either the supervisor or the staff member, and he was frustrated by how the conflict was distracting the rest of the team from its performance. Still, the process of finding resolution involved some painful moments, such as how emotionally taxing the workshop proved to be. But by going through the workshop, the staff began to see that each of them was a warm-blooded human being who brought this humanity to work. This powerful insight led them to start treating one another with increased care and compassion. George noted that the experience has helped him and his team to be responsive, for example, "when someone is hurting from overload or because of a family matter like a serious illness or a death." It reconstituted the team into a much more caring and connected community than it had been before.

Perhaps most important, the experience ensured that the work of toxin handling would be shared among all the members of the team, rather than relegated to just one person. It also restored health and vitality to the team's experience of work. The pain of one became the concern of the others, so that they no longer talked in terms of, "Let them sort it out. Just leave us to get on with our work." They laugh and they have fun, and their morale and productivity has improved.

Working through Setbacks

Of course, not all the efforts of leaders who recognize and use the lens of pain as an entry into problems will necessarily end so happily. There will be occasions when a manager cannot solve a problem through attention to the pain alone. Nevertheless, a focus on pain will often yield valuable lessons about the emotional condition of those involved, or of those left behind if there are losses along the way. Had George lost one of his key people, even after his efforts, knowing the emotional dynamic of everyone involved still would have shown him a path to recovery. At the very least it would have helped him avoid the same kind of problem in the future.

Even so, such healthy outcomes are not fixed in time; there are no "happily ever after" endings. Life goes on. New sources of toxins emerge. The system needs to be maintained continuously. The production of emotional toxins is an ever-present component of life at work (much like the production of toxins in the human body), and at times these toxins will create "infections" and illnesses that require urgent or prolonged attention. When managers and leaders understand this, they are much less likely to be complacent about their staff. They are better tuned to the emotional well-being of their staff and their organization, and they recognize the need to take action when toxicity occurs.

The health of the manager as a toxin handler, of course, is all-important. We have noted many of the emotional and physical costs associated with working unprotected with emotional issues. In this case, George felt an emotional lift after resolving his problem successfully. Still, he'll likely need to access the kinds of tools and attitudes for self-protection identified in this book if he is to build bridges of understanding and support within his organization.

The Healing Power of Human Connection

Simply put, we need one another.

—Edward Hallowell, *Connect*

I began this book with a focus on the toxin handler, and I included in chapter 1 the story of a nurse who helped an old man cope with the indignities of cancer. I'll close now with a story of another nurse in a different hospital, handling a painful situation associated with a set of newborn twins.[3] Kyrie and Brielle Jackson were born on October 17, 1995, at the Massachusetts Memorial Hospital in Worcester, Massachusetts. Each of the twins weighed all of two pounds at birth. Though Kyrie was putting on a bit of weight in the days following her arrival, Brielle was not doing as well. On one particular day, she had such a hard time breathing that her face was blue. She cried continually. Her intensive care nurse, Gayle Kasparian, tried to comfort her, wrapping her in a blanket, holding her, and even suctioning her nose. But nothing worked.

That's when Kasparian decided to try a procedure that she'd heard was practiced in Europe. Going against the hospital's standard practices, she put Brielle in the incubator with her sister, Kyrie. Almost immediately, Brielle snuggled up to Kyrie. Her blood-oxygen saturation levels, which had been frighteningly low, soared. She began to breathe more easily. The frantic crying stopped and her normal pinkish color quickly returned. Over the next weeks, her health improved steadily in her new, less lonely quarters. In time, the twins went home with their parents and, when last heard from, were healthy preschoolers.[4]

Here, then, was a nurse who observed her patients, cared for them, and—apparently overcoming resistance from her organization—created a successful intervention, a healing space that made a difference. This moving illustration of the power of human connection reminds us of the positive—and often life-altering—effects that toxin handlers can have on the people around them.

Kasparian is a toxin handler. She sees the human trauma unfolding, feels the suffering of both Brielle and her parents, and acts to try to alleviate or remove the pain. Like the nurse in chapter 1, and the many compassionate managers discussed in this book, she has good professional skills. She does what needs to be done to help those in her care to do well. The additional impact of her emotional attunement to the pain involved propels her to seek more creative and more human solutions that are not "in the manual." She reaches for an intervention that attends to the emotional as well as the physical state of the twin, and she argues for the support of her colleagues and her organization to do what will solve the problem.

Organizations need such toxin handlers as George and Nurse Kasparian in their systems. They are crucial to the health and success of their enterprises. They do work that carries with it a high risk of burnout, given the intensity of ongoing efforts to deal well with emotional toxins at work. Because of this risk and because of the important—though often unseen—contributions that handlers make, it is essential that these pain managers receive recognition, support, and opportunities for renewal by their organizations. A burnt-out Kasparian would have been too mentally and emotionally numb to have come upon her inspired solution—and too physically drained to have done the lobbying likely needed to convince the rest of her team to let her try her idea.

Toward a More Compassionate, Healthy, and Productive World of Work

There is no shortage of good days.
It is good lives that are hard to come by.

—Annie Dillard, *The Writing Life*

WORK IS THE PLACE where many of us live out much of our lives. Whether or not this is a healthy development hasn't been a focus of this book. But given this trend, much of what we hold dear and a great deal of what happens in our lives takes place at work, or spills into or out of our time there. Having this reality acknowledged, respected, and compassionately "handled" makes this intense and essential part of our lives immensely richer and more productive.

I believe that people in organizations help others in pain first and foremost out of concern for the sufferer's welfare. When they do this work, toxin handlers aren't normally thinking about the bottom line—even though the organization's success often depends on how well toxicity is handled. Indeed, when toxin handlers work in an environment that acknowledges and supports them, the types of positive outcomes multiply for everyone involved—including loyalty, commitment, and effort toward bottom-line results.

Ultimately, however, leaders need to give more systemic attention to emotional pain in organizations and to how it is handled. Leaders need to do this, because they have the vantage point of seeing the emotional pain in the system. Indeed, they often have a role in creating that pain. While every leader won't possess the skills of the toxin handler—and indeed, shouldn't necessarily be expected to have those skills or even be able to learn them—every leader *can* take steps to better recognize and address the pain in the system in a compassionate way. Paying attention to the emotional dimension of work, treating others with respect, and drawing on the competencies of the toxin handler are all things that leaders can do. Organizations, for their part, can minimize the risk of toxicity at work, and they can intervene and even facilitate recovery through their policies and practices. They can support their leaders and others—in management and in the grass roots—who emerge to deal with the unpredictable yet reliably painful consequences of change, trauma, and personal tragedy.

We live in times where there is much pain and suffering in and around organizations. There is much to be learned about toxicity in organizations and how best to handle it. This book is but a beginning. But my vision is for managers and their organizations to take up the challenge to safeguard the health and well-being of their people, and to offer compassion to those who hurt—something that is both a noble undertaking and eminently practical.

NOTES

Prologue

1. Joan Borysenko, *Minding the Body, Mending the Mind* (New York: Bantam, 1988).

2. Borysenko, "The Power of the Mind and Spirit to Heal," (workshop, Hollyhock, Cortes Island, B.C. Canada, July 1997).

3. Larry Dossey, *Healing Words: The Power of Prayer and the Practice of Medicine* (San Francisco: HarperCollins, 1993).

4. Dossey, *Be Careful What You Pray for . . . You Just Might Get It: What We Can Do about the Unintentional Effects of Our Thoughts, Prayers, and Wishes* (San Francisco: HarperCollins, 1997).

5. Daniel Goleman, *Emotional Intelligence* (New York: Bantam Books, 1995), 115.

6. Elaine Hatfield, John T. Cacioppo, and Richard L. Rapson, "Primitive Emotional Contagion," in *Emotion and Social Behavior,* ed. Margaret S. Clark (Newbury Park, CA: Sage Publishers, 1992), 151–177; Janice R. Kelly and Sigal G. Barsade, "Mood and Emotions in Small Groups and Work Teams," *Organizational Behavior and Human Decision Processes* 86, no. 1 (2001): 99–130; Arnold B. Bakker and Wilmar B. Schaufeli, "Burnout Contagion Processes among Teachers," *Journal of Applied Social Psychology* 30, no. 11 (2000): 2289–2308; Daniel Goleman, Richard Boyatzis, and Annie McKee, *Primal Leadership: Realizing the Power of Emotional Intelligence* (Boston: Harvard Business School Press, 2002).

7. See for example, William N. Grosch and David C. Olsen, *When Helping Starts to Hurt: A New Look at Burnout Among Psychotherapists* (New York: W. W. Norton, 1994).

8. When I first developed these ideas, I originally used the term "toxic handler"—the term that appeared in the *Harvard Business Review* article (Peter J. Frost and Sandra L. Robinson, "The Toxic Handler: Organizational Hero—and Casualty," July–August 1999, 96–106). I used the term "toxic" (rather than "toxin") because the person who does the work of handling toxins, the emotional pain of others, frequently gets sick and in fact becomes toxic. I intended to convey this double message through this term. Over time, it has become apparent that the term "toxic handler" confuses some people who "get" the image of the handler as toxic, but interpret this to mean that this is someone who causes the toxicity in the first place—quite the contrary to our message. So, for clarity's sake, I relinquish, rather reluctantly, the evocativeness of the former term for the unambiguity of the term the "toxin handler" and use this latter term throughout this book.

Chapter 1

1. In many examples used throughout this book, the names have been changed or otherwise disguised.

2. Jill Andresky Fraser, *White-Collar Sweatshop: The Deterioration of Work and Its Rewards in Corporate America* (New York: W. W. Norton, 2001).

3. Doc Lew Childre and Bruce Cryer, *From Chaos to Coherence (The Power to Change Performance)* (Boulder Creek, CO: Planetary Publications, 2000), 17.

4. Joel H. Neuman, "Injustice, Stress and Bullying Can Be Expensive!" (Presentation at Workplace Bullying 2000 Conference, Oakland, CA, January 2000.)

5. F. Analoui, "Workplace Sabotage: Its Styles, Motives and Management," *Journal of Management Development* 14, no. 7 (1995): 48–65.

6. Michael D. Crino and Terry L. Leap, "What HR Managers Must Know About Employee Sabotage," *Personnel* 66, no. 5 (1989): 31–32, 34–36, 38.

7. Ibid.

8. Alan B. Krueger and Alexandre Mas, "Strikes, Scabs and Tread Separations: Labor Strife and the Production of Defective Bridgestone/Firestone Tires," working paper, Princeton University, January 2002; also reported in Wessel, "Capital—The Hidden Cost of Labor Strife."

9. David Wessel, "Capital—The Hidden Cost of Labor Strife," *The Wall Street Journal*, 10 January 2002.

10. Neuman, "Injustice, Stress and Bullying Can be Expensive!"

11. C. Brady Wilson, "U.S. Businesses Suffer from Workplace Trauma," *Personnel Journal* 70, no. 7 (1991): 47–50.

12. Jane E. Dutton, Peter J. Frost, Monica C. Worline, Jacoba M. Lilius, and Jason M. Kanov, "Leading in Times of Trauma," *Harvard Business Review*, January 2002, 61.

13. Richard M. Ryan and Edward L. Deci, "Self-determination Theory and the Facilitation of Intrinsic Motivation, Social Development, and Well-being," *American Psychologist* 55, no. 1 (2000): 68–78.

14. L. Ganzini, W. S. Johnston, B. H. McFarland, S. W. Tolle, and M. A. Lee, "Attitudes of Patients with Amyotrophic Lateral Sclerosis and Their Caregivers toward Assisted Suicide," *New England Journal of Medicine* 339, no. 14 (1998): 967–973.

15. Daniel Goleman, *Emotional Intelligence* (New York: Bantam Books, 1995), 14.

16. Ibid.

17. Recent research indicates that "fight-or-flight" may be a phenomenon found primarily in males, rather than females. For more on females' "tend-and-befriend" behaviors, see box 4-1, "Stress and Gender."

18. Elisabeth Kübler-Ross, *On Death and Dying* (New York: Macmillan, 1969).

19. Ryan and Deci, "Self-determination Theory and the Facilitation of Intrinsic Motivation, Social Development, and Well-being."

20. Edward M. Hallowell, "The Human Moment at Work," *Harvard Business Review,* January–February 1999, 59.

21. Hallowell, "The Human Moment at Work," 60.

22. Hallowell, 63.

23. Pamela Kruger, "Make Smarter Mistakes," *Fast Company,* 11 October 1997, 152.

24. Amy Zipkin, "The Wisdom of Thoughtfulness," *The New York Times,* 31 May 2000.

25. Bender describes this as an emotional attunement to the person or situation. Patricia E. Benner, Christine A. Tanner, and Catherine A. Chesla, *Expertise in Nursing Practice: Caring, Clinical Judgment, and Ethics* (New York: Springer, 1996), 149–151.

26. Daniel Goleman, Richard Boyatzis, and Annie McKee, "Primal Leadership: The Hidden Driver of Great Performance," *Harvard Business Review,* December 2001, 42–51; P. Salovey and J. D. Mayer, "Emotional Intelligence," *Imagination, Cognition and Personality* 9 (1990): 185–211.

27. Bruce Cryer, interview with author, 15 March 2002. Other examples of compassionate organizations are discussed in chapters 7 and 8.

28. Adapted from research reported in Monica C. Worline, Jane E. Dutton, Peter J. Frost, Jason M. Kanov, Jacoba M. Lilius, and Sally Maitlis, "Creating Fertile Soil: The Organizing Dynamics of Resilience" (paper presented at the Academy of Management National Meetings, Denver, CO, 2002).

29. The Watson Wyatt studies can be viewed online at <http://www.watsonwyatt.com> (accessed 25 July 2002).

30. Jeffrey Pfeffer and John F. Veiga, "Putting People First for Organizational Success," *Academy of Management Executive* 13, no. 2 (1999): 37–48.

31. Pfeffer and Veiga, "Putting People First for Organizational Success," 39.

32. Peter J. Frost and Sandra L. Robinson, "The Toxic Handler: Organizational Hero—and Casualty," *Harvard Business Review,* July–August 1999, 97.

Chapter 2

1. Marcia Lynn Whicker, *Toxic Leaders: When Organizations Go Bad* (Westport, CT: Quoram Books, 1996).

2. Bennet J. Tepper, "Consequences of Abusive Supervision," *Academy of Management Journal* 43, no. 2 (2000): 178–190; Peter J. Frost and Sandra L. Robinson, "The Toxic Handler: Organizational Hero—and Casualty," *Harvard Business Review,* July–August 1999, 97.

3. George Fieldman, "Work Stress," *New Scientist* 173, no. 2324 (2002): 11.

4. Indecision over issues that are sensitive or urgent or ambiguous can lead to a build up of "toxic decision processes" in organizations. Tasks mishandled by managers (for example, by ignoring warning signals, avoiding making hard choices, or miscommunicating key information) can detonate, causing anger or indignation, and contribute to a volatile and dysfunctional workplace. For more information on toxic decision making see Hakan Özçelik and Sally Maitlis, "Toxic Decision Making: The Mismanagement of Emotional Issues in Organizations" (paper presented at the Academy of Management Annual Meeting, Washington, DC, 2001).

5. Cary L. Cooper, Philip Dewe, and Michael P. O'Driscoll, *Organizational Stress: A Review and Critique of Theory, Research, and Applications* (Thousand Oaks, CA: Sage Publishers, 2001).

6. Daniel Goleman, Richard E. Boyatzis, and Annie McKee, *Primal Leadership: Realizing the Power of Emotional Intelligence* (Boston: Harvard Business School Press, 2002).

7. The survey, published in 2001 by human resource specialist Watson Wyatt, was cited in Kathryn May, "Human Rights Agency Faces Staffing Exodus: Employees Say Management Abusive: Report," *National Post,* 12 May 2001.

8. Jim Beatty, "Women in Pants Can't Answer Telephones at Enquiry B.C.: Government Contractor's Dress Code Offensive, Former Employee Says," *Vancouver Sun,* 1 February 2001.

9. Jill Andresky Fraser, *White-Collar Sweatshop: The Deterioration of Work and Its Rewards in Corporate America* (New York: W. W. Norton, 2001).

10. Gerry Bellett, "Digital Depression, Computer Rage Start to Boil Over: Studies Show 83 Percent of IT Managers Have Experienced Enraged Workers Who Damaged Computers," *Vancouver Sun,* 2 June 2001.

11. Eric Auchard, "Technology Imperils Privacy in the Workplace: Three-quarters of U.S. Businesses Now Electronically Monitor Employees in Some Fashion," *Vancouver Sun,* 4 August 2001.

12. American Management Association, "2001 AMA Survey: Workplace Monitoring and Surveillance: Policies and Practices" (New York: AMA, 2001).

13. Oren Harari, *The Leadership Secrets of Colin Powell* (New York: McGraw-Hill, 2002), 13.

14. Michael Useem, *The Leadership Moment: Nine True Stories of Triumph and Disaster and Their Lessons for Us All* (New York: Random House, 1998), 65–93.

15. Or at the very least they sense the problem later (often in one of those "3 A.M. waking moments" that so many leaders experience), and they'll cycle back to deal with it later. For example, a project leader like Eugene Kranz may go back to his staff after a crisis and help them talk through their feelings about being replaced at a critical point in the process. Or a leader may call on a staff member the day after a tense meeting in which the employee was cut off in mid-sentence, acknowledge the unfortunate intervention, and help the staff member redress the discomfort. Pain that is toxic, then, can actually become generative—mobilizing and empowering people to resolve issues themselves. The problem comes when managers create pain frequently and without resolution—because they are simply chronically toxic or because their abusiveness,

indecision, and inconsistency are unrelenting, pervading the daily life of people in the organization.

16. Christine M. Pearson, Lynne M. Andersson, and Christine L. Porath, "Assessing and Attacking Workplace Incivility," *Organizational Dynamics* 29, no. 2 (2000): 123–137.

17. Ibid.

18. Pearson et al., "Assessing and Attacking Workplace Incivility," 130.

19. Ibid.

20. Gary Namie, "Campaign Against Workplace Bullying, 2000 Hostile Workplace Survey," (Bellingham, WA, September 2000) <http://www.bullybusters.org/home/twd/bb/res/surv2000.html> (accessed 1 July 2002).

21. Hugh Davies and Paul Marston, "Rock Star Cleared in Drunken Air Rage Incident," *Vancouver Sun,* 6 April 2002.

22. Arlie Hochschild, *The Managed Heart: Commercialization of Human Feeling* (Los Angeles: University of California Press, 1985), 7.

23. Ellyn Spragins, "LOVE & MONEY: When Numbers Cease to Matter," *The New York Times,* 7 October 2001.

24. Steven Edwards, "UN Drug Agency 'Demoralized and Paralyzed': Official's Resignation Letter Accuses Boss of Breaking Promises," *National Post,* 22 January 2001.

25. Carola Hoyos, "Annan Tells UN Drugs Agency Head to Go," *London Financial Times,* 24 July 2001.

26. Ibid.

27. Jack Welch with John A. Byrne, *Straight from the Gut* (New York: Warner, 2001), 328.

Chapter 3

1. Walter Wangerin Jr., *Ragman: And Other Cries of Faith* (New York: HarperTrade, 1984), 3–4.

2. This is not the only or necessarily the safest way to perform this role, but taking on pain, as well as taking away another's pain, are frequent outcomes of the work of toxin handling. In chapter 4 I will discuss the hazards to the toxin handler of taking on the pain of others.

3. Peter J. Frost, "Why Compassion Counts!" *Journal of Management Inquiry* 8, no. 2 (1999): 127–133.

4. Jean Baker Miller and Irene Pierce Stiver, *The Healing Connection* (Boston: Beacon Press, 1997).

5. William A. Kahn, "Caring for the Caregivers: Patterns of Organizational Caregiving," *Administrative Science Quarterly* 38, no. 4 (1993): 539–563; Jane E. Dutton, Monica C. Worline, Peter J. Frost, and Jacoba Lilius, "The Organizing of Compassion," working paper/unpublished manuscript 2002.

6. Jay Conger and Nancy Rothbard, "Orit Gadiesh: Pride at Bain & Co. (A)," Case 9-494-031 (Boston: Harvard Business School, 1993), 15.

7. William A. Kahn, "Relational Systems at Work," *Research in Organizational Behavior* 20 (1998): 44.

8. Patricia E. Benner, Christine A. Tanner, and Catherine A. Chesla, *Expertise in Nursing Practice: Caring, Clinical Judgement, and Ethics* (New York: Springer, 1996).

9. Kahn, "Caring for the Caregivers: Patterns of Organizational Caregiving," 546.

10. See Ronald A. Heifetz, *Leadership Without Easy Answers* (Cambridge and London: Belknap Press of Harvard University Press, 1994); and William A. Kahn, "Holding Environments at Work," *Journal of Applied Behavioral Science* 37, no. 3 (2001): 260–279 for further discussion of holding space for others. Heifetz talks about leaders "managing the holding environment" in a relationship. The term holding environment was first used in psychoanalysis to capture the relationship between a therapist and a patient. "The therapist 'holds' the patient in a process of developmental learning in a way that has some similarities to the way a mother or a father hold their newborn or maturing children" (104). In Heifetz's model of leadership, the notion of this environment can be applied to any relationship in which "one party has the power to hold the attention of another party and facilitate adaptive work" (104–105). Holding space this way works because it "contains and regulates the stresses that work generates" (105). William Kahn discusses holding environments as a means to helping workers manage debilitating stress and anxiety.

11. Conger and Rothbard, "Orit Gadiesh: Pride at Bain & Co. (A)," 15.

12. Joyce K. Fletcher, *Disappearing Acts: Gender, Power and Relational Practice at Work* (Cambridge, MA: MIT Press, 2001), 59–60.

13. Deborah M. Kolb, "Women's Work: Peacemaking in Organizations," in *Hidden Conflict in Organizations: Uncovering Behind-the-Scenes Disputes,* eds., Deborah M. Kolb and Jean Bartunek (Newbury Park, CA: Sage Publishers, 1992): 80.

14. Jane E. Dutton, "The Making of Organizational Opportunities: An Interpretive Pathway to Organizational Change," in *Research in Organizational Behavior* 15, eds., B. Staw and L. L. Cummings (Greenwich, CT: JAI Press, 1993), 197.

15. David Crisp, interview with author, 15 June 2001.

16. David Cooperrider, "Positive Image, Positive Action: The Affirmative Basis of Organizing," in *Appreciative Management and Leadership: The Power of Positive Thought and Action in Organizations* (San Francisco: Jossey-Bass, 1990), 91–125.

17. Shelley E. Taylor, Margaret E. Kemeny, Geoffrey M. Read, Julienne E. Bower, and Tara L. Gruenewald, "Psychological Resources, Positive Illusions, and Health," *American Psychologist* 55, no. 1 (2000): 99–109.

18. Fletcher, *Disappearing Acts,* 56.

19. Daniel Goleman, *Emotional Intelligence* (New York: Bantam Books, 1995).

Chapter 4

1. Peter J. Frost and Sandra L. Robinson, "The Toxic Handler: Organizational Hero—and Casualty," *Harvard Business Review,* July–August 1999, 97–106.

2. Joyce K. Fletcher, *Disappearing Acts: Gender, Power and Relational Practice at Work* (Cambridge, MA: MIT Press, 2001).

3. Hans Selye, *Stress in Health and Disease* (London: Butterworth-Heinemann, 1976).

4. Bruce S. McEwen and Eliot Stellar, "Stress and the Individual. Mechanisms Leading to Disease," *Archives of Internal Medicine* 153, no. 18 (1993): 2093–2101.

5. Lauren Heist, "Cease and De-Stress," *Fast Company,* May 2000 [magazine online]; available from <http://www.fastcompany.com/feature/stress.html> (accessed 6 May 2002).

6. Ibid.

7. G. Rein, R. McCraty, and M. Atkinson, "The Physiological and Psychological Effects of Compassion and Anger," *Journal of Advancement in Medicine* 8, no. 2 (1995): 87–105.

8. Shelley E. Taylor, Laura Cousino Klein, Brian P. Lewis, Tara L. Gruenwald, Regan A. R. Gurung, and John A. Updegraff, "Biobehavioral Responses to Stress in Females: Tend-and-befriend, not Fight-or-flight," *Psychological Review* 107, no. 3 (2000): 411–429.

9. J. A. Bosch, E. J. de Geus, A. Kelder, E. C. Veerman, J. Hoogstraten, and A. V. Amerongen, "Differential Effects of Active versus Passive Coping on Secretory Immunity," *Psychophysiology* 38, no. 5 (2001): 836–846.

10. Doc Lew Childre and Bruce Cryer, *From Chaos to Coherence (The Power to Change Performance)* (Boulder Creek, CO: Planetary Publications, 2000), 80.

11. Peter J. Frost and Sandra L. Robinson, "The Toxic Handler, Organizational Hero—and Casualty," *Harvard Business Review,* July–August 1999, 102.

12. Daniel Goleman, *Emotional Intelligence* (New York: Bantam Books, 1995).

13. Robert C. Solomon, "The Moral Psychology of Business: Care and Compassion in the Corporation," *Business Ethics Quarterly* 8, no. 3 (1998): 515–533.

14. Ram Dass and Paul Gorman, *How Can I Help? Stories and Reflections on Service* (New York: Alfred A. Knopf, 1985).

15. Dass and Gorman, *How Can I Help?* 201.

16. Dass and Gorman, 189.

17. Solomon, "The Moral Psychology of Business."

18. Pamela Kruger, "Betrayed by Work," *Fast Company,* 29 November 1999, 184.

19. In 1993, Dr. Greg Passey, a retired lieutenant-commander of the Canadian Armed Forces, conducted a sweeping study of the psychological stress endured by soldiers returning from peacekeeping duty in violent overseas conflicts, and concluded that 12 percent of them suffered post–traumatic stress disorder (PTSD), "four times the estimated number of civilians who suffer from it." Said Dr. Passey: "[Peacekeeping] extracts a high toll in terms of death, suicides, injury, diminished health, broken relationships and disrupted families." James Cudmore, "Peacekeepers Pay High Price, Doctor Says: Army Accused of Neglecting the Troops," *Toronto National Post,* 30 March 2001.

20. Carol Off, *The Lion, the Fox, and the Eagle: A Story of Generals and Justice in Rwanda and Yugoslavia* (New York: Random House, 2000).

21. Off, "General Breakdown," *Saturday Night,* 28 October 2000, 28–36.

Chapter 5

1. Carl Ransom Rogers, *Carl Rogers on Personal Power* (New York: Delacorte Press, 1977).
2. Bill Moyers, *Healing and the Mind* (New York: Doubleday, 1993), 351.
3. Jim Loehr and Tony Schwartz, "The Making of a Corporate Athlete," *Harvard Business Review,* January 2001, 120–128.
4. Loehr and Schwartz, 122.
5. Ibid.
6. Loehr and Schwartz, 120–128.
7. Loehr and Schwartz, 123.
8. Laura Lee MacLean, "What Helps or Hinders Toxic Handlers in the Performance of Their Jobs" (master's thesis, University of British Columbia, 2000).
9. Loehr and Schwartz, "The Making of a Corporate Athlete," 124.
10. Loehr and Schwartz, 125.
11. K. Yaffe, D. Barnes, M. Nevitt, L. Y. Lui, and K. Covinsky, "A Prospective Study of Physical Activity and Cognitive Decline in Elderly Women: Women Who Walk," *Archives of Internal Medicine* 161, no. 14 (2001): 1703–1708.
12. Loehr and Schwartz, "The Making of a Corporate Athlete," 125.
13. Andrew Vickers and Catherine Zollman, "ABC of Complementary Medicine. Massage Therapies," *British Medical Journal* 319 (1999): 1254–1257.
14. T. Field, G. Ironson, F. Scafidi, et al., "Massage Therapy Reduces Anxiety and Enhances EEG Pattern of Alertness and Math Computations," *International Journal of Neuroscience* 86 (1996): 197–205.
15. R. A. Lippin, "Alternative Medicine in the Workplace," *Alternative Therapies in Health & Medicine* 2, no. 1 (1996): 47–51.
16. Anne Underwood, "The Magic of Touch," *Newsweek,* 6 April 1998, 71–72.
17. Loehr and Schwartz, "The Making of a Corporate Athlete," 124.
18. MacLean, "What Helps or Hinders Toxic Handlers in the Performance of Their Jobs," (2000).
19. Ibid.
20. Norman Cousins, *The Healing Heart: Antidotes to Panic and Helplessness* (New York: W. W. Norton, 1983).
21. Martin E. P. Seligman, *Learned Optimism* (New York: Alfred A. Knopf, 1991), 173.
22. Ibid.
23. Toxin handlers could benefit from reading Martin Seligman's *Learned Optimism,* in particular the exercises for building/restoring optimism (exercises such as identifying your ABCs—what is the *adversity* you are dealing with, what are your *beliefs* about it, and what are the *consequences* of those beliefs).
24. Seligman, *Learned Optimism,* 15.
25. Tom Spears, "Fake Medicine Can Work the Same as Real Drugs: Study: Placebos Sometimes May Even Work Better Than the Real Thing," *Vancouver Sun,* 10 August 2001.
26. Ibid.

27. Important work on this topic can be found in Barbara L. Fredrickson, "The Role of Positive Emotions in Positive Psychology," *American Psychologist* 56 (2001): 218–226.

28. William C. Taylor, "The Leader of the Future," *Fast Company,* 25 June 1999, 130.

29. Phil Jackson, *Sacred Hoops: Spiritual Lessons of a Hardwood Warrior* (New York: Hyperion, 1995), 48–49.

30. David Crisp, interview with author, 15 June 2001.

31. Jack Kornfield, *A Path with Heart: A Guide Through the Perils and Promises of Spiritual Life* (New York: Bantam, 1993).

32. Loehr and Schwartz, "The Making of a Corporate Athlete," 126.

33. MacLean, "What Helps or Hinders Toxic Handlers in the Performance of Their Jobs," 47.

34. Moyers, *Healing and the Mind,* 328.

35. Ibid.

36. See Kornfield, *A Path with Heart,* for more detail on meditation practice.

37. Jackson, *Sacred Hoops,* 125.

38. See, for example, Stephen R. Covey, A. Roger Merrill, and Rebecca R. Merrill, *First Things First: A Principle-Centered Approach to Time and Life Management* (New York: Simon & Schuster, 1994).

39. Covey, Merrill, and Merrill, *First Things First,* 37.

40. David Crisp, interview with author, 15 June 2001.

41. Jackson, *Sacred Hoops,* 120.

42. Taylor, "The Leader of the Future," 138.

43. Doc Lew Childre and Bruce Cryer, *From Chaos to Coherence (The Power to Change Performance)* (Boulder Creek, CO: Planetary Publications, 2000).

44. André L. Delbecq and Frank Friedlander, "Strategies for Personal and Family Renewal," *Journal of Management Inquiry* 4, no. 3 (1995): 262–269.

45. MacLean, "What Helps or Hinders Toxic Handlers in the Performance of Their Jobs," 42.

46. "The Gambler" written by Don Schlitz; sung by Kenny Rogers, United Artists Records original album release, 15 November 1978.

47. Loehr and Schwartz, "The Making of a Corporate Athlete," 127.

48. Moyers, *Healing and the Mind,* 351.

49. William N. Grosch and David C. Olsen, *When Helping Starts to Hurt: A New Look at Burnout among Psychotherapists* (New York: W. W. Norton, 1994), 1–3.

50. Ibid.

51. Kornfield, *A Path with Heart,* 176.

52. Christina Maslach and Michael P. Leiter, *The Truth about Burnout: How Organizations Cause Personal Stress and What to Do about It* (San Francisco: Jossey-Bass, 1997).

Chapter 6

1. Debra E. Meyerson and Joyce K. Fletcher, "A Modest Manifesto for Shattering the Glass Ceiling," *Harvard Business Review,* January–February 2000, 126–136.

2. Fletcher, *Disappearing Acts: Gender, Power and Relational Practice at Work* (Cambridge, MA: MIT Press, 2001).

3. Fletcher, *Disappearing Acts,* 121.

4. Daniel Goleman, Richard Boyatzis, and Annie McKee, "Primal Leadership: The Hidden Driver of Great Performance," *Harvard Business Review,* December 2001, 42–51; Goleman, *Working with Emotional Intelligence* (New York: Bantam, 1998).

5. Fletcher, *Disappearing Acts,* 123.

6. Karl E. Weick, *The Social Psychology of Organizing,* 2d ed. (Reading, MA: Addison-Wesley, 1979).

7. Fletcher, *Disappearing Acts,* 126.

8. Fletcher, 130–131.

9. Peter J. Frost and Sandra L. Robinson, "The Toxic Handler: Organizational Hero—and Casualty," *Harvard Business Review,* July–August 1999, 96–106.

10. Bill Moyers, *Healing and the Mind* (New York: Doubleday, 1993), 317.

11. David Spiegel, *Living Beyond Limits: A Scientific Mind-Body Approach to Facing Life-Threatening Illness* (New York: Crown, 1993).

12. Frost and Robinson, "The Toxic Handler," 103.

13. Ibid.

14. André L. Delbecq and Frank Friedlander, "Strategies for Personal and Family Renewal," *Journal of Management Inquiry* 4, no. 3 (1995): 262–269.

15. Frost and Robinson, "The Toxic Handler," 1999.

16. Meyerson, "If Emotions Were Honored: A Cultural Analysis," in *Emotion in Organizations,* ed., S. Fineman (Thousand Oaks, CA: Sage Publishers, 2000), 171.

Chapter 7

1. Stanley Coren, *Sleep Thieves: An Eye-Opening Exploration into the Science and Mysteries of Sleep* (New York: Free Press, 1996).

2. Oren Harari, *The Leadership Secrets of Colin Powell* (New York: McGraw-Hill, 2002).

3. Gordon Pitts, "Neutron Jack's Softer Side," *The Globe and Mail,* 5 September 2001.

4. Phil Jackson, *Sacred Hoops: Spiritual Lessons of a Hardwood Warrior* (New York: Hyperion, 1995), 119.

5. Jackson, *Sacred Hoops,* 117.

6. Charles A. O'Reilly and Jeffrey Pfeffer, *Hidden Value: How Great Companies Achieve Extraordinary Results from Ordinary People* (Boston: Harvard Business School Press, 2000), 68.

7. William C. Taylor, "The Leader of the Future," *Fast Company,* 25 June 1999.

8. Jennifer M. George, "Emotions and Leadership: The Role of Emotional Intelligence," *Human Relations* 53, no. 8 (2000): 1045.

9. Alan M. Webber, "Danger: Toxic Company," *Fast Company,* 19 November 1998, 152.

10. Patricia E. Benner, Christine A. Tanner, and Catherine A. Chesla, *Expertise in Nursing Practice: Caring, Clinical Judgment, and Ethics* (New York: Springer, 1996), 145.

11. Mary Gentile and Todd D. Jick, "Donna Dubinsky and Apple Computer, Inc. (A)," Case 9-486-08312 (Boston: Harvard Business School, 1986).

12. Elliott also noted that it took awhile for him to recognize how much of the organizational pain he had taken on, through the period of downsizing and the project. "I was taking it into my gut. I was taking things very personally. I was concerned for everyone." He added: "The redesign of the workplace was itself very draining physically. But it was so successful that it later became hugely energizing."

13. Jack Kornfield, *A Path with Heart: A Guide Through the Perils and Promises of Spiritual Life* (New York: Bantam, 1993).

14. My thanks to psychiatrist and medical director Sid Perzow for sharing this concept of professional intimacy with me. I may use it differently than he intends, but hope I have honored his insight.

15. George, "Emotions and Leadership: The Role of Emotional Intelligence," 1033.

16. George, "Emotions and Leadership," 1027–1055.

17. Benner et al., *Expertise in Nursing Practice,* 149–151.

18. Daniel Goleman, Richard Boyatzis, and Annie McKee, "Primal Leadership: The Hidden Driver of Great Performance," *Harvard Business Review,* December 2001, 49.

19. I am grateful to Open Space consultant Chris Corrigan for suggesting this framework.

20. Benner et al., *Expertise in Nursing Practice,* 143, 144.

21. Taylor, "The Leader of the Future."

22. O'Reilly and Pfeffer, *Hidden Value,* 80.

23. Jane E. Dutton, Peter J. Frost, Monica C. Worline, Jacoba M. Lilius, and Jason M. Kanov, "Leading in Times of Trauma," *Harvard Business Review,* January 2002, 59.

24. Debra E. Meyerson and Maureen A. Scully, "Tempered Radicalism and the Politics of Ambivalence and Change," *Organization Science* 6, no. 5 (1995): 585–600.

25. Meyerson, "Radical Change, the Quiet Way," *Harvard Business Review,* October 2001, 95.

Chapter 8

1. Charles A. O'Reilly and Jeffrey Pfeffer, *Hidden Value: How Great Companies Achieve Extraordinary Results from Ordinary People* (Boston: Harvard Business School Press, 2000), 9.

2. Ibid.

3. O'Reilly and Pfeffer, *Hidden Value,* 37.

4. O'Reilly and Pfeffer, 89.

5. O'Reilly and Pfeffer, 79, 93.

6. Management consultant Dale Sands, personal communication with author, March 2002.

7. Sandra L. Robinson, "Trust and Breach of the Psychological Contract," *Administrative Science Quarterly* 41 (1996): 574–599.

8. O'Reilly and Pfeffer, 43.

9. Roger Lewin and Birute Regine, *The Soul at Work: Listen . . . Respond . . . Let Go* (New York: Simon & Schuster, 2000), 119–120.

10. O'Reilly and Pfeffer, *Hidden Value,* 107–108.

11. O'Reilly and Pfeffer, 34–35, 146–147.

12. Jane E. Dutton, Peter J. Frost, Monica C. Worline, Jacoba M. Lilius, and Jason M. Kanov, "Leading in Times of Trauma," *Harvard Business Review,* January 2002.

13. "An Alternative to Cocker Spaniels," *The Economist,* 25–31 August 2001, 49–50.

14. Andrea Rohmeder, PR Manager, ICM, Siemens AG, personal communication with author, October 2001.

15. Diana B. Henriques, "Horrible Year Ends on Up Note at Cantor," *The New York Times,* 3 January 2002.

16. Dutton et al., "Leading in Times of Trauma," 57.

17. Ibid.

18. This framework first appeared in Dutton et al., 58–59.

19. Dutton et al., 57.

20. Elisabeth Kübler-Ross, *On Death and Dying* (New York: Macmillan, 1969).

21. Dutton et al., 57.

22. Dutton et al., 58.

23. Of course, it is possible that when an organization makes no initial response to a traumatic situation, its leaders might be going through the "denial" stage of their own cycle of grief—and may soon in fact respond. If, however, those same leaders never issue a response of any kind, even well after the traumatic event is over, this places the organization at risk for creating a toxic situation.

24. Frost, Dutton, Worline, and Annette Wilson, "Narratives of Compassion in Organizations," in *Emotion in Organizations,* 2d ed., ed. Stephen Fineman, (Thousand Oaks, CA: Sage Publishers, 2000), 25–45.

25. Dutton et al., "Leading in Times of Trauma," 59.

26. Dutton et al., 60.

27. Dutton et al., 61.

28. Ibid.

29. Richard M. Ryan and Edward L. Deci, "Self-determination Theory and the Facilitation of Intrinsic Motivation, Social Development, and Well-being," *American Psychologist* 55, no. 1 (2000): 68–78.

30. Sandra L. Robinson, personal communication with author, March 2002.

31. Kathleen M. Sutcliffe, "Leading with Resilience in the Face of the Unexpected," University of Michigan, Leading in Trying Times Web site; <http://www.bus.umich.edu/leading/Leading_with_Resilience.htm> (accessed 26 April 2002).

32. Karl E. Weick, "Leadership When Events Don't Play By the Rules," University of Michigan, Leading in Trying Times Web site; <http://www.bus.umich.edu/leading/Leading_with_Resilience.htm> (accessed 26 April 2002).

33. James Pennebaker, personal communication with author, January 2001.

34. Weick, "Leadership When Events Don't Play By the Rules," 3.

35. Rosamund Stone Zander and Benjamin Zander, *The Art of Possibility: Transforming Professional and Personal Life* (Boston: Harvard Business School Press, 2000), 57.

36. Sutcliffe, "Leading with Resilience in the Face of the Unexpected."

37. Ibid.; Debra E. Meyerson and Joyce K. Fletcher, "A Modest Manifesto for Shattering the Glass Ceiling," *Harvard Business Review,* January–February 2000, 126–136.

38. Barbara Beck, formerly VP Human Resources, Cisco, October 2001. As of June 2002 this program has been extended for another six months.

39. Weick, "Leadership When Events Don't Play By the Rules."

40. Frost and Robinson, "The Toxic Handler: Organizational Hero—and Casualty," *Harvard Business Review,* July–August 1999, 105.

41. Paula J. Caproni, *The Practical Coach: Management Skills for Everyday Life* (Upper Saddle River, NJ: Prentice-Hall, 2001).

42. Robinson, "Trust and Breach of the Psychological Contract," *Administrative Science Quarterly* 41 (1996): 574–599.

Chapter 9

1. Edward Wong, "A Stinging Office Memo Boomerangs," *The New York Times,* 5 April 2001.

2. Ibid.

3. This story initially appeared on the Internet in April 2000 and the now-famous photograph of the infants, taken by Chris Christo of the *Worcester Telegram & Gazette,* has been published in *Life* magazine and *Reader's Digest.*

4. "Rescuing Hug," <http://www.snopes.com/glurge/hug.htm> (accessed 25 July 2002).

Index

About the Author

PETER J. FROST holds the Edgar F. Kaiser Chair in Organizational Behavior in the Faculty of Commerce and Business Administration at the University of British Columbia. For the past twenty-five years he has studied and written about issues of leadership, with particular attention to organizational culture and to emotions in the workplace. His work has been published in the top academic and professional journals in his field, and he is the author or editor of more than a dozen books on organizational issues and practices.

His has wide experience as a practicing manager, a university administrator, a consultant, and as a researcher. He has taught seminars and workshops for executives in Canada, the United States, Australia, Brazil, Europe, and South Africa.

Dr. Frost has received international teaching recognition during his career, including a 3M Teaching Excellence Fellowship, the CASE Canada Professor of the Year Award, the *Financial Post* "Leaders in Management Education" Award, and the Academy of Management's "Distinguished Educator" Award. He is a Fellow of the Academy of Management.